Born in York, Mike Pannett joined the London Metropolitan Police in 1988, and became one of the youngest officers in service to be given his own patch. He went on to serve on the Divisional Crime Squad, Robbery Squad, Murder Squad and the TSG (Riot Police), where he was also trained in surveillance.

Missing his native land, Mike transferred to the North Yorkshire Police in 1997, working as a Rural Community Beat Officer and eventually, as a Wildlife Officer. Mike became one of the highest commended officers – for intelligence gathering, drug seizures and bravery, to name but a few examples. In 2005 he starred in 26 episodes of the BBC's *Country Cops* series. Mike and his wife Ann, who is still a serving police officer, live with their three children in a small village in the shadow of the North Yorkshire moors.

"Now then Lad . . ."
Tales of a Country Bobby

PC Mike Pannett

CONSTABLE • LONDON

This book is based on real events; some names and locations have
been changed to protect the identity of those involved.

Constable & Robinson Ltd
3 The Lanchesters
162 Fulham Palace Road
London W6 9ER
www.constablerobinson.com

Published by Constable,
an imprint of Constable & Robinson, 2008

A copy of the British Library Cataloguing in Publication
Data is available from the British Library

ISBN: 978-1-84529-811-1

Printed and bound in the UK by CPI Mackays, Chatham ME5 8TD

7 9 10 8

For Ann

*With great thanks
to Alan Wilkinson
and also Algy, Soapy, Walter
and all of the other characters
– you know who you are*

· One ·

Christmas was a memory. They'd slung the trees out a week since, taken the decorations down and now it was a matter of counting the days – and weeks, and months – until spring. To tell the truth, though, I was busy counting the hours till I would get home to a nice warm bed that icy January night. It was minus seven by the patrol car thermometer as I sat overlooking the lake at Castle Howard in the moonlight, its edges rimmed with ice, when blow me if a fox didn't come trotting up from the tangle of last year's flags and bulrushes with a fat mallard in his mouth. I almost choked on my cheese and chutney sandwich as he trotted across the pasture and slipped quietly into the woods. Then I started thinking about how long it was since I'd eaten duck myself. It must have been the time me and the ex treated ourselves to a dinner in that posh place over by Kirkham Abbey. It was the last wedding anniversary we ever celebrated, and it needed to be: the food may have been great but they don't half know how to charge you out there.

You get like that some nights, when there's nothing doing and even your jobbing burglars have decided to stop home by the fireside. Your mind wanders. You sit there looking at the stars, and thinking. Then maybe you'll see a big white owl flit noiselessly down to grab some little creature from a hedge bottom, and you yawn and check your watch again. Ten past three. All of five minutes since you last looked.

Oh well, only a couple of hours to go and I could wend my

way back to the station. I drained the last drop of tea from my flask, closed the lid on my bait tin and set off up the long straight avenue, the light of a full moon flickering at me from behind the bare lindens. To tell the truth, I'd not had any particular direction in mind; just keep the engine running warm and the car nice and snug.

I decided I might as well take a tour round Sheriff Hutton. If I timed it right I might catch John, the milkman. He usually started out on his rounds about this time. That was some pretty strong cheddar I'd picked up from the Farmers' Market in Malton and I was still thirsty. Maybe I'd get a drink off the back of the float. John was one of my most useful contacts on that part of the beat: always on the look-out, keen as mustard; had all our numbers on his mobile – me, the lads from Malton and the other two who covered Kirkbymoorside, Helmsley and Pickering. He was dying to set me up with a decent arrest.

I timed my run perfectly; entered the village and was just passing the school when I saw him, swinging a crate of empties into his truck, right under the street-light, his breath coming in a white cloud. He was wearing a bright red felt hat, the sort of thing only a married man could get for Christmas.

'Now then, John. Give us an orange, will you?'

'I'll sell you one.'

'Aye well, if you must.' I dug my hand into my pocket as he passed me a bottle. Don't believe what you hear: there aren't many perks on this job, not in North Yorkshire at any rate. They have deep pockets out here. 'What's new, then? Apart from this daft thing?' I pointed to his hat.

'Hey, I may look like a bloody pixie, but at least I'm warm.'

I shivered as the icy juice hit my front teeth. Have to see about them some time, I was thinking – except that I hate dentists. 'So, is there anything happening?'

'Tell the truth, I was on the point of calling you. Seen a car parked in Church View there.'

2

'Oh aye?'

'Aye, and there's someone in it.'

'What's he doing?'

'Reckons to be sleeping, but you'd want a fair drop of beer to make you drop off on a night like this, don't you reckon?' He scratched the thick white rime on the pavement with his boot. 'Old car too. Doesn't belong round here by t'look of it.'

'Okay,' I said, slinging the empty bottle into a crate. 'I'll check it out. Cheers now.'

•   •   •

It was a Cavalier, ten years old. No frost on the roof, nor the bonnet. He hadn't been there long: windows weren't even steamed up. I pulled in behind him and got out. He was squirmed right down in his seat, head tilted theatrically to one side. Doing his best, I suppose. I tapped on the window.

'Now then, young man.' He reached for the handle and started winding. 'What are we up to then?'

Of course, he had to do a pretend yawn and stretch. But he looked more dozy than sleepy. 'Oh, it's okay officer. Bin on a night out, like. Tired, tha knows.'

'Where've you been?'

He had to think about that, just for a second. What he came up with wasn't very original. 'Er . . . Scarborough.'

'Scarborough? In January? So how'd you end up in Sheriff Hutton?'

'Oh . . . got lost, like.'

'You're very lost, sunshine. On your own, are you?'

'Aye.'

'And where's home?'

'Barnsley.'

'Barnsley, eh? And you're quite sure you're alone?'

'Aye.'

3

'Because the milkman reckons he's just seen a couple of lads out and about in the village. 'Bout your age too.'

'Nah, I'm on me own, honest.'

I didn't like the way he kept rubbing his face. He was edgy. He was lying to me.

'You got a job, mate?'

'Aye.'

'Well, what is it?'

'Er, I'm an electrician like.'

'Who d'you work for?'

'Missen.'

'Mind if we take a look in your boot?' He didn't like that, but he had no choice. I'd reached into the car and removed the keys from the ignition. Didn't want him doing a runner. 'What you got in there then?'

'Tools and stuff.'

'Okay, you sit there while I take a look.'

Tools, he'd said. And he wasn't wrong. It was stuffed full of them. A super big Stihl saw – that was several hundred quids' worth on its own; a nice set of Stanley chisels, good as new with their little plastic caps still on the cutting edge; a Bosch drill. It was quality gear. And of course, when I asked him what make they were he couldn't quite remember. But they were his, he assured me, and he was still quite sure he was on his own.

'Right, my friend, I'm placing you under arrest on suspicion of burglary.' I slapped the handcuffs on him and put him in the back of my patrol car.

I now had a problem. I'd nabbed him, but where were his mates? By rights I should take him back to the station, call my oppos – opposite numbers – from Pickering or Malton, and let them take over while I took me-laddo into custody as soon as possible. But that would mean processing him in York, and we all hate that – working away from our own base. You never know where the papers are, nor can you count on regular cups of tea and coffee; and when it's all done and dusted, there's the long drive back to Malton before signing off. Besides, if I did trail across to York with him, why, I'd miss out on two more possible arrests – those mates of his that he wasn't admitting to. Not to mention a chase. And I know I shouldn't say it, but I quite enjoy a chase. Gets the old adrenalin pumping.

I didn't think about it too long. Should've done, but didn't. I called the Malton lads: they were double-manned – I was on my Jack Jones. Here was a chance of grabbing three villains in one go. You have to take your chances. I learned that in the Met. Pity York City haven't got the message yet.

I decided I'd better radio York, ask them for a van to come and collect the prisoner. Then, with me-laddo in the back, I cruised slowly around the village. No two-tones, no blue lights, nice and quiet. Every few minutes I checked the Cavalier, just in case. Nothing. Maybe they'd spotted me and weren't coming back.

It was past four when I called York again. 'Where's this van got to?'

'They're in the area, but they can't find you.'

'Bloody typical. You let a townie out and first thing he does is get lost.'

I'd no sooner said that than I saw a pair of headlights approaching. It was my mates from Malton, Ed and Jayne. 'What have you dragged us out here for?' they asked. 'Can't you manage?'

'Why, were you wanting to be left alone together?' Ed had a thing about Jayne. God knows why, but he did. I thought he was happily married – perhaps he was just married.

No answer. 'Anyway,' I said, 'I think you'll find it's policy not to have three prisoners in one car.' They knew that, of course, but none of us could resist a bit of banter. The fact is that you don't ever want more than one prisoner at a time. The less chance a couple of villains have to talk to each other the better.

'But you ain't got three prisoners.'

'You're right, Jayne, my old Cockney mucker, but it's only a matter of time, mate, only a matter of time. You stick with me and we'll have one each. And I'll save the good-looking one for you. Now look, why don't you take the west of the village and I'll cover this side.'

● ● ●

It didn't take long for the bad guys to break cover. Five minutes later I was passing the Highwayman pub when I heard the squeal of tyres a couple of streets away. The Malton lads were on the radio right away, calling out my number. 'Ten fifteen! Ten fifteen!'

'Aye, go on.'

'Two young males in an Escort, in a hell of a hurry.'

'Heading which way?'

'Terrington, it looks like.'

'I'll be right behind you. Over.'

I spun the car around. 'That'll be your mates,' I said to the lad in the back, but he was still in denial.

'I told you, I'm on me own.'

I soon caught sight of the blue light, maybe half a mile away across the fields, heading north. And beyond that the rear lights of the fleeing villains, flashing red as they braked on the bends. They wouldn't know these roads. But I did, like the back of my hand. 'Your mates are going to be in dead trouble if they don't slow down,' I said, over my shoulder. 'Way they're going, they'll roll it. You see if they don't.'

'You wanna watch it. They're a bit barmy, them two. They won't wanna stop for you.' He was frightened now – both for himself, as I hurled the car round the bends and bumped into the dips – and for his mates. The ones who didn't exist ten minutes ago.

We were racing up the steep bank that leads into Terrington. I was doing 60 plus, but easing back on the accelerator. There was a T junction at the top – stone wall in front of you. 'They'll ditch it here if they don't bloody slow down.'

My own tyres screeched as I took the 90-degree turn. In the headlights I could see two black furrows where they'd ploughed right across the frost-white verge. Even above the noise of the engine I could hear my prisoner shivering. He was rattled; no doubt about that.

The villains were out of the village now and speeding through Ganthorpe, 70 plus, the Malton lads hard on their tail, and me keeping a safe distance. 'Another T coming up, matey. They'll be straight through the hedge.'

The luck some people have. They re-arranged the verge, whacked a flower-tub, but still made the right turn at the top, and were hurtling through Bulmer, heading back towards Sheriff Hutton. 'Now they've had it,' I said. And this time I was sure. Any second now and they'd pass the badger set. After that the road really takes a dive – one in four, I'd say. Then wallop – the hairpin bend at the bottom. At this speed they'd have no chance. I hit the brakes, braced myself against the seat, and grabbed the radio mike. 'Back off! Back off!' I shouted. Did the lads in front hear me? No idea. Next thing it was them shouting at me: 'Crash! Crash! Crash!' The Escort had hit the bend, slewed off the road, rolled over twice, and was on its side in the hedge bottom, wheels spinning, tail lights still aglow. The Malton car had only missed it by veering right and shooting 50 yards beyond it.

• • •

You dread going to a scene like that, especially with a full stomach. You never know what you're going to find. But these blokes had been riding their luck all night, and they'd got away with

7

it again. As I yanked the hand-brake on and opened my door, blow me if one of them wasn't stumbling out of the upturned car. He was making for the hedge when I grabbed hold of him, but he still wasn't going to come quietly. He swung a fist and grazed my forehead before I caught him in the stomach and winded him. It took three of us to get the handcuffs on him.

'Well, where's his mate got to?' I was looking in the car but he wasn't there.

As the other lads looked around I fetched my Dragon light from the squad car. I soon caught him in the beam, about 20 yards away, trying to fight his way through the hedge. I hesitated to go after him. It was blackthorn, ten feet high and almost as thick, with a couple of strands of barbed wire on the other side. 'Give over, lad. You'll rip yourself to shreds!' I shouted after him, but by the time I realized that he really didn't care, he'd wriggled through to the other side. Credit where it's due: the lad was a trier. I did manage one swing with my ASP, but I got more hedge than villain, and there he was, racing across the moonlit field like a mad March hare.

The other lads had got prisoner number two into their car and were standing looking at the wrecked Escort, half-heartedly rocking it as if they were going to right it. 'Never mind that,' I panted, waving an arm at the fleeing suspect. 'What about him?'

'He won't get far.'

'I don't know so much. He hasn't done badly up to now.' I ran along the hedge to where there was a gate, all the while playing my beam into the field. 'I'm going after him.' I could still see him, heading downhill, dodging a tuft of dead thistles and leaping over a low wall. The land belonged to Mick Easterby, the racehorse trainer, and as I galloped after the fugitive I was thinking, 'If Mick's looking for a staying hurdler he could do worse than check this lad out.'

By now I'd reached the bottom of the field where it runs into

Bulmer Beck. It's a only a narrow little thing, but I'd fished in it many a time as a lad. I stopped and listened. At first all I could hear was my own pulse pounding in my ears. Either I needed to get back to the gym or find myself a desk job.

I stood there holding my side. Maybe he'd got away after all. Maybe the other lads were right to let him go. Why bust a gut? He was bound to show up when he got cold enough. I was just about to turn back when I heard an explosion of noise – ducks and geese, what sounded like dozens of them, all going off at once, squawking and flapping as if there was a fox in the coop. There was a little lake up the rise – I knew it well; caught a four-pound carp in it, back in my school days.

There was nothing for it now. If that's where he was, I had to cross the little beck. Would I make it? Well, matey had, and who the hell was he? A common criminal – from bloody Barnsley, too. I simply ran at it, fast as I could, and took off. I managed to get one foot on the far bank okay. The other landed just an inch or two short, where the water was a couple of feet deep, and just a couple of degrees above freezing. Call it a draw.

A minute later I was standing by the lake in the yard. No sign of the fugitive, but it was suddenly lit up like Scarborough sea-front: automatic security lamps, yard lights, bedroom windows, and finally a door opened and I was dazzled by a torch shining right in my face.

'What the bloody hell— oh, it's you, Mike!'

It was Pete Jowett, one of our Countryside Watch team.

'We're after a burglar, mate. Chased him all the way from Sheriff Hutton.'

'Right.' He switched off his lamp. 'Which way'd he go?'

'Across that next field, I reckon.'

'Give us a second. I'll fetch t'Land Rover out. We'll have the bugger.'

Next thing we're bumping over the pasture, Pete at the wheel, me with my head stuck out the window, half blinded by tears, telling him the tale as I swept the frozen landscape with my lamp.

'Barnsley?' He was outraged. 'Bloody rogues from Barnsley on the loose in our patch? Can't be doing with that. One thing being robbed by local villains, but bloody South Yorkshire? You wanna tell 'em to stop home and steal from their own folk.'

'If we find him, Pete, you can tell him yourself.' But for the moment there wasn't a thing we could do. The bird had flown. Half an hour later we were back at the farmhouse, frozen stiff and empty handed. 'Well,' I said to Pete, as he passed me a cup of hot tea and glugged a generous measure of brandy into it, 'we've got two of 'em. That'll have to do us for now . . . and whoa, that's enough brandy. I'm still on duty, you know.'

●　　●　　●

It was well after six, and in theory I should have been thinking about home, but we still had one or two loose ends to clear up. Anyway, our sergeant should be on duty any minute, and we could now make this a legitimate Ryedale capture. So we shipped the two suspects back to Malton, where we briefed the early turn who then set off to continue the search for the third member of the gang. It didn't take them long to get a result, and they didn't have to try very hard. They hadn't been in Sheriff five minutes when a youth, half frozen to death, crept up to the car and just managed to stop his teeth chattering long enough to say, 'I think you're looking for me.'

The Bulmer Three, it turned out, were well known to the Barnsley force. Well, two of them were. The driver had been roped in against his better judgement. He'd had no more than a caution to his name prior to that night's events, but his record would make more interesting reading now. As for the other two, they already had form, and now they had four charges of burgling premises in Sheriff Hutton. For us, they were three good arrests, especially as we were able to return all the stolen hardware to the rightful owners.

Back at the station I was going over the circumstances of the arrest with the duty sergeant. 'Now,' he said, 'you apprehended the first youth at what time?'

'Three forty-five, sarge.'

He repeated the words as he keyed it in. 'Three . . . forty . . . five.' Then he looked at his watch. 'Well, what the bloody hell have you been pratting about at till half past seven?'

I sighed. 'Don't ask, sarge, don't ask.'

I finally got off duty at lunchtime, but not before I'd been spoken to by a reporter from the *Mercury* – and got myself into more hot water. It must have been a combination of fatigue and exhilaration that prompted me to say – well, this is what came out in the paper the following week:

Malton Bobby's Warning to South Yorks Criminals. Stay off our patch or we'll have you! If they think they can come and do as they please in Ryedale, I say let's see you try. You'll have Mike Pannett to deal with.

Fatigue? Exhilaration? Perhaps I should put it down to Peter Jowett's brandy.

· **Two** ·

Driving to work and back – for ten years it had been something to be endured, a regrettable part of an extended working day, a pain in the neck. Five days a week I'd nudge the old Astra along the Balham High Road – accelerator, brake, accelerator, brake, grind my teeth, pop another Rennie in my mouth – then skirt the west side of Clapham Common, queue up at the lights to cross Lavender Hill, dip down into the dark underpass beneath the railway lines outside Clapham Junction before heading north in fits and starts towards the river along Battersea Bridge Road. It was three and a half, maybe four miles from my gaff to the police station up there. I always meant to measure the journey, but I never did. What was the point? The only thing that mattered to me on my daily drive to work was the traffic. Would I get a nice clear run, as I might on the night shift, and make it in a quarter of an hour? Or would I get stuck amongst the shoppers, delivery vans, cabs and roadworks, as I might on the afternoon run, meet the occasional 'incident', and spend the thick end of an hour edging forward in first and second gear, swearing to myself that I could've cycled it in half the time if the rain hadn't been coming down like stair-rods?

I couldn't help thinking about that daily grind as I sped along the deserted lane towards Bulmer, the bare hedgerow flashing by. It may have been coming up to midwinter, but the sky was a beautiful pale blue, the trees were thickly rimed with white frost, and with every little stirring of the air it showered

13

down like so much desiccated coconut, glinting in the bright sunlight. As I swooped down the hill and approached the beck I looked at the clock on the dashboard: twenty-five to nine – bags of time. I pulled over on the roadside, got out and leaned over the side of the little stone bridge, peering through the tangle of woodbine into the slow-moving water. On the low parapet, sheltered by a dense overhang of elder, the moss was damp and soft under my hands. On an impulse I brushed aside a glistening dead alder leaf and pressed my face against the green cushion. The chill sensation, the vague scent of wintry dankness, took me back to my childhood days when my mate and I used to fish for brook trout off this very bridge. And we caught them too. They may have been no more than a pound in weight, but to a couple of ten-year-olds they were whoppers. At the end of the day, when we'd drunk all our fizzy pop and eaten the last of our meat-paste sandwiches, we rushed home with our trophies, gutted them on the back step and got my Mum to grill them for our tea with a pile of bread and butter.

Back in the car, I drove on with the window wound down. It was that kind of day, the air deliciously cold, the sun in my face as I headed east, warming my spirits if not my body. I wondered whether my new job would give me time to take in the odd day's fishing. Perhaps I should make sure it did. At the crossing with the Castle Howard road I checked the time again, swung north and followed the long straight avenue past the house and the lake, then took a right turn through the tiny estate village of Coneythorpe and climbed the gentle gradient that took me up to where the Moors were visible to one side, the Wold tops to the other. It was an unnecessary diversion, adding a mile or so to the trip, but I wanted to absorb the full beauty of this perfect winter's morning.

I entered the town a few minutes later, passed the hospital, then cut through the back roads to Old Maltongate. What had I done, ten miles? I checked my watch – 19 minutes including those few moments' day-dreaming on Bulmer Beck. Welcome to the grind of daily commuting, North Yorkshire style.

As I swung into the driveway I told myself that I must remember to bring a camera to work one day. I wanted to take a picture of the police station to send to the lads at Battersea Bridge Road. They wouldn't believe it. I've heard people say it could pass for a vicarage. To me it was more of a parsonage, perhaps a Victorian country house – tall, imposing, faced with pale stone and set back from the road amidst sweeping lawns, with a proper old-fashioned shrubbery softening its lines. Vicarage, country house, parsonage, manse – whatever it looked like, it was the sort of place where you could imagine Miss Marple snooping around in pursuit of a suspect butler, or a philandering, monocled toff in plus fours having his wicked way with a parlour-maid.

The first appointment in my diary was with the Super-intendent. I ought to explain about ranks in the police force. In the Met it was all very laid-back. Your Sergeant was one of the lads, and you'd be on first-name terms with him. (Or her, of course.) The same went for your Inspector – unless you were in trouble, in which case he or she might insist on a degree of formality. When it came to your Super – well, they were definitely higher up the evolutionary scale, but they were still ten a penny. You knew who they were and what their rank was but if you stopped to salute every time you met one as you walked through Battersea cop shop you'd never make it from one end of the corridor to the other. A nod of the head would do in most cases. If a Chief Superintendent happened to come by when you were at your desk, well, that didn't happen every day. I'm not saying you'd note it in your diary, but you'd cert-ainly expect to stand up. Anything higher than that and you'd salute – at least, if you were outside you would. Indoors you'd maybe stand up and give a nod, or push your shoulders back. There was no mistaking the serious big-wigs, because they generally swept along the corridors and through the office like visiting politicians, flanked on either side by cronies and clipboard-clutching wannabes, and you always worried that they'd jot your number down if you failed to honour the Chief in the approved manner.

Malton was different. As PC Ed Cowan told it, my move north had taken me back in time to the good old days. I'd been assigned to Ed's shift, and he had been told to show me the ropes and take me on a tour around our beat over the next few days. 'Just to put you in the picture, mate,' he told me as he pointed out the essential facilities – washrooms, photocopier, teapot and coffee machine – 'your Sergeant is "Sarge", your Inspector is "sir"—'

'Bloody hell.'

'Just take note of what I'm saying, Mike. When in Rome . . .'

'Aye well, fair enough. So what's the Super?'

'He's God. And he lives out the back there, in the Wendy House.' He put his hand to the kettle, and withdrew it sharply. 'Ah, we're in luck. Fancy a brew?'

'Cheers.'

He glanced up at the clock on the wall. 'You've got ten minutes before your appointment with the Almighty. Here' – he picked up a file and dropped it in my lap – 'you can familiarize yourself with a few local villains.'

As he fiddled about at his desk and the tea brewed in the big brown china pot – we never had one of those in Battersea – I looked through a sheaf of papers containing details of various 'wanteds'. I've a good memory for faces, and I like to keep up to date with the latest memos, especially if we have a decent photo. A lot of the lads I worked with down south would spend all their spare time playing cards or chewing the fat. They used to take the mick out of me for always studying the mug-shots; called me a Yorkshire geek. But once in a while it paid off. You just never knew.

'Right, sup up, buddy. Time to go and meet your Maker.'

I was glad I'd had Ed's little tutorial. It put me in the right frame of mind for my introductory talk with the resident deity.

'Well, PC Pannett,' the Super said, offering me a seat at his huge antique desk as he lowered himself into a leather wing-chair and flipped open a beige folder, 'I see you've come to us from the Met.'

'That's right, sir.'

'So you'll know all about policing. Modern methods, psychological theories, task forces. And I see you've done time in the TSG, what the public like to call the, ah, Riot Police.'

'Yes, sir.' I didn't know quite where this was leading, but if I'd learned one thing from my dealings with top brass over the years it was to restrict myself to one-word answers wherever possible. They hate being de-railed when they're trying to get a point across. Also, of course, the shorter your answer, the less chance you'll put your foot in it.

'Well,' he said, 'you'd best forget most of what you learned in the Met. Country policing is another matter altogether.' He threw the folder on to the desk between us. 'But that's an impressive record, and one or two fine commendations, so I'm assuming you're a fast learner.'

'Yes, sir.'

'Any experience of country life, Pannett?'

'I grew up just down the road, sir.'

'Ah, really.' He didn't sound that interested. 'Well, you'll know that North Yorkshire is unique – and so is its police force. I expect that in London you guarded your privacy somewhat jealously.'

'You mean not telling people what I did, sir?'

'Exactly so. And I should imagine you were particularly careful where the criminal fraternity were concerned.'

'Indeed so, sir.' I love the way some of the high-ups talk. Sort of Dickensian. I often wonder whether they send them on a

17

course – how to sound important. And the funny thing is they soon have you imitating them.

'Up here, let me tell you, if you do a good job as a policeman, just about everyone – all your local malefactors, that is – will know precisely who you are, what your nickname is, and probably where you live too. They'll be on first-name terms with you. You will be known to all and sundry. You will have a reputation – and that reputation will be no more and no less than a reflection of the kind of policeman you are. In short, you will be remembered for the way you treat people – be they criminals or ordinary law-abiding citizens.'

I kept expecting him to let me say something, but it slowly occurred to me that this wasn't an interview. It was a pep-talk, a lecture, and it was going to be a short one. In no time at all he was out of his chair and opening the window, as if to let an unpleasant smell out of the room.

'If I ever see you in this office again, PC Pannett, it'll be for one of two purposes.' He nodded at my folder. 'Either you'll be here to be congratulated on receiving another of those commendations, or' – he was at the door now and I was on my feet, heading towards it – 'or you'll be on the carpet for a bollocking.'

'Very good, sir.'

Back in the main building, Ed wanted to know how I'd got on. 'Er, he made himself painfully clear.'

'Meaning?'

'Well, you know him better than I do. Basically, I have it all to learn, from scratch.'

'And he's right, buddy. Come on, let me drive you around your new patch.'

We got in his squad car and headed into town. 'We'll do the eastern part today,' he said, as we drove down to Malton's solitary set of traffic-lights. 'Leave the rest for tomorrow.'

Bear in mind that in Battersea we patrolled a square mile,

perhaps two. I realized that Ryedale was a large area, most of it rural, but it had never really occurred to me to consider just how huge it was – and that even on a good day there would be no more than four or five of us on a shift to cover every square inch of it, and that if there was something so simple as an RTA (road traffic accident), it could tie up every man jack of us. We were soon out of town and heading along the A64, and within 20 minutes were on the outskirts of York, approaching the roundabout on the ring-road.

'This is where our patch starts,' Ed explained.

'So that's what, about 15 miles?'

'From Malton? More or less.' We circled the roundabout and headed back the way we'd come. 'We'll meander through a few villages south of the main road, give you an idea. You've got a map with you, I take it?'

'No. But I come from around here.'

'Oh. Local lad, eh?'

'Aye, I grew up in Crayke there. Used to get around this area a fair bit on my bike.'

'Well, just bear in mind that we're looking at half of the area you'll be patrolling.'

'You mean there's more?'

'Hell, aye. If you go from York, Malton's about halfway to the far end – and all we're looking at today is the half that lies south and east of the main road.'

'So you mean when we call for back-up . . .'

Ed knew what I was going to say. ''S right, buddy. It can be anywhere from 30 to 40 miles away. You could be stuck out in a field with a gang of poachers from Warrington, ugly bastards without a scruple between the lot of 'em, and the nearest squad car is half an hour away dealing with an RTA. And the best of it is, the bloody villains know it. Now, most of the baddies round here are fairly respectful.'

'Meaning?'

'Well, if you pull 'em over or stop 'em in the street, like, they'll co-operate.'

'That'll make a change. In the Smoke they'll pull a knife on you.'

'Aye, but . . . you cop 'em out in the wilds and they know bloody well you're single-handed. So they can take liberties. Which they do.'

• • •

I was struggling to take in the fact that this was to be my new working environment. We were driving through places I knew from my youth: Bossall and Howsham, where the road crosses the Derwent; up past Howsham Woods and down towards Kirkham where the ruined abbey stands beside the river and the railway line to Scarborough snakes its way between the wooded hillsides. We used to lark about on the weir there. Now my job would be to stop kids from doing likewise and endangering their lives.

We were soon back on the main road, speeding along the Malton by-pass and looking out over Eden Camp, where a Second World War Spitfire stands guard over the museum, once a POW camp.

'So where we off to now?' I asked.

'Far end of the beat. 'Bout 17 miles.' By that he meant the Staxton roundabout, where the road forked: Filey in one direction, Scarborough in the other.

'And how big did you say this patch is, in total?'

'Ooh, now you're asking.' Ed drummed his fingers on the wheel as he slowed down for the lights at Rillington. He was quiet for a moment, then, as we passed the Coach and Horses, he said, 'This is where I grew up. Had me first pint in there.' He paused again, then said, 'Aye, sweet 16. The lads dragged me in after I'd played my first game for the village footie team.'

'Oh aye?'

'Mind, they weren't up to much by then – not like their glory days.'

'What glory days?'

'When we won the Scarborough League Cup. 1967.'

'But that's 35 years since. How old are you?'

'Not that bloody old, bud. No, I heard all about it from me Dad. He was there watching 'em. Shoulda been playing but he hurt his foot harvesting. We had a picture of 'em with the cup. Pride of place, right next to me Mum and Dad's wedding picture on the sitting-room wall.'

Ed was smiling distantly. As we cruised through the village and by the broad pastures and stately cedars of the Scampston estate, he recited the whole team in measured tones. 'Watson, Johnson, Bramley B, Oxendale, Bramley K, Blanchard, another Johnson, Whitty, Temple B, Temple A, Christie. I think I've got that right; have to ask me brother. Aye, they played Old Scarborians in the Final at Scarborough Town's ground. Two goals to one we beat 'em. Temple and Christie the scorers. And here's one for the pub quiz – Oxendale was booked in first minute, which was a rare occurrence in them days. Guess what for?'

'You'll have to tell me, mate.'

'He entered the referee's little black book . . . for smoking while the game was in progress. Smoking. Now then, how often d'you think that's happened in the history of the game?'

I was still chuckling to myself when he went on, 'He was built like a pony, skinny body and great stout legs, hard as a shithouse wall. And his shirt – I'll show you the picture some time – his shirt stands out paler than the others; he used to boil it after every game. He was always squinting through his eyes, on account of always having a fag on. My Dad reckoned he always lit a fresh roll-up as the game kicked off – to see him through to the break. So there he was, crunching into the tackle with a half-smoked ciggy between his lips. According to

Dad, one time he even got up and scored with a header while he was still puffing on it. Then he flicked the tab end away as he ran back to his position – and the bugger dropped right down the opposing centre-half's shirt and burned half the hair off his chest. Spent the rest of the game chasing after old Oxendale, miles out of position of course, and when he caught him he chopped him down in the box and gave away a pen. Got a right bollocking off his team-mates.'

'You should write a book, matey.'

'That's what they used to tell me Dad,' he said quietly. 'And then it was too bloody late.'

· · ·

We were in Heslerton, East or West, one of them, when Ed suddenly said, 'Call it 600.'

'Eh?'

'I'd say we cover 600 square miles.'

'Oh . . . our patch, you mean. Now I see why you asked about maps.'

'Yep. You'll want a full set. There's too many ways of getting lost on a beat this size.'

'Where do I get 'em from?'

'From the bloody shop, like the rest of us.'

'What, and then claim for 'em, like?'

'You can try claiming against tax, but you'll get bugger all off North Yorkshire Police, buddy.'

As we drove back by the scenic route I realized that maps – even if they were at my own expense – were top of my shopping list. I was well out of my depth, and suddenly aware that despite having grown up in North Yorkshire there was a whole world of tucked-away villages and farms, a huge network of by-ways that I'd never got to know. Hell, I'd left for the big city when I was barely an adult. I'd certainly never ridden my bike as far as

Foxholes or Butterwick, nor explored the wonderful dry valleys on the Wolds, like Thixendale, where the lady who kept the post office stores sold home-made honey, post-cards, bundles of rhubarb in season, or plums from her garden. I'd never seen, either, the fantastic views from Leavening Brow, which was where Ed parked up so that I could have a quick smoke. You can see fifty, sixty miles and more, south to the power stations at Drax and Eggborough, west to the Pennine chain, north to the Moors, with the effluence of Teesside forming a grey-green stain over the northern horizon.

• • •

'Hell fire,' I said. We were in a gateway, looking out over a field of winter wheat, brilliant green in the low sunlight. Across the far side, where it dipped towards a stand of bare, grey-green ash trees, a man in a deer-stalker hat and wellies was walking a couple of black Labradors, a shotgun in the crook of his arm. 'It's going to take some getting to know.'

'Well, as I said, buddy, this is a whistle-stop tour of the eastern half of our beat. Really, we haven't started yet, certainly not on the good stuff.' He pointed to the north. 'There's Kirkbymoorside, Helmsley, Pickering – you can see 'em all from up here. Then the Moors yonder – Bilsdale, Farndale, Rosedale, Newtondale and all the rest of them, right across the other side to Grosmont and Goathland. Take you a year or two to get settled in, I'd say. Find your way around, then show the Super what kind of reputation you can build up.'

As it happened, I started to make a name for myself that very first week. And the funny thing was, I was off duty and well away from my new home patch. It was my first rest-day, and I'd decided to pop over to York and look around for some new hiking boots. Now that I was back in Yorkshire I was determined to make the best of it and get out into the hills as much as I could. As well as wanting to enjoy the countryside, I was on a bit of a campaign to get fit – although that didn't stop me popping into my favourite restaurant before I hit the shops. The way I look at it, what some people call retail therapy is a stressful business, and for a professional Yorkshireman, always in search of a bargain, you need your wits about you. No good trying to strike a deal with a wily salesman when your blood sugar is depleted. What I needed was a decent start – and for that there's no better place than Betty's, world renowned for a number of good reasons, not least among them its cooked breakfasts.

So there I was, strolling down Coney Street, and all was well with the world. Full stomach, nice charge of caffeine flowing through the veins, cash in my pocket, and whistling a happy tune. I was weaving my way through the crowds, about to pop into one of the record stores when I spotted a familiar face. Vaguely familiar, and definitely not friendly. He was actually walking beside me, faster than everyone else, and the reason I turned to look at him was that he'd nudged me as he went by. In fact, I could've sworn I felt his hand rub against my hip pocket. This was nothing to do with the pressure of the crowd – it wasn't that busy yet. No, my first instinct – and I've learned to trust my gut feelings over the years – was that he was a pick-pocket and he'd been looking for my wallet, although I learned a long time ago not to keep it back there.

I let him get a few yards ahead, then followed him, and as he turned to mutter something to a passing woman I got a better look at him. He had a thin sort of face, bony, with reddened eyes darting everywhere. He looked decidedly edgy – and to my mind that spelled trouble. I was sure he was up to no good; he was probably on drugs, I wouldn't have been surprised if he'd turned out to be armed.

Despite the crowds, and although he was only of average height, it was easy enough to follow him. He walked on the balls of his feet, and turned his head to look at people as they passed, not casually, but giving them a steady stare. It really was quite menacing. He looked the sort of person you'd cross the road to avoid. I followed him as he passed British Home Stores and turned left, which gave me another look at his face. That's when it clicked. He'd been in the 'wanted' file that Ed had given me when I was waiting to see the Super. Top of the bloody list – burglar, drug user, and violent with it. He was wanted for three separate assaults, one on a police officer. But here I was, off duty, and in mufti. What should I do?

If I'd had my mobile with me it might've turned out differently, but I didn't. Never did at that time; I preferred to be inaccessible when I was off work. I had to think fast – although to my surprise the suspect had now stopped and sat down right outside Mothercare, just behind an open door where he was almost hidden from view. I walked on past, nice and steady, to where I could keep an eye on him, then turned to face the shop window a few yards away. I could hardly believe what I saw next as he rolled up his trouser leg, pulled a needle from his coat pocket, and injected himself just above the ankle. Christ, he must be desperate – dangerous too. I turned away – if he saw me watching there was no telling what he might do. Some of these people will stab you with a used needle as soon as look at you, never mind whatever else he might be carrying.

I don't know whether I look like a copper or not – that's for other people to decide – but you hear plenty of criminals saying they can spot one a mile off. And since I've already admitted that I follow my gut feelings, who am I to say that a criminal's instincts are any less reliable?

Still, when the Good Lord gave me a healthy nose for sniffing out a bad 'un he also touched me on the head and said, 'You will always be a seriously lucky bugger, Pannett' – and there on that crowded street I suddenly got very lucky indeed. Amongst the hats and bare heads, through the shifting tide of shoppers, barely 15 yards away I saw a policeman's helmet bobbing along.

I wove a path through the crowd. 'Thank God for that,' I said. 'Listen. we've got a potentially dangerous situation here.' He was staring at me, his mouth open. 'Oh, sorry, matey. My name's Mike Pannett, I'm a PC at Malton, Ten fifteen's me number. I'm off duty, but look – I've just spotted a man who's wanted for assault and theft.'

'You sure?'

'Yep. I can't give you a name, but I've seen him on the circulars. He's got drugs on him right now and the way he's going on I think he's on a bit of a shoplifting spree.'

'Well if he spots me he'll do a runner. Can you watch him while I get back-up?'

'Don't worry, I can still see him from here.'

PC Crouch was on his radio immediately, but just as he did so me-laddo got to his feet and looked our way.

'Shit, he's seen us.'

'Okay, Mike, here goes,' – and Crouch shoved his way through the crowd towards the shop doorway. I hesitated – my instinct was to go with him, but I was off duty. Better if I stayed put – unless things got nasty. The law says that even when you're off duty you're a copper, and you're expected to behave as one; in reality you like to give the on-duty lad first crack. For one thing, he's equipped for crime-fighting, you're not. As Crouch moved in, our friend surprised us both. Instead of legging it he went for the officer, going in low and shoving him to one side, knocking his helmet off in the process. He thought he was away, but he hadn't seen me. As he raced towards me he smacked into a young lass with two little kids. Down she went, and as I stuck out a leg, down he went, flat on his face. I was on him immediately, my knees in his back as I grabbed his wrists and pinned them behind him. There was a sharp hiss as Crouch sprayed CS gas in the guy's face then got the cuffs on him.

In London, even when you have an incident as dramatic as that, most people walk right by. They don't want to be involved. Or they're just too laid back to be impressed: they've seen worse. If a crowd does gather it's usually an ugly one – gang members, family, neighbourhood kids – ready to wade in at the drop of a hat. That's when you really need back-up – and fast. But here on the streets of York on a Saturday afternoon we'd attracted a tight circle of people eagerly watching us, the word 'fight' on everyone's lips. For a moment it felt like being back in the school playground, but by the time I'd handed over to Crouch and checked that the lass who'd got knocked over was okay, the squad car had arrived, the suspect was inside and the crowd had melted away.

●　　●　　●

PC Crouch had made the arrest – and he was welcome to it – but he must have given me a hell of a write-up, because a few days later I was back in the Wendy House to pay my respects to the Super. 'Ah, PC Pannett,' he said, 'back so soon?'

'But hopefully not for a bollocking, sir.'

'Ah . . . no.' He picked up a letter from his in-tray. 'Sit down. Tea or coffee?'

'Er . . . tea please, sir.'

'No, I've received a glowing report from the Chief Superintendent over in York. It seems you're like our friends the Pinkertons.'

He'd got me there. I didn't know what he was on about.

'The Pinkertons, a celebrated private detective agency in the United States. Motto: The Eye Never Sleeps.'

'Ah, right. I see. You mean, always vigilant and alert, sir.'

'Precisely – always on the look-out, even when off duty in another town.'

It turned out I'd received another commendation. He read it

out to me as I sat there supping tea from one of his china cups. As Ed said when I got back in the office, 'Bloody hell. You don't hang about, do you? Haven't even taken over your duties officially and you're over there having tea with the Super. I hope you put a good word in for us ordinary mortals.'

'I gave you an honourable mention, matey. Told him you were doing your best, given your limitations.'

'All right, all right.' Ed had a think, then he said, 'I tell you what, though.'

'What?'

'I think you've arrived, buddy.'

'I think you're right,' I said, re-reading my copy of the commendation.

· **Three** ·

I'm not sure I knew what I expected to find when I left the multi-cultural streets of Battersea and my contacts among the Afro-Caribbean and Asian communities – not to mention the enclaves of Ghanaians, Yemenis, Kashmiris, Polish, Cockneys, Irish, Nigerians and Australians – and headed north to sleepy old Malton, where you still meet people who've never been outside Yorkshire in their entire lives. One thing I wasn't expecting was a base like ours, set back off the road behind a lawned garden, overshadowed by mature trees and protected by a long privet hedge which had been painstakingly trimmed to form the words Malton Police Station.

This was a country town in a large rural area, and a wealthy area at that. There was little unemployment: there were always plenty of jobs at the bacon factory, and the town was a trading and commercial centre that served the needs of a lot of very wealthy people, some of whom were to become my friends as time went by. I first realized just how much money was around when I got chatting to a salesman at one of the car dealerships that operated on the outskirts of town. He told me that their annual sales of BMWs were the second highest in the entire country. And when I looked around on a Tuesday morning and saw the line of shiny new four-wheel drives parked end to end around the weekly cattle market, the superb strings of racehorses being exercised along the lanes and gallops that surround the town, it began to make sense. I'd grown up in villages not far from Malton, but my parents came from fairly ordinary working families. My Dad was actually a chartered mechanical engineer; he designed the sights on the Challenger tanks. So – not exactly simple country folks, but they did have their feet very much on the ground, and we were certainly never well off. I grew up having no idea about how much money there was around this part of the country.

When I was leaving the Met all my friends had cracked jokes about me going to live in the back of beyond, donning a flat cap and clogs, and huddling over a coal fire on a night-time. Nice joke, I told them, but you haven't a clue. It wasn't until I got into my new job that I realized I didn't either.

As I said, I wasn't sure what to expect, but I did know what I was hoping for in my new life: plenty of wide open spaces and the opportunity to enjoy them – both on the job and during my leisure time. As for policing, I think I expected a more traditional set-up within the force, and a slower pace on the streets. The rape and murder cases, the serious assaults, the gun crime, the major league drug-dealing, the Yardie gangs – all of that I was leaving behind. This 600 square miles of God's Own Country, surely, was a different world.

I think the whole thing started to come into focus one morning when I found myself in Yates' hardware store, looking at the various delicacies they keep in the bins there next to the sacks of pet food. I was wondering what my old mates in Battersea would say if I told them you could pick out a roasted pig's ear – all translucent like a piece of underdone crackling – or a marrow bone for your dog, and that when you went to pay you might be standing alongside some farmer in a tattered gabardine raincoat with a frayed bit of baling twine for a belt, that he might be holding a length of metal link chain, or a pick-axe, or handing a wonky spade over the counter to have a new wooden handle put on it. And what would they say if

I then told them that the farmer was worth four million at present-day land prices?

I'd been in Yates' to have a natter with their bicycle repair man. There had been a few thefts in the area recently. There were the usual cheap little bone-shakers that get nicked from outside a village pub and turn up a few days later, tyres flat, front wheel buckled, down by the riverside. Then there were the more up-market machines. You can easily spend £1,000, maybe twice that, on a decent mountain-bike, and you can just as easily have it stolen. The difference is that the kind of person who nicks one of those isn't the sort of opportunist who's looking for a ride into town to collect his benefit cheque. He's a pro, and he's looking to sell it on as quickly as he can and make a nice bit of cash. And instead of waiting for a car boot sale, there was always the chance he might just bring it into a repair man to try and sell it. Well, I had to start somewhere, but the lad upstairs at Yates' emporium assured me he hadn't had anything of that sort offered to him.

I must admit I dawdled a bit on my way out. You don't get many shops like Yates' these days. They sell a bit of everything: hardware, farm supplies, kitchenware, boots and shoes, outdoor clothing and every type of tool you can imagine. You can buy a pair of bathroom scales, a set of fire-irons, a galvanized dustbin, a washing-machine, a cement mixer or a packet of jam-jar covers. You can buy new deck-chair canvas by the yard, rope by the metre, galvanized iron clouts by the pound, pickling onions by the bag and a hundred different types of garden spray. Or, if you're stuck for something to do while the wife's ferreting amongst the Pyrex dishes, you can stand and watch the caged zebra finches, whose cries were once described to me as being like the creaking of aged bed-springs. All human life is in that shop: an elderly housewife looking for a pie funnel; a stooped allotment holder weaving a path to the counter with an ergonomic wheelbarrow; giggly children looking for goldfish food; campers in search of methylated spirits; and the odd policeman, recently transferred from the Met, smiling to himself as he remembers the Saturday markets south of the river. They certainly had some exotic items on sale there, but nothing quite like this.

●　　●　　●

A policeman's lot – it would be a great deal simpler were it not for the criminal fraternity. But so long as there are wrong-doers on the loose, there'll be no peace for us. As I stepped out into the sunlight the radio was chattering away. Would I investigate a report from a dog-walker up in Old Malton. Suspicion that two youths were selling drugs. In a public open space.

It took me several minutes to extricate myself from the crush of cars nosing their way through town. It'd be the level crossing, of course: every time the gates come down the traffic backs up to the lights at the main crossroads and there's not a thing you can do except wait, and wait, and wait, and this time some idiot pulling a trailer full of pigs for the bacon factory had managed to get halfway across the intersection with the Pickering road and was stranded in the middle of the yellow box, stopping the job completely.

By the time I got up to the old Roman camp there was nobody much to be seen. Hardly surprising in the middle of March, and on a raw old day too. It's an odd sort of spot, a large expanse of grassland barely a quarter-mile from the town centre, with some fine mature trees dotted about, but more or less deserted most of the time. People drive by on their way to Flamingoland or the museum at Eden Camp and seem unaware that they're passing the site of a major Roman settlement where a garrison of fighting men were stationed almost 2,000 years ago. Maybe it needs a visit from *Time Team*. Quiet as it is, it's a strange place for someone to get up to mischief. I found it hard to believe

32

that anyone would be trading in narcotics just across the road from the police station in broad daylight – that sort of thing didn't happen on my patch in Battersea.

I got out of the car, put my top-coat on and strolled across the wet grass. I'd seen a woman sitting at a picnic table, smoking a cigarette while her dog went about its business under the trees that bordered the adjacent field. I asked her if she'd seen any-one else around the place. 'Oh aye, couple of youths, heading down the bottom towards the river. But that was 20 minutes since,' she said, and now, beyond the low humps that marked the outline of the Roman ramparts, the park looked empty. I drove back through town, swinging left just before the bridge and heading along Sheep's Foot Lane towards the soft drinks factory that borders the other side of the camp. With a bit of luck I might catch them as they headed back over the bridge to Norton – because I was willing to bet that's where they came from. A search of their persons might prove fruitful.

• • •

From what I'd observed since I moved up from the Met, they weren't that keen on 'stop and search' procedures in North Yorkshire. Perhaps I mean they weren't that switched on to it. Their techniques were, to put it bluntly, naïve. With nine years in the Met, where stopping and searching suspects in the street was routine, I'd found it to be a valuable tool in crime prevention, and I'd learned some pretty effective methods – you had to.

First, you learned to tell at a glance whether someone had been using drugs, or whether they had something else to hide, like a concealed weapon. That first glance could be crucial. It would tell you, as often as not, whether the person you were about to apprehend was carrying something they didn't want you to find. Body language, a sudden nervousness as they saw you slow the car down, a change of gait, a shifting of the gaze, a hand dipped into a pocket to dispose of something incriminating. And you soon learned to pick up the other clues, like that tell-tale redness in the eyes if they'd been smoking dope.

As for your approach, you needed to plan that carefully. 'The Met way' we called it: make sure you get the person under your control right away, and have their hands where you can see them – all the time. You don't want them whipping a knife out from their pocket, or their waist-band, or from inside a sock. Down in my part of London I should say 50 per cent of the street robbers I stopped were carrying knives. And I've seen enough people stabbed to know it's not worth taking a chance – ever.

I suppose we had no choice down there but to be quick on our toes, and sharp-eyed too. It became a habit, so I was shocked when I moved back to Yorkshire, because what I found amongst my new colleagues was a surprising degree of naïvety. It was a rural thing, I suppose. In a city like York, as far as I could see, and even in Scarborough, they were relatively switched on. But out in Ryedale they just didn't have enough experience of stop and search. They'd give a suspect far too many opportunities to escape, whereas I instinctively had them leaning against a wall, or the car, hands out in front of them, and always making sure that something – again, the wall or the car – stood between them and a quick getaway. Otherwise they'd be off, like shit off a stick.

By and large, the techniques my Ryedale mates used struck me as naïve – although it wasn't just my fellow police officers who seemed unsophisticated – it applied to the criminals themselves. In London a suspect only had to see the car slow down and he'd be off. Approach a group and they'd starburst – everyone shooting off in a different direction. If half a dozen had been involved in robbing someone, the first thing they'd do would be to swap clothing, which would make a nonsense of the descriptions we'd been given – or any CCTV images. And of course, face to face, there was always that fear that they'd pull that knife on you. As for the search, that didn't really bother them. They'd all been through it before, dozens of times in some cases. They were prepared – give them a five-second warning of your approach and you could bet they'd be clean as a whistle.

In North Yorkshire it was different – very different. Stop someone in the street here and they stay stopped. This has never happened to them before: they've never felt a copper's hands patting their pockets and armpits and running down their legs. They'll probably be in shock, certainly in awe. They assume that if you've approached them you know who they are and, by implication, where they live. Which you often do. They aren't going to run because you'll be round their house in five minutes waiting for them. Their attitude is like something out of a 1940s black-and-white film – it's a fair cop and all that. It's not London, where everyone's a stranger and a beat copper takes months to work out where all the narrow back streets and alleyways connect up. But it wasn't simply a matter of technique; it was more about practice. In Battersea we'd be investigating ten or a dozen street robberies a day – and that alone often gave us adequate cause to stop suspects in the street and search them. Up here I was hardly coming across one a month.

So, this was a new type of policing I was getting used to. But at the same time the bad guys were having to get used to me. I was different – I was more direct, more authoritative, and I didn't take any risks. I had a mission. The fact is that as much as I was surprised at the difference between policing methods on my new patch and the way we'd done things in the Met, I was more shocked at the way in which illegal substances were being touted and consumed on the streets of a small country town. I mean cannabis and ecstasy at this time, not the harder drugs;

they came later. But, from the word go, I'd find that in casual conversation it would come out that so-and-so was a dealer who operated at such-and-such a place or time. And you could more or less go and watch them at work. They had no fear, and why should they? Nobody had ever sorted them out. They'd never been stopped and searched. I used the word 'naïve'; you could almost call it innocent – were it not for the fact that the law was being broken and young lives endangered. Well, that was about to change. Drug dealing in broad daylight? Not on my bloody patch.

● ● ●

I found the two youths where I hoped I would, loping through the grass towards the lane that led to the bridge. They checked their stride, looked nervously to left and right. Were they about to make a dash for it? I saw one of them slip a hand in his pocket. In London I would have been thinking 'knives'. Here it was more likely 'dispose of the evidence' – or swallow it – but either way, with their general demeanour, and the call we'd had from the dog-walker, I knew I'd be on safe ground if I decided to search them.

You have to be careful with stop and search. It's a procedural thing. In the Met we had to remember six basic steps in the procedure, and we remembered them by using a mnemonic, GOWISE. Most important is G, Grounds for suspicion, which in this case I already had. A member of the public had called in. Next was O – Object of search: what do you think the suspect might be carrying? Today it was drugs. Then W: show your Warrant Card if you're in plain clothes, which of course I wasn't; I – Identification: the requirement that you give the suspect your name; S, the station you're attached to, as if they'd be in any doubt in a small town like this; finally E – letting the suspect know his Entitlements under the law.

In reality the suspicion part often comes down to another G, Gut feeling – and that comes with experience. As well as a person's mannerisms and demeanour there's the fact that in a small community you soon get to know who the users and dealers are. You get to know the type of places they hang out. They don't realize how obvious they are half the time. As soon as you approach them they'll go red or start shaking, particularly the less experienced ones. Some of them might just as well fly a big flag with 'Guilty' embroidered on it.

As it happened, my two lads at the Roman camp were clean – either that or they'd disposed of anything they might have been carrying. I wasn't about to crawl through a great tangle of dead nettles and brambles to look for it, not this time. And, in fairness, I only had the suspicions of a member of the public to go on. She may have just overheard a snatch of conversation. Still, as far as I was concerned I'd got a result of sorts just by stopping them. They now knew who I was, and I knew them. As I said to them, with a smile on my face, 'Don't worry, lads, I'll get you next time.' It's the sort of warning I like to give people, especially when I know they're bent. It keeps them on their toes. These two, though, thought they'd got away with something. They couldn't resist giving me a bit of lip.

'You can't touch me, copper. I'm too clever for a bloody flat-foot.'

There's no law against cheeking a policeman. You just have to take it. The days of clipping them round the ear are gone. All the same, I was entitled to ask the lads their names and addresses.

'Eastwood,' one of them said. He was a tall youth with a mop of dark curly hair and a complexion like a cheap supermarket pizza.

'Aye, and we call him Clint,' his mate chipped in.

''Cos I ride into town and do whatever I want, me.'

'Clint, eh?' I had my notebook out and was getting the details down.

'Aye, Clint Eastwood. Ya get it?'

'Oh I get it all right,' I said. 'I'm good with names, as well as faces. So here's one for you. I'm PC Pannett, and I'm a big fan of Clint Eastwood. Seen all his films. In fact, where I come from they call me Harry, Dirty Harry. And I'm telling you that things have got too slack in this town, and I'm going to make it my mission to clean the place up. Do I make myself clear, punk?'

I should never have said it, I suppose; but I couldn't resist it. Within days it was all over town. There were youths at the skateboard park, kids playing football up against the wall behind the bowling club, even a gaggle of Girl Guides outside the swimming-baths. 'Here he comes, Dirty Harry.'

It didn't take long to get back to the station either.

'Now then, Harry . . . or do we call you Clint? Or the Enforcer?'

I could handle a bit of mickey-taking from Ed. We'd got on well from the day I first walked in and he'd driven me around the patch. We'd become quite matey, and often stopped for a pint together after a shift.

'Oh, so word's out, is it?'

'Small-town life, buddy. You did well to get back to the station before the story broke.'

'Well,' I said, 'now that it's out, maybe I need to find a way of living up to my reputation.'

'Oh aye,' he said, 'and what do you mean by that? You going to rampage through the streets of Malton with a .44 Magnum? Freeze, ass-hole!'

'Listen,' I said. And, credit where it's due, he did. As far as I could see, drug dealers had free rein in the town. As a force we knew plenty of them by name, and if we applied a few Met techniques to the problem we could surely arrest the most high-profile offenders and drive the others underground.

But Ed wasn't keen. 'That's CID territory,' he said. 'I mean, that's what they're for.'

'The suits?' I said. 'They're a joke.'

'Careful, Mike. You're new in town and walls have ears.'

'I can trust you, can't I?'

'Sure you can.'

'Well, do you think they pull their weight? Poncing about all day in plain clothes and unmarked cars?'

'You aren't the first to say that.'

'Well, and what do you say?'

'I'd say you aren't far off the mark.'

'Half of 'em think they're in an American movie, on some kind of stake-out. I mean, Ed . . . new as I am up here, I've seen 'em with me own eyes parked up outside the secondary school, watching the bloody dealers as the kids come out. "Oh no, we can't move in. We're gathering evidence." Gathering evidence, while 14-year-olds are being sold marijuana right outside their school? You know I'm right, don't you?'

'We all know what goes on . . . but, like I say, it's CID territory.'

'As I see it we all have a duty as policemen to go after criminals. If they're selling drugs on my patch I'm going to have 'em . . . and CID be buggered. I mean, come on, Ed. You've got kids – how long before they want to start going out on a night?'

'Well, big one's coming up to 14.'

'Right, so she'll already be wanting to hang out with lads.'

'Aye, right enough.'

'And cast your mind back. How old were you when you first started going out drinking?'

'Sixteen.'

'And how old were the lasses you met up with?'

'Oh hell . . . 14, some of them. High heels, big dollop of mascara. They could get served well before we could.'

'Precisely, mate. And where do these dealers ply their trade,

39

once they've done the bloody school run? They're down that pub where all the youngsters gather.'

I didn't need to rub it in. He knew I was right. 'Go on, then,' he said. 'What's your plan?'

'Ah,' I said, 'I haven't got a plan . . . but you and me, Ed, I bet we can knock sommat up.'

'And then what?'

'Then we take it to the mountain top.'

•   •   •

It never goes down well in a hierarchy like the police when someone vaults over the entire set-up – shift leader, Sergeant, Inspector – and goes straight to the Superintendent. Least of all the CID. But as far as I was concerned things were in a right state out there on the streets – streets on my beat, streets I was meant to patrol – and what was I supposed to do about it? Turn a blind eye?

We cobbled together a simple plan over a cup of tea. It was a real back-of-an-envelope job. 'What I reckon', I said, 'is we use the old Met tactics. Get stuck into anyone and everyone who we think is using or dealing.'

Ed agreed. 'We must have a fair few names between us.'

We did – and we knew where to find most of them.

'If we call at their homes, their hang-outs, or stop them on the street . . . search them, we'll rattle a few cages, let 'em know we mean business. And act fast, before they have a chance to work out what's going on. Out of that we'll surely make a few arrests, and they'll give us enough intelligence to find the more serious dealers.'

'You hope.'

'Aye, I hope. Come on, mate, think positive.'

I reckoned – and here, to be fair, I was taking a bit of a punt – that we needed a fortnight.

'Two weeks?' Ed wasn't sure.

'Well, if we go to the Super and ask for a month he's gonna say no. We're already a man short, aren't we?'

'Aye, and they still haven't advertised the vacancy.'

'But then again the holiday season hasn't kicked off yet. Let's go for two weeks.'

We pitched it nice and simple. Ed and me to take a late turn, an unmarked car, wear plain clothes and work as much overtime as it took – because if we did any good we'd generate a ton of paperwork. Then we'd be in business. It was just a matter of convincing the Super – and that, when it came to it, was a piece of cake.

He listened to our plan, which took me about as long to explain as it did to write it. 'Well,' he said, 'you've got the experience, you've got the desire, and you seem to have a plan. And we certainly have a problem on the streets. Let's see what you can do.'

Of course, as soon as word got out, there was trouble. We were expecting it and we got it – from our mates the CID. People have the wrong idea about the CID. They think that (a) they're above us ordinary coppers, (b) they're super-intelligent, and (c) they live a glamorous life, kicking down doors, doing high-speed car-chases, tracking down the Mr Bigs of the criminal world, and meeting top-flight journalists in secret locations to tell their stories. In fact, the CID are no different in rank from beat coppers. They think they're superior; we know they're not – at least, not in small towns. London is a different case: the CID there – and I've worked with them on a number of cases involving Yardie gangs and the like – do some terrific work.

Even so, there's still a rivalry between the uniformed branch and the plain-clothes boys. To them, we're wooden-tops; to us they're idle buggers in suits. Their work involves the kind of routine information gathering that would drive a beat copper nuts: endlessly checking facts and figures, going through lists of names, addresses and phone statements, sitting and watching doors and windows or parked cars, hour after hour, day after day, and eating horrible takeaways. Personally, I think it dulls their minds – the grub as much as the tedium. It gives them wind too, serious wind. They see us out and about engaging with the public, having something like a life, and wonder why the hell they ever put in for CID in the first place. So when they find a jumped-up bobby, fresh up from the Met to sleepy old Malton, setting out to bust the drug scene open, they don't like it – at all. What they didn't realize was that in London I'd planned an operation that netted the largest ever seizure of crack cocaine at that time. I knew what I was about.

● ● ●

'What the f*** do you think you're up to, Pannett?'

'Me? I'm doing what I'm paid to. Policing the streets, matey.'

'Listen, you four-eyed pillock, we do the drugs busts in this town.'

'Oh, you do, do you? So what about the lad that operates outside the secondary school, in that Y-reg Fiesta every afternoon?'

'Don't you worry, we've got his number.'

'Aye, and so have half the kids in Year 11.'

'We're collecting evidence.'

'And the kids in Year 11 are collecting a stash. I presume you're poised for the kill then?'

'In our own good time, flat-foot.'

'So that's what I'm to tell the parents who ask me how the hell their kids are managing to get hold of ecstasy at knock-down prices in a quiet market town in broad daylight. That what you're saying?'

'We'll have 'em, sunshine, don't you worry.'

'Aye, but when? That's the bloody question.'

Not that I really cared what the answer was. It couldn't be soon enough for me. As far as I was concerned, Ed and I had a job to do, and two weeks in which to do it. Unlike our friends in suits, we couldn't afford to hang about.

We kicked off by stopping any vehicle that we suspected – or in some cases knew – was involved in the drug scene. As soon as we spotted one out and about we got after it and pulled it over. We worked as a team, jumping out and grabbing hold of the occupants before they could run – which we fully expected them to do. If there were more than two in the car we'd target the driver and front-seat passenger, and warn the remaining occupants to stay where they were. They were like lambs to the slaughter. Just like the stop-and-search lads, they weren't used to this sort of thing – they froze. We were mostly stopping users at this stage; we still had to get to the dealers. There was no resistance from the kids we arrested, no fighting, no knives, no back-chat, no bleating on about solicitors. All we did was arrest them, take them back to the station and interview them, building up a database of names and contacts – and frightening the living daylights out of them.

The business about solicitors surprised me. In London everyone was wise to that as a stalling tactic: 'I'm not saying a word till my lawyer gets here,' and all that. Or if they were in a really chatty frame of mind, 'no comment'. Here I felt I was meeting up with the good old-fashioned 'honest crook'. They accepted they'd been caught and they came clean. Within days we were getting a picture of the Malton drugs scene, and the picture was of a town dominated by a particular gang, most of whose names we now had.

The gang had eight main members. With the exception of a couple of 20-year-olds, they were all teenagers. One was as young as 15. Prominent among them was the kid called Eastwood.

'Had him in mind from the word go,' I told Ed as we sat in the office late one night typing up our reports. 'He's the little twat they call Clint – the one where I said my name was Dirty Harry.'

Ed liked that. 'Well,' he said, 'just make sure I'm there with you when you pull him in. Tell you what, you do the "Do you feel lucky, punk?" and I'll do that other line.'

'What's that, Ed?'

'You know the one. "This gun will blow your f***ing head clean off." That a deal?'

'Yeah, yeah, yeah.'

As it happened, Ed was with me when we almost got our hands on the lad – almost, but not quite. It was early evening, and the sun was just going down. We'd been cruising around town wondering where the hell everyone was. We were on our way back past the police station. It seemed extraordinarily quiet.

'Is there a game on, or what?'

'No, England play tomorrow. Maybe it's that big showdown in *Celebrity Big Brother* or something.'

'Bloody amazing what some people'll watch.'

'Hey, if it keeps the criminals off the street . . .'

'Now, there's an idea.'

'What?'

'Round up all the bad guys, stick 'em in a secure house and do 24-hour CCTV surveillance.'

'We already have that, Mike.'

'Have we? I've not seen it. Mind you, I don't watch much telly these days.'

'It's called prison, you prat.'

Trust me, it gets that bad when you're double-manned and there's nothing going off. You run out of things to talk about. But although you can slump into that sort of idle chat, and you're so bored you feel as if you could just pull over, curl up in your seat and take a crafty nap, you know bloody well that everything can change in the time it takes for your radio to crackle into life. In this case, though, we didn't need the radio.

We were barely 400 yards from the station, just doubling round the back where there's a footpath that leads past a row of old cottages and down towards the by-pass. You get dog-walkers, courting couples going down there – and the odd chancer scouting around for an open shed or a bike parked without a lock on it. As we drove by we saw a skinny tall youth climb over the stile.

'It's that bugger Collins.' His name was on our list of gang members.

'Right, let's have him.'

He'd looked over his shoulder as he mounted the stile, but of course he didn't recognize the unmarked car. We gave him a second to disappear, then pulled up and went after him. As soon as we were a few yards along the pathway we saw four of them, just ahead of us. But by this time they'd seen us, and legged it. 'Green jacket . . . I'm sure that's that bugger Eastwood,' I panted as we dashed along past the back-garden hedges and wooden sheds, the overhanging brambles lashing at our faces. We could see them, plain as you like, emptying their pockets into the hedge bottom before swinging left across the bare field with Eastwood several lengths to the good.

'Nippy little bastard,' Ed gasped as we gained on the other three.

We caught them at the far side of the field. I wrestled one of them to the floor, a second stood there frozen, but his mate was all for taking Ed on.

'Come on, copper, I'm ready for you!'

'I think not, m'lad.' Ed bent down, went in low, and had him over his shoulder in a flash. He dumped him unceremoniously in the thorn hedge and turned to slap the cuffs on the other two. I looked around for the lad Eastwood but he'd vanished.

Ed radioed for assistance. I hoped it wouldn't be long. It'd soon be dark and we had the hedge bottom to search.

Half an hour with our Dragon lights and we'd collected nearly two pounds of cannabis resin for our three captives to explain. So there we were, three of the main suspects in our care and a nice stack of evidence. All we lacked was a positive ID on the fourth lad, the one who'd got away. I knew damn well who it was, but, as they like to say these days, where was the evidence? All I had to go on was that green jacket. And fair play to his mates – they weren't obliged to incriminate him, and they never did – even when all three went to prison for 18 months. So now we had to wait for 'Clint' to come to us, as he surely would, because as far as we knew he had no means of support other than his trafficking.

• • •

Ed and I had a spectacularly successful fortnight. We made 27 arrests, of which half a dozen led to prosecutions that resulted in terms of imprisonment. They weren't all spotty youths either – and one case showed us just how far reaching the drug problem had become in the town. We'd received information from one of the many stop and searches that a middle-aged woman was supplying drugs at lunchtimes from a fish-and-chip shop car park.

'That can't be right,' I said to Ed. 'Operating from a car in broad daylight?'

'Well,' he said, 'we'd better check it out. We know what car it is?'

'Aye, a little black Peugeot.'

We drove into the car park at midday and sure enough, there was the suspect vehicle, and inside it was a woman answering the description we'd been given.

'Are we going to watch her or what?'

'No. Why bother? If she's dealing we'll have all the evidence we need.'

It was almost surreal. We simply parked a few yards away, and walked up to the car. She wound down her window and looked at us enquiringly and I showed her my warrant card.

'Bloody hell,' she said, and gave a great sigh.

'Look at that,' Ed said. And there on the passenger seat right beside the woman was a pile of £10 and £20 notes, some loose change and several lumps of cannabis resin – about an ounce each – as well as a little set of scales and a wad of plastic zip-lock bags. It was a regular little retail set-up. We arrested her and charged her. She didn't argue. What was the point? It was a sad tale, really: a single mother trying to make ends meet; three kids, and a husband serving time for fraud. They treated her leniently – 12 months community service – but the main thing was we'd put her out of action.

● ● ● ●

Towards the end of Operation Clean Sweep we started to get lucky, catching a couple of fish in the net more by accident than design. We'd gone to look for a youth who was wanted on warrant for failing to appear in court to answer a charge of theft. We decided we might as well pay a visit to the lad's home address. 'Why not?' Ed said. 'He's probably daft enough to be sat there watching the telly.'

'Aye,' I said, 'but let's not make it easy for him. I've had dealings with his mother. If we show up at the front door she'll stall us while he nips out the back.' We decided that if the lad was at home we'd sneak up from behind. Which explains how we ended up climbing over a neighbour's fence a few doors down and working our way along to his place through one garden after another. We soon caught the familiar smell of cannabis, coming from an old greenhouse. Creeping towards it, we could see the wanted lad sitting on the floor, apparently half asleep. And who should be there with him but our pal in the green jacket – Clint Eastwood, sitting on a chair smoking a joint, his head back and his eyes half closed. They were high as kites, the pair of them.

I nudged Ed and beckoned him to follow me. The door to the greenhouse squeaked horribly as we opened it, but the lads were quite oblivious. I was able to walk right up to Eastwood and take the joint out of his mouth. As he sat there impersonating a goldfish I informed him that he was under arrest for possession of drugs – at which point his brain re-established contact with his tongue and I was treated to a torrent of obscenities, as well as the usual litany of threats as to what he would do to me if and when . . . 'Forget it, matey,' I said. 'You're going to be out of circulation for quite a while.'

I don't usually keep a score. I'm more proud of the work I do in preventing crimes than in the numbers of arrests I can make. But in this case I really did feel we'd chalked up a couple of good ones. Not only had we got the lad who was wanted on warrant, but we'd collared Eastwood, done for possession – and he would later answer further charges relating to his dealings with the drugs we'd found in the hedge bottom a few nights earlier.

Ed and I wound up our temporary partnership late on a Friday night, congratulating ourselves on a job well done. More gratifying than that was what happened when one of the CID men walked into the hotel where we were having a few beers. We could tell he wanted to insult us, and we were all ready to insult him back, but – hell, this was the weekend coming up. Besides, he was on his own. What was he going to do against us two? We were on top of our game, full of it. 'Sit down, have a pint,' Ed said. 'We're celebrating. We can call this one up for the police, can't we?'

'Aye, go on then,' he said, parking his arse next to me and

downing the first half of his pint in a single gulp. It took him a second pint to relax, and he was into his third before he enquired, politely, how things had gone with our project. He was halfway down his fourth, and struggling, but in the end he could contain his admiration no longer. He was, he admitted, impressed. 'I tell you what,' he said, 'there ain't many – and I don't mean you any disrespect, y'understand – but there ain't many wooden-tops could do what you've done. Me and my mate were . . . well, I wouldn't say we were wrong like, but we weren't as right as we'd like to be.' He drained his glass and went to get another round in. When he came back from the bar he was looking thoughtful. 'You lads, you ever thought of joining the CID?' he asked.

· **Four** ·

Spring had properly arrived at last. After a week of cold and rain, the wind had dropped and the clouds had broken up. The hawthorn hedges were greening up nicely, the grass was gleaming under a warm April sun and all over my patch inquisitive lambs were managing to wriggle their way through wire fences in search of the rich grazing along the verges. So there you had them: gaggles of lost youngsters scampering along the roadside butting the fence, their thin bleating answered with a deeper call from across the pasture. I'm always amazed at how they manage to find their way back, and how on earth they pick out their mothers from the dozens of ragged ewes scattered over a 40-acre field. Because they do – somehow or other. Once in a while, if you're lucky, you can help shove one of them through a gap, but there are casualties. Some are hit by the cars and vans that hurtle along the lanes at 60 and 70, regardless of the sharp bends and sudden gradients; others fall victim to people who have an appetite for fresh meat and no scruples about grabbing an opportunity. I like a bit of lamb myself – to my mind there aren't many more appetizing sights than a roast shoulder coming out of an oven all spiked with rosemary and surrounded by a few overdone shallots. And the smell! Unforgettable. And quite unmistakable.

● ● ●

It was a Sunday, the early shift. Not a lot doing. We'd been out on the Wolds to see a farmer who reckoned someone had been at his diesel tank in the yard, except that he couldn't be quite sure how much he should've had in it, so he couldn't be positive how much, if any, he'd had stolen. I told him to keep a check on it and let me know if any more went missing.

From there we followed the old gypsy race along the valley that leads out towards Foxholes. It rarely sees any water these days. It's little more than a shallow depression that courses along beside the road through East and West Lutton, Weaver-thorpe and such places. But once upon a time it was a proper little beck – at least in a wet season. I was in my element, sound-ing off about my younger days when I used to bike around the Wolds and go fishing along the Derwent. I'm saying 'we' – I had a captive audience with me: Jayne was riding shotgun, so to speak. This was when she first came to us, as a graduate from police college. They like to farm probationers out to get a bit of practical experience before they're let loose on an unsuspecting public. Three months working with one of us to show them the ropes and so on. You might say it's our job to blood them, ease them into the routine as well as some of the more unpleasant tasks we get from time to time. Mind you, I wasn't expecting any action on a day like this, although I should've told the lass what I tell most people about this job: always expect the unexpected.

I quite like having company from time to time, especially a new young copper. To be honest, I think I've a bit to offer the raw recruits. Here they are in the wilds of North Yorkshire, learning about a rural beat, and after I've given them the low-down on the wildlife, the game-keepers, the farmers who act as my eyes and ears, my tea stops and so on, I start throwing in a few stories from my days in the Met. And then there's what you might call style. There's more than one way of policing a beat, and these young recruits will meet plenty of coppers who take the heavy-handed approach. Wade in, take charge, terrify the buggers. Well, that's simplifying it a bit. They'd call it a 'no-nonsense' approach. I call it the easy option. Anyone can do that. I prefer to tread softly, get to know the criminal fraternity if I can. I believe in looking for the best in everyone. Give them the benefit of the doubt, I say. The quiet word of warning, the bit of friendly advice. 'I know what you're up to, so why don't you make it easy on yourself by stopping right now because otherwise I'll have you.' That kind of thing. I'm not saying it's the best way, or the only way, but it's my way. And I like it when I get the chance to pass it on to a young constable who hasn't had time to formulate an approach to the job, hasn't got set in their ways and turned cynical.

I'd not really met Jayne before. I think she'd been with us a couple of weeks but she'd been assigned to one of the other lads at Malton – one who had what you might call a more fundamentalist approach to the job. Sort of copper who would go out of his way to nail a motorist for a minor speeding offence, chalk them up on his hit list and then quiz you as to how many arrests you'd made last month. However, that particular officer was off on some sort of training scheme. Perhaps it was a course on non-confrontational policing, perhaps not. He was good at finding courses to go on, and would disappear for months at a time. He'd done a course about trans-gender issues and followed that up with one on negotiating skills. You couldn't blame the lad for trying.

Anyway, the upshot was that I had another pair of hands – and someone to talk to. So there I was, telling Jayne the tale: my love of the countryside, my fishing exploits, my drug-busting escapades in London. Poor lass, she had no choice but to listen. And then I got on to sheep – and looking back it's a wonder she didn't nod off, except that I was letting her drive. We were back on the tops now and I was looking at the ewes dotted all over the hillside while their lambs explored the edges of the pasture in little gangs of four and five. Jayne was a townie, and a southerner. She came from Peterborough, and when I started telling her about the problems we were having with rustlers she was all ears.

'Rustlers?' she said. 'You mean like in cowboy films?'

'Well, aye, you could put it that way.'

'What, with lassoes and that?'

'Now then, don't be daft.'

'Only joking.'

'Thing with sheep is they're pretty much left to look after themselves a lot of the year.'

'Fair enough,' she said. 'I mean, all they do is chomp away at the grass all day long.'

I let that pass. I can never tell with southerners. 'Anyway,' I said, 'we've had farmers come out in the morning and find half the flock missing. 30, 40 sheep – gone. One of them reckoned he lost 80 odd in a single night last year.

'Well, he would, wouldn't he?' Jayne said. 'I mean, it's a classic one, that'

'You what?'

'A hundred sheep? It'll be the old insurance job.'

'Oh aye, they'll be insured all right.'

'No, I mean a scam. You know – "I could swear I had 100 sheep when I went to bed last night and now there's only 20 left."'

'How old are you?' I said, pressing myself back in my seat as she attacked the descent towards Wintringham at about 40.

'Twenty-two,' she said.

I shook my head. Here she was, still a probationer, and sceptical as one of the old lags. 'Gangs,' I said. 'It has to be. Drive over from the West Riding or somewhere in a big wagon and herd 'em in. We've got the odd eye-witness report, livestock wagons cruising the lanes at dead of night; we've seen the tyre marks in the gateways, but we've never got near making an arrest. However,' I said, 'as it happens we're off to investigate a spot of possible rustling right now. Head down to the bottom and turn right, will you?'

There was no gang involved in this case, and no mystery vehicle, and not that many sheep. The farmer who'd called the station told me he had 150 in one field, 80 odd in the other. He couldn't be quite certain, but he insisted he'd kept a careful watch on his lambs. Just getting ready for market, he said, and now they were starting to disappear, one by one. And he was adamant that the gypsies who were parked on the roadside down at the bottom of his land were responsible. Same trouble every spring, he reckoned.

The encampment consisted of an assortment of Transit vans, trailers and a single old-style wooden caravan.

'They shouldn't be here, by rights,' I said.

'Can't you just move 'em on?' Jayne asked.

'Well, live and let live,' I said, as I put on my cap and opened the car door. 'They're no real trouble. And they'll be on their way in a few weeks.'

'But what about all that? You going to make 'em clear up before they go?' Jayne was looking at the roadside where a skinny sort of whippet was dragging a big red-streaked bone from a pile of plastic bags full of rubbish and had got it all tangled up in a length of baling twine.

'Aye, they're not the tidiest, are they?'

There were two families, probably ten or a dozen travellers all told; a couple of women and a handful of kids sitting on the steps of their caravans, three or four men sitting around a half-hearted sort of fire fringed with scorched tin cans and stinking of burnt rags. They appeared to be finishing off a meal. There were a couple of ponies too, threadbare types lying on their sides on the grass, soaking up the spring sunshine. 'See that?' I said. 'We once had someone call in to tell us there were two dead horses on the roadside. They thought they only slept standing up.'

55

'Is that right?'

'Aye, got quite excited about it. Said we should have the knacker down there to clear them away.'

'No, what I mean is, do they really sleep standing up?'

'You don't know a lot about country life, do you Jayne?'

'Well, no. I mean, Peterborough . . . it's . . .'

I was out of the car now and approaching the men around the fire. There was another smell in the air, roast meat – lamb. No question about that. Quite fragrant it was. The men looked ill at ease as I approached, staring at the sickly yellow flames rather than looking at me, stroking their chins, pulling their flat hats down over their eyes, coughing as the smoke wafted across their faces. One of them was working away with a tooth-pick. Another speared a last potato and popped it in his mouth before putting the plate on the ground. Behind him the dog had settled down to gnaw his bone. Another one, a puppy, made a move for the plate but was shooed away.

'Now then,' I said, stepping towards the fire.

The man with the tooth-pick got up, wiped his chin, then rubbed his hand on his dark track-suit bottoms. He was about 60 and wore a sort of trilby hat. He was only short, but he was obviously the spokesperson for the group. 'What can I do for you, officer? 'Cos we've done nowt wrong, you know.'

'No, I'm not after anyone. Just wondering whether you can help us.'

'We don't snitch on nobody neither.' There was no doubt about it – he'd been eating that meat I'd smelled. His chin and his hands were covered in grease.

'No, I'm not asking you to do that. Just that we've had reports of a couple of sheep gone missing.'

'Sheep, you say? Ooh, we don't know nowt about that,' he said. Behind him the other men stared fixedly at the fire. One of them glanced up and shook his head.

'Well, I thought you might have seen something. You know

how they get loose and then can't get back in through the fence, and—'

'I told you, we don't know nowt, officer.'

I looked at the plate on the ground. There was a layer of grease, already congealed, sort of white and hard – and if my memories of school dinners served me right that was lamb fat I was looking at. I bent down and picked the plate up. There was what looked like a smear of mint sauce there.

'What have we had,' I said. 'Sommat nice?'

'Chicken, officer.' You had to admire his nerve. Standing there with his arms folded across his chest, staring me right in the eye as if he was daring me to taste the congealed gravy on the empty plate. 'We kill our own.'

'Chicken, eh?' I looked around the site, and there were indeed a couple of scrawny hens settling in the grass under one of the vans. And a duck. But you can tell when people are lying through their teeth. It's the way they stand there, jaw set, not a muscle moving. As if they've had to take a deep breath to get the lie out and then don't dare breathe out in case their face colours up.

'Well,' I said. 'If you hear owt, or see owt, maybe you'd let us know.'

'We've done nothing, officer.'

'Course not. I wouldn't expect honest travelling folks to do something like that. They're not daft enough to get involved in that sort of caper. No,' I said, putting the plate back down beside the fire, 'I've had no complaints about any travelling folk on my patch and I don't expect I will.'

'That you won't, sir, that you won't.'

Back in the car I could sense that Jayne wasn't happy. 'Bloody hell,' she said, 'he was lying through his teeth.'

'Aye,' I said, 'you're not wrong. But what was I going to do? How could I prove they hadn't bought some chops in town? I mean, when there's been slaughter the first thing you need is a body, and I think they've disposed of just about all the evidence. Them and the dogs between them.'

'Yeah, but . . .'

'Come on, let's swap over. I'll drive.'

As I turned the car around I caught sight of one of the women, hurrying back to her van with the dirty dishes. 'Look, Jayne, the way I see it, we know they've had a lamb or two, and they know that we know. And they know that if we get another report of any livestock going missing we'll be straight back to see them. Anyway,' I said, as we headed out of the village, 'let's see how we're doing along the Scarborough road.'

●　　●　　●

In the winter the A64 flows pretty steadily, but as soon as the better weather comes along everyone wants to be to the coast. 'Delays can be expected,' as they say on the radio – and sure enough the eastbound traffic was pretty heavy as we headed against the tide to make a routine call on the outskirts of York, right on the edge of our beat. I was doing Jayne a favour. A couple of days earlier she'd been called to a 'damage only' accident – that is, no injury to anybody involved. The car had been more or less a write-off, but now she had to go and check it over to see that the tyres were in good order, that it had a valid tax disc and hadn't been stolen. As I say, routine stuff, and three-quarters of an hour later we were heading out of town once more, wondering whether it was time to grab a spot of lunch. There was a cafe on the road just towards Sand Hutton and I thought we might pop in there, get a hot drink and eat our sandwiches in the car.

We were just about within sight of the place, in a steady stream of traffic travelling at about 40 when I saw a car some way ahead of us swerve sharply towards the central white line, then cut back in as one car after another slammed their brakes on.

'Can you see owt?' I pulled the car over towards the verge to give Jayne a better view.

She was leaning out of the window. 'Bleeding hell, some poor sod's on the deck,' she said. 'Looks like a biker.'

Blue lights, two tones: I snapped into action and pulled out to the right of the now stationary line of cars. The good news was that nothing was coming towards us – although at the same time it was obviously bad news. Whatever had happened up ahead it had stopped everyone in their tracks.

It took seconds to get to the accident. Right outside the cafe, in amongst all the tables where people had been sitting having a drink a man in black leathers was lying on the ground, face up. Before I even opened the car door I was on the radio calling for an ambulance. It was obvious from the shape of his body that he was in a bad way. His head was right up against a flower pot of some sort – although as I put my yellow jacket on and walked across the rough tarmac, I could see that it was a big, heavy stone tub all covered with algae. It would've stopped a tank. There was a scuff-mark on the side where the white concrete was exposed. And there on the biker's helmet was the tell-tale streak of green.

Jayne was hovering. She seemed uncertain as to what to do. 'Don't let anyone touch that,' I said. The bike was lying on its side about 30 or 40 yards away, a big gleaming red and white thing shimmering in the bright sunlight. To one side of it was the car I'd seen swerve out into the road a few moments earlier. A Nissan Micra. 'In fact, why don't you go and take the keys out of it.' I knew I had to keep her busy.

I looked down at the man on the ground. Just a glance told me he was in a very, very bad way. His eyes were slightly open but his face was purple. Worse than that, there was blood seeping out from under his helmet, not a bright red but a darker, frightening shade soaking into the white silk scarf around his neck and spreading, visibly, as I stood there. He was dead. I knew it, and

I knew there was nothing I could do for him. I felt that familiar helplessness, but at the same time I knew that everyone on the scene, seeing my uniform, expected me to do something. But there was no getting away from the fact that he'd gone. From where the bike was lying he must have been thrown 30 yards and more. The impact with the flower-tub had probably broken the poor guy's neck. His head was pressed right down against his left shoulder, and his legs were twisted and limp.

'Oh God.' It was a young woman, hurrying away from me dragging a young girl with her. Couldn't have been more than four years old. The girl kept looking back, but the woman kept tugging at her arm. A man was standing over me. He was wearing a T-shirt and jeans, his dark glasses pushed back on his shaved head. 'The wife and I were sat right there,' he said, pointing to a table where the woman had put the child on a seat with her back to us and was picking up bits of broken china off the ground. 'We just heard a bang, and there he was . . . just . . . shooting across the forecourt and . . .' He shook his head. 'Hell of a crack. He was heading straight for our table till he . . .' He looked at the planter and tailed off.

'Right, well . . . I'll be asking for witnesses when I've got the situation under control, my friend.'

He glanced at his wife and the kid, then towards the road where one or two people who'd pulled over were getting out of their cars, standing there on the verge in the warm sun with their doors open not knowing whether to come forward or hang back, some of them already jabbering into their mobile phones as one or two drivers tried to edge their way past. The man was saying something about not going anywhere in a hurry, but I was looking at the bystanders, wondering whether anyone would dare start taking pictures with their phones. You get that these days. Next thing it's on the Internet.

I looked for Jayne. I hoped she'd be up to this. To be honest, I was glad I had her to watch out for. That fact is I hate dead bodies. Don't get me wrong – nobody likes them; most people find them upsetting, but me, I cannot abide them. They simply rattle me. I know I'll never get used to them. It's always a shock, for everyone. For me there's that added element of terror – this is what I'll be one day. Dead. I could feel my body react. My heart was thumping, my mouth was dry. But this is where you're glad of all your training. What you have to do is go into procedural mode. Let your training and your experience take over for you. Training school . . . mnemonics . . . accident . . . COW. That's the one. C for Casualties, O for Obstruction, W for Witnesses. So the first thing is to remember is that this is a Casualty, and that means first aid. So even if you know the guy's dead you need to check the vital signs – and let the public see you do it. I knelt down, unzipped the front of the man's jacket. He only had a T-shirt on underneath it. I pressed my ear to his chest. Nothing. I pulled off one of his red leather gloves, tugged back the sleeve on his limp wrist and felt for a pulse. Christ, that's the bit I really hate – the flesh still warm, even though the living part has gone. Nothing.

Jayne was standing there looking at the body. I couldn't read her expression. I was braced for anything – I've seen them collapse in tears; I've seen them go nauseous; I've seen them grin stupidly – and I can't blame them for any of it. None of us knows till we are faced with it how we'll react, then or after-wards. I've seen a lot of dead bodies, and I remember them all. It's that first sight that sticks with you. Someone once said to me that you lock them all in a box in your head. That makes sense, because whenever I see another one the old ones are all there, staring at me.

'What do you want me to do?' Jayne had her notebook in one hand, a pen in the other. I doubted that she really meant to write anything in it. But I remember doing that myself, more than once. If your hands are full there's less chance you'll be asked to touch the body.

I stood up. 'Right, first off we need to stop the traffic, both ways. You stay there with the . . .' I wanted to say 'body' but I stopped myself in time. 'Stop with the patient,' I said. You have to be so careful. People were coming out from the cafe, from their stationary cars, and sort of milling around, listening to everything we said. 'Take names and addresses of any witnesses, and tell them to stick around. We'll be requiring statements.'

I hurried back to the car. There were a few daft pillocks still trying to drive around the stationary traffic. Clever buggers. What people don't realize is that there's a lot of evidence at the scene of an accident – glass fragments, skid marks, scuff marks on kerbstones, that kind of thing. The accident investigators need to have all of those things preserved so that they can recreate what happened, measure it all up, and work out the probable speeds involved, and so on. Someone has died, and it may be someone's fault – just like a murder.

'Whoa!' I shouted as a man in a BMW tried to do a three-point turn. 'There's been a serious accident, mate. I'm going to have to stop the job right here.'

'But I'm meeting a train in York. I'm late already. I'll go back and cut across through Stockton on Forest.'

'I'm sorry, sir, but I can't let you go. This side's blocked as you can see and I need the other side clear to let the emergency services through.'

I left him banging his hands on the steering wheel in frustration, got into the car and swung it right across the westbound lane with the blue lights flashing. The thing is, as soon as you know there's been a fatality – or if you suspect there might be one – an accident scene is treated just like a crime scene. Keep everything as it is, hang on to any witnesses, take statements as soon as possible, and give priority to any casualty. The motorbike would have to stay precisely where it was. I radioed in for back-up and was assured that a traffic patrol would be with me in 10 or 15 minutes. Then I went to the back of the car and pulled a blanket out from under my wellies. As I did so I heard the ambulance racing up behind me. I had to get in the car and ease it back to let him through.

Back outside the cafe there were still people sitting at the tables. Some of them had been eating and drinking when the accident happened and looked pretty shaken up. Some were toying with their food. One or two were crying. Others had drifted inside or were sitting on their cars, anything to get away from the figure lying on the tarmac. The paramedics were kneeling over the victim doing the ECG test. It was obvious they'd get nothing on their screen but the flat line, and as soon as they were done I covered the guy over with the blanket. I felt the weight ease from my shoulders then. I hate it when there's some poor soul lying there and you just know that one or two of the bystanders are curious enough to come and have a look. Can't say I blame them. It's natural enough I suppose, but at the same time it's undignified. Get him covered up, I say.

Jayne had been busy with her notebook. People were blurting out their stories uninvited, pointing to the little Nissan which had collided with the motorbike. It was still out in the middle of the road, straddling the white line, the driver sitting inside. A young girl, 20, maybe 22. 'Come on, Jayne,' I said, 'let's have a word.' As we approached her, the girl wound her window down. Her face was streaked with tears. 'I was just coming to work. I work here. On the till. I never saw him.' She opened her mouth to say something else, but she was shaking uncontrollably and all I got was her teeth chattering.

'Listen, love, are you hurt?'

'No.'

'Quite sure now?'

'Yeah, I'm sure.'

'Right, well why don't you let my colleague and me take you across to the cafe and get you a cup of tea.' I opened the door and she stepped out. She was very slightly built, and seemed terribly young. Jayne had to put an arm round her to keep her steady. 'I was just turning in,' she said, shivering and drawing a thin jacket around her. 'Got into the middle like you're supposed to – indicate, wait for a gap – you know.'

'I'm sure you did,' I heard Jayne say. I looked at the pair of them. Like a couple of kids. The girl had probably only been driving a year or two, and now this. 'And there was this horrible bang. Then I saw him like . . . just . . . flying.' But she couldn't go on.

'And you'd just come from home, had you?' Jayne asked.

'Aye. For the afternoon shift. I work on the till.'

'And have you had anything alcoholic to drink before you set off?'

She looked surprised. 'No, course not. Didn't get up while 11.'

'No, well, I didn't think so, but I have to ask you . . . and I shall have to ask you to take a breath test. Are you okay to do that?'

In some way the routine questions seem . . . what's the word . . . banal? But they do help. Gives an accident victim some-thing to concentrate on. Gives us something practical to do while we're waiting – in this case for the ambulance crew to finish, then the traffic police to sort the road out. As to the lass herself, I think she might have gone to pieces if she hadn't had to go through the motions. As it was, by the time Jayne had got a few details off her she'd had a cup of tea and was a little bit calmer. She even wanted to check her car over, see what the damage amounted to. I left her with Jayne and went to where a knot of people were standing by the table nearest to the flower-tub. 'I'm telling you,' someone was saying, 'he shot by like a bat out of hell. I were doing 50 like, and he come by me as if I were bloody parked on t'roadside.'

Before I could get started on statements the traffic lads

showed up. 'You've got a queue backed up ten miles already,' they told me.

'That's not surprising,' I said, 'day like today.' And so we set to, organizing diversions. Again, something practical – keep yourself busy, no time to brood. It's not too bad re-routing traffic off the Scarborough road, but you still have to rustle up a car to police each junction where you're diverting people. Still, there are enough back-ways through the villages and it wasn't long before we had things moving, albeit slowly. Gradually, that side of things would calm down – and when it did there would be what I call the eerie part, when you're there on what is normally a busy main road, you and the various teams going about their business, and the wrecked vehicles and the victim – and nothing's moving; no familiar roar of traffic, no cars flashing by, and it's all quiet. You hear fragments of conversation, the crunching of boots on gravel, radio chat, even birdsong.

The thing with an incident like this is you can't rush things. A lot of people have jobs to do, thoroughly, and they will all take their time. After about half an hour the Accident Invest-igation Unit showed up from Tadcaster and set to with their tape measures and chalk marks, reconstructing the whole incident. It was no wonder the young lass in the Nissan hadn't seen him – by the AIU chaps' reckoning he'd hit her and been catapulted 30 feet through the air before making contact with the concrete plant container. As they filled me in on this, the undertaker showed up. This is what people don't realize about an accident scene. They really think you cart the casualties away and everything goes back to normal, but it isn't like that. There are a lot of procedures to go through, and as I said, I'm often glad of that. Less time to brood on what you've seen. Amongst other things the accident investigators ran a back-ground check on the deceased biker. He was a York lad, well known around the area as a bit of a tearaway. Married with a family, but still addicted to speed. Somebody would have the unpleasant task of knocking on his door and telling the next of kin. But that wouldn't be us, thank goodness; it was a job for the York police.

Somebody brought me a glass of water and I was standing there drinking it when the undertaker beckoned to me. He wanted to show me something I'd missed. Under the biker's blood-soaked scarf, on the back of his helmet in really small print, was written 'If The Police Are Reading This, I'm Probably Dead.' I wondered what kind of man would write that, but I didn't say anything. I could feel myself getting weary – things like this take a lot out of you, and the procedures have a way of dragging on. By the time we finally realized we were just about there, that we'd cleared up all the loose ends, sent the witnesses on their way and removed the diversion signs, it was 5 p.m. 'How you feeling?' I asked Jayne as I rolled the blanket up so that the blood stain was on the inside, and stowed it in the back of the car. 'Shattered,' she said, 'and starving.'

'Me too. Funny how it never hits you till you stop. When did you last eat?'

'Now you're asking. Bowl of cereal at six, I suppose . . . oh, and I had a Twix bar when we were with them gypsies.'

'Well,' I said, 'we're in luck. The duty sergeant's just called to say he's sent out for fish and chips.'

•   •   •

I was surprised at that. It's not a thing North Yorkshire Police usually think of, in my experience. It's more a Met thing – down there it's seen as a way of having an informal de-briefing. It's encouraged because what doesn't get said right after an incident like that will probably never get said. The details get buried by the next case, and the one after that. Some of the lads on the scene there would be straight off to attend to other emergencies. If they had anything to get off their chest this would be their only chance.

And so we sat there, eight, ten, twelve of us all told, scoffing out of paper wrappers and drinking cans of Coke in the late afternoon sun. Out on the road it was all back to normal, people were driving to and fro and getting angry with each other for going too fast, too slow, or just for being on their bit of road. On the cafe forecourt people were sitting at the tables and ordering meals, quite unaware of what had happened a few short hours before.

'He had a family,' I said.

'Who's that?'

'The biker.'

'Oh aye?'

'Two kids. Living with their Mum.'

'Well, at least it was quick for him.'

'Aye, if you've got to go . . .'

'Sod that. I wanna die in my bed.'

'From what I hear of your love-life there's every chance you will.'

'Very droll, Pannett.'

'I dunno so much. Nice sunny spring day. Riding your bike. It could be worse.'

'Aye, he wouldn't have felt much, would he?'

I glanced at Jayne. She was peeling the batter off what remained of her fried cod. 'That your first?' I asked.

'First what?'

'First dead body.'

'Yes, it was.'

'Well, at least you didn't have to handle it.'

'No.'

Young Jayne and I hardly spoke as we drove back to the station. There was no atmosphere, nothing like that. I think it was just that everything had been said that needed to be said.

67

And the adrenalin was wearing off. So long as you're on the job, at the scene, you can keep going, even if you are hungry or tired. But once it's over, you slump. And in a way you welcome it, because if your shift isn't over, you may well get called to another job – which is all the more likely when everyone's been called out to a fatal like that. Sometimes they're stacked up and waiting for you. And even if your shift's up you know you'll have people asking questions back at the station. So at least you've had your quiet spell on the way back, and at least you don't go charging into the next situation with adrenalin surging through your body.

I don't think the accident was mentioned again, just our Inspector walking past us as we were leaving the building. 'That was a bad fatal out at Sand Hutton,' he said.

And before I could open my mouth Jayne said, 'Yeah, bleeding horrible.' Then she turned to me. 'Cheers, Mike,' she said. 'And thanks.'

· Five ·

'Enjoy a bit of liver, do you?'

It was the vicious-looking knife in his right hand that would have caught your eye. Then, as he pushed his cap back, there was his blood-soaked left hand wiping a dark red smear across his forehead.

'Just killed her this morning.' He gave a dark, toothless grin. 'Still warm, she is.'

'Walter,' I said, kicking off my wellies, 'I've had nowt but a bowl of Weetabix and me head's still aching from last night. Now, are you going to invite me in or have I to go elsewhere for a cup of tea?'

'She was a beauty, mate. Nice and plump. I cut a bit of haunch off for you.'

'Aye go on then. But first off—'

'What is it?'

'Pop your teeth in, will you? You'd frighten the dead. And get that kettle on.'

• • •

I first met Walter shortly after I was appointed Rural Community Beat Officer. Quite a title that, and a bit of a mouthful, but it was music to my ears. When I first opened the letter I practised saying it aloud. It took me two or three goes to get it right. But it was worth it. To my mind it had class. Even the

69

paper it was written on felt somehow superior. It was slightly stiff, and you could see the watermark without holding it up to the light. It was a bit like a new red £50 note, or a cheque. I would've framed it if I'd had a place to hang it, but I was still flitting from one place to another at this stage and most of my things were in boxes. But this cheered me up. After all those years in the Met, I'd not only worked my ticket back to North Yorkshire but landed the sort of posting I used to lie awake at night dreaming about.

My new job amounted to a licence to embrace a rural community made up of 30 odd villages, countless farmhouses and cottages, not to mention a country estate or two, all of them sprawled out across a huge area which encompassed parts of the Vale of York and the Wolds. This was where I'd grown up. I'd fished, walked, cycled, picnicked, gone scrumping, even done my courting in these woods and fields and streams. Then I'd left home and gone off on my travels. Now, all these years later, I'd come back to Malton – getting this job really felt like coming home.

When I sat down and thought about it, though, I realized I needed a strategy. I may have grown up in the area, but I'd been away so long I might as well be a stranger. I needed to make myself known around my new patch without making myself a nuisance. And believe me, any newcomer who starts putting himself about in the North Riding and asking questions will soon enough make enemies. I needed to make haste slowly, as the old saying goes, and I needed to recruit one or two willing helpers as soon as I could. Eyes and ears, because working a rural beat, every bit as much as patrolling the mean streets of Battersea, you're only as good as the information you can gather. Don't set too much store by all those films about sharp-witted detectives working on clues, analysing forensic evidence and coming up with great leaps of deductive imagination. It's a lot of nonsense. Good detection starts with good local knowledge.

And if you want to get your hands on reliable information you have to work at your relationships.

So, I asked myself as I spread out my Ordnance Survey maps and feasted my eyes on my new kingdom, how was I going to cultivate contacts in these parts? Everyone I'd known as a kid had either left the area or departed this life. As it would turn out, I may have been in alien territory as regards knowing people, but I would soon find out that the locals knew plenty about me. It didn't take me long to realize I could drive for miles and not see a soul, yet the minute I pulled in at a village shop they knew exactly where I'd been half an hour ago, how long I'd stopped there, could even tell me which route I'd taken to get to where I was. As often as not they had their answer ready before I'd asked the flaming question.

In the end, I didn't need to try too hard – not in Walter's case, at least. Walter, it turned out, had been waiting for me to call. He was anxious to get to know me. He'd lived in that same house on the edge of the Wolds all his life and he felt he ought to know everybody within his field of vision – which was quite extensive, because if you looked out across his field you could see several hundred square miles. More with a following wind, as he liked to say. In fact, I would later find out that if I ever mentioned some chap I'd been talking to in an isolated farm cottage up an unmade road, someone who hadn't been that long in the neighbourhood, he'd fret and fuss and shove that old cap to the back of his head and furrow his brow until he could work out who it was, who he paid his rent to, who his Dad might be and who he used to be married to. The way Walter felt about his bit of country – well, you might say it was proprietorial. There was I thinking it was my patch. The truth was it was his.

It was a late spring morning, maybe half past eight. I'd been in the new job a matter of a week or two. I'd left Malton, driven up past the gallops and was making my way through the Birdsall estate, pondering my strategy. To tell the truth, I didn't quite know what I was doing those first few weeks. I had to rely on there being a few enquiries to follow up, calls to make. Something to give a bit of a framework to the day. But some mornings I simply had to go out and make things happen, as it were. It would get easier as I got to know the patch, and I'd made a start with calling in at village shops, post offices and the like. I'd arranged meetings with community groups, youth leaders, vicars, primary school head-teachers. I'd made contact with the district nurses, the postmen – people who get out and about and see things. I'd even started to find out who the estate game-keepers were. But there was no question about it: I was still feeling my way.

That morning a report had come in – in fact, a number of reports. Sheds had been broken into, lawnmowers had gone missing: rotovators, that kind of thing. It had happened over at Leavening, Thixendale and one or two other places. All in one night. It's the sort of caper the thieves will get up to in springtime. With the grass suddenly growing like crazy, there's a ready market for a cheap mower or strimmer; hedge-cutters too. The question in my mind was where to start. In fact, I was weighing up the options when I almost ran smack into the Middleton hounds, out exercising. Forty odd eager-looking dogs with their tails all erect, being promenaded past the Hall with a whipper-in at either end. What I could do with, I thought, as I swerved by them and waved an apologetic hand to the men on bikes in their long brown coats, was a nice tea-stop. There isn't much that draws us Yorkshire folk together and gets us chatting better than a cup of tea. Unless it's a nice pint of bitter, of course.

I'd got to the crossroads at the top of the hill, under the tall stand of beech trees there. They face west, and take the brunt of the wind that sweeps in across the valley and up the Brow. Their leaves had just come out, and it was a glorious sight.

There's nothing quite like beech-leaves in the spring: they're a lovely pale green and the sun shines right through them, delicate as tissue, not at all like they are later in the year, leathery and tough. If you can't spare a few moments to take in a sight like that once in a while, well, what's the point? That's what I say.

Anyway, I parked up for a minute and had a think. If I turned left I could drop down into Thixendale. It's a right pretty run, and there was a lady there who ran a little cafe just past the post office. She could natter like a good 'un. And there was the post office itself, of course, but once you got talking to her, you never got away. She knew everything and everybody. And if she didn't she'd send you to someone who did. Lovely lass, and she told a good tale, but she would wander off the subject. Of course, they were all good at chatting down there. Had to be – the hills that enclose the valley are so steep they couldn't receive TV until cable arrived. There were more than one or two disgruntled newcomers who'd paid big money for a house down there only to find their kids in uproar because they couldn't get *Neighbours*.

Nope, I decided, I'd leave Thix for later on and drop down into Leavening, although first I just had to take a minute or two to survey one of the grandest views in all of North Yorkshire. All across the Vale of Pickering the fields were bursting with life: the wheat was an almost iridescent green in the sunshine, the yellow rape was in full bloom, and there was a barley field just starting to take on that feathery look as it comes into flower. I love the way the wind ripples across its surface pushing it this way and that as it turns from pale green to silver and back. When I was a kid I used to I imagine I'd got a giant hand and could stroke it, as if it were a huge green fur coat. Way over the other side the moors were sharply outlined against a clear blue sky. Above me one or two ragged bits of cloud came scudding in on a brisk westerly breeze. I realized it was a while since I'd been out that way. Maybe this weekend if it stayed fair we could do a nice hike up in Rosedale or somewhere.

Well, I said to myself, this won't do, and I slipped her into gear and headed down the hill.

I was vaguely aware of Walter. His house stood alone on the road to the village, and I'd already seen him once or twice as I passed by, always busy with something, and always wearing his black boots, brown corduroy trousers tucked into his socks, a green body-warmer and a crumpled flat hat. Perhaps it was because I almost felt I knew him that I slowed down when I spotted him out the front that morning. The postman had just driven off and he sort of hesitated, glancing in my direction. As he caught my eye he lifted the wrought-iron gate half of its hinges, shoved it forward and stepped outside.

'Now then,' I said, braking and winding down the window. 'Grand morning.'

'Aye,' he said, 'what's left of it.'

That could've been that. He could just as well have waved goodbye and gone back indoors, but he didn't. And I could've said something like, 'Oh well, can't stop here all day nattering,' but I didn't. Next thing, and I swear I don't know how it happened, I was in through his gate, and helping him shift a pile of logs into his lean-to. I say I helped him – what I mean is, he stood there and watched me do it. I believe he did mention something about his back playing up.

'That's right good of you,' he said as I slotted the last load into the little shed. 'Come in and clean yourself up.' Inside his kitchen he passed me a towel. 'Here you are. I'll put kettle on. Nowt spoiling out there, is there?'

I scrubbed my hands at the hot tap while he filled the kettle at the cold. 'Course, t'other lad used to call by regular and help me out,' he said as I dried my hands and hung the towel back on the rail of an antique Rayburn.

'What other lad?'

'T'other . . .' he took a deep breath, 't'other Rural Community Beat Officer. That's what they call you, in't it?'

'It is. If you can get your tongue round it.'

He sat me down at an old-fashioned scrubbed table and set a china plate and a mug in front of me. 'You make yourself at home, young fellow-me-lad,' he said, as he fetched a packet of biscuits from a wooden cupboard set in the alcove beside the stove, then twisted the kettle on the hot-plate. 'You have to watch there's no coal dust under it,' he explained. 'Else it teks an age to boil.'

It still took long enough, and while we waited he showed me round the place – well, downstairs at least. He showed me into his sitting-room. It was low ceilinged and dark. There was a hearth with the remnants of a log fire in it, a couple of old easy chairs piled with embroidered cushions, a dark wooden bureau, lid down, papers strewn all over it, and right there under the window was a cock pheasant in a glass case. 'Me Grandad shot that, back in about 1910. Grandmother said she were sick of plucking game birds, so the old feller had it stuffed. Now then,' he went on, taking a picture down from the wall, 'here's a photograph of the house, taken about the same time, I reckon.' You could tell it was the same place, even though the two ladies standing outside it carried parasols and wore long Edwardian dresses with shoulder-of-mutton sleeves. 'Course, we hadn't built the extension out the back, but see the gate?' The gate was the same one he'd opened to let me through. 'Mind, it hung a bit straighter back then.'

He took me back into the kitchen. This was clearly the hub of his operations. With the old range ticking away in the corner – 'I keep her going all year,' he told me – it was nice and snug. 'Course, this used to be the outside wall,' he said, placing his calloused hand on the rough stonework above the table. 'And this,' he stamped on the stone slab floor with his black work-boots, and I noticed for the first time his laces: one red, one blue, 'this were all outbuildings. That corner, that's where we used to keep the pig. Took nigh on ten years for t'smell to disappear after we built on.' He pointed up at the low ceiling and the bowed wooden beams. 'And when we'd dealt wi' him we'd hang the hams from those hooks up yonder.' Reaching up, I felt the steel tips. Heck, they were sharp.

'What's that?' I asked. Tucked away in the corner I'd spotted what looked like a little old blackboard, the sort a child would have.

'It belonged my Dad. Must be 80 year old, that. No, mek it 90, 'cos I'm coming up 70 and he had it when he were a lad.'

'Sort of an heirloom, is it?'

'Aye, I reckon it is, now that you mention it, but I still have a use for it.'

'Oh? What's that?'

He dragged it out from its corner. 'It's me bulletin board. Any dodgy-looking characters going by I jot down their numbers, see? Used to save 'em for your predecessor.'

'I see.' He'd actually got some numbers on the board, but he didn't seem to want to show me. 'So whose are those?'

Even as I asked he was rubbing one of them out with his sleeve and giving an embarrassed little laugh.

'Shouldn't I be asking?'

'Aye well, it'll be common knowledge by now, I should reckon. I were out the front there, early morning, and I saw this car go by in a bit of a hurry. This were last week, mind. Didn't recognize it. Anyway, next morning, same car shot by me again.'

'How early was this you're talking about?'

'Ooh, four, maybe half past.'

'You always get up that early?'

'Always been an early riser, 'specially in summertime. Up wi' the sun. There's a lot goes on that folk don't see, that time of day.'

'Well, are you going to tell me about it?' I motioned towards the blackboard.

'Why, it were a bit of scandal really. My mate who works in the pub tipped me the wink. It were one of the lasses in the village, her fancy man scooting off home before her hubby got back off night shift in town. I thought it had been maybe a burglar scouting around.'

'And what's the other number?'

'That? Now then. That was just night before last. That's what I wanted to talk to you about. A blue Transit. Not from round here. Hull plates, I reckon. AKH. Clapped out old thing. Came coughing and spluttering up the hill about two o'clock time, burning oil. Didn't half smell.'

'Hang about, you said you get up at fourish . . .'

'Aye, I do. But that night I were up late.' He looked at the floor, and I could've sworn he blushed. 'Seeing someone home, you know.'

There are times when you're better off saying nothing.

'Anyway, it were in a hell of a hurry. Three lads squashed in the cab, and a whatsit hanging out the back door.'

'A whatsit?'

'Aye, a length of flex, like.'

'Cable?'

'Aye, that's it.'

'Couldn't have been off a Flymo, could it?'

'Why, do you know, it could have. Orange it were. Aye, that'd be it.'

I think we recovered 22 mowers and half a dozen other bits and pieces thanks to Walter writing down that number. I passed it on to Humberside Police and they got back to me within the day. The van belonged to a gang they'd been after for quite a while. They were so grateful they even volunteered to bring the stuff over. Well, they probably fancied an afternoon out in the country, and who could blame them, weather like that?

• • •

So that was how I met Walter. From that day on he was my main tea-stop, as well as being one of my most useful sources of information. He was also my main supplier of game birds and fresh meat – which explains what he was doing that autumn morning with an offensive weapon in his hand and all covered with blood.

'Here,' he said, when I'd got inside and put the kettle on. And he thrust a newspaper parcel into my hand. It was about the size of a decent chicken and it wobbled alarmingly.

'What's this?'

'Liver – off that deer I shot this morning.'

'I don't need the whole blooming thing, Walt. This'll keep me going all week.'

He ignored me. 'Is there owt else you want? My freezer's bung full of stuff. Rabbits, pheasants, pigeons. There's only myself to feed.'

'And the odd lady friend, perhaps?'

'Aye well . . .'

'No road-kill this time?'

Walter chuckled. He was glad I'd steered the conversation away from his personal life.

'Aye, road-kill,' he said. We'd sat there talking one time about all the various things he'd eaten in his life and he'd confessed to scraping the odd animal off the road. 'Why, so long as it isn't mangled and you fetch it in quick.'

He'd eaten hedgehogs in his younger days, he told me, and squirrels, crow too. 'Nowt wrong with a crow pie,' he said. 'My mother said you haven't to be particular when there's a family to feed. Do you know, she reckoned that old song, "Four and twenty blackbirds baked in a pie", she reckoned that were crows. You wouldn't make much of a pie out of blackbirds, would you now?'

He'd eaten some very strange things. 'Course,' he said, 'you wouldn't do it these days, but when I were a lad we'd eat whatever we could get. And one time my Dad brought home these badger cubs . . . well, he called 'em hams. Tender and succulent they were. Made smashing gravy.'

As the months went by I started to get to know Walter. To look at him, in his work-boots and flat cap, his blackened fingernails, you'd think nothing of him. He could be just another retired farm worker poking about in his garden, reminiscing to anyone who'd listen about the old days when they worked the land with horses. But I was to find out there was a lot more to him than that. Not only was he to become a crucial part of my intelligence network, he was to become a friend, a confidant and a support in times of trouble – because there was going to be plenty of that.

· Six ·

I like night shifts. I'm one of those lucky people who can kip anywhere, any time. So coming home at seven o'clock on a summer's morning with the sun blazing and the birds all shouting at the top of their voices has never stopped me from collapsing into bed and getting a solid eight hours' beauty sleep – which, they'll tell you at the station, is good news for them, as well as for the public at large.

You look forward to certain things on a night shift. Midweek there's often a lull in the early hours, and if you're around the station you can catch up on a bit of paperwork without being interrupted by the to-ing and fro-ing of fellow officers, or calls from your general public about kids playing football up against their side wall, dogs fouling the footpaths or old ladies losing their purses, as well as all the other minor problems they'll ring up about in the daytime. When the phone goes at night it tends to be something a bit more exciting – or should I say serious. The other big plus on nights is that the bosses tend to work the day shift, so they aren't getting in your hair. As for patrolling, I look forward to being out and about in the small hours. Three in the morning when it's all quiet I have real sense of everyone being tucked up in bed with just me out there to protect them. I like that. It gives me a sense of purpose, of being some sort of guardian of the community – because to be honest that's what I feel about my job, and my patch, that they're my people and it's my duty to look after them.

If you're lucky enough to be out in the country at night you see some spectacular sights. I've sat in my car and watched hares boxing in a moonlit field at Scagglethorpe. I've seen a mother deer with twin youngsters stepping watchfully out of the woods at dawn up above Rosedale. I've seen foxes creeping around rabbit warrens at North Grimston as the sun comes up, waiting for something plump and furry to emerge. I've seen many an eclipse of the moon; I've seen meteor showers, watched the Hale-Bopp comet track across the sky in 1999, and I once thought I'd seen a UFO – except that I don't believe in all that. I was over Staxton way – it must have been a military aircraft, although it wasn't like any I'd ever seen.

The eeriest sight, though, was one night in early autumn when I was over at Lastingham, near Hutton-le-Hole, right in the shadow of the moors. There's a fabulous old church there with a crypt that dates back to Saxon times, and someone thought they'd seen a stranger prowling about in the cemetery in the dark. I went to investigate, poked around amongst the gravestones, but couldn't see anything. I walked around the village to see if anyone was out and about. Not a soul. Still, I thought it was probably worth sticking around for a bit, just in case. I sat in the car up there by the graveyard and poured myself a cup of coffee from the flask. It was a clear, cold night with no moon, so the stars were all out, and in between the black outlines of the yew trees the Milky Way was clearly visible as a great swath across the sky from north to south. I was sitting there thinking about the mysteries of the universe and how far it stretched, where it ended, and if it did end what was beyond it – you know how it is when you get started on that train of thought – when I noticed a strange glow in the sky. My first thought was that it was just the lights of Teesside, but of course you only see that when there's a layer of cloud to reflect it. So maybe the pale red veil I was looking at might be some sort of film on my windscreen. But what?

I opened the door and stepped out. The only sound was the chomping of a few sheep working their way along the edge of the neighbouring field. And there it was again, a great wash of scarlet, shifting slightly and seeming to flicker on and off as if there were a faulty connection up there in the sky. I looked around at the outlines of the gravestones, some of them dating back two or three hundred years, some covered in ivy, some leaning wearily, all of them suddenly looking quite ghostly. Maybe I was seeing things, but when I looked up at the sky again, there was this same strange glow, shifting slightly and looking more and more like a translucent drape of some sort. That's when it dawned on me – the Northern Lights. Nowhere near as spectacular as you'd see in the Arctic Circle, of course, but a breath-taking sight all the same. And even as I realized what it was, it started to fade. Within minutes it had gone.

It occurred to me that the inhabitants of the cemetery would have been much more familiar with such a sight, and would have seen things that are hardly ever revealed to us, living as we do in towns and surrounded by artificial lighting. The thought made me all the more grateful to have been there that night. Privileged, you might say. Put it down as another perk of the job.

• • •

You need nights like that. They're the counter-balance to some of the really ugly aspects of modern life you have to deal with when it gets towards the weekend. Because on a Friday and Saturday the night shift often kicks off with a bang. I don't know how it was in the good old days that we hear so much about – because I'm sure people got falling-over drunk then just as they do now – but I can't believe there was so much random violence 30 or 40 years ago. It doesn't always happen, but it's always a possibility, and you have to be prepared. Sometimes a police presence defuses a situation before it gets out of hand; other times just being there seems to aggravate it. You've no way of predicting how it'll work out, but my approach tends to be softly, softly – perhaps because I'm confident that if it does get rough I'll be able to handle myself.

It was a Friday, late June as I recall, and I'd been running around like the proverbial blue-arsed fly. I was double-manned, which you would normally appreciate on a weekend, but in this instance my side-kick was Jayne. Having said that, I appreciate having her with me when we're required to get stuck in. I mean, if there's a crowd and one or two trouble-makers need to be collared, she's always up for it – and very effective, I have to say. She frightens people. I'm no shrinking violet when it comes to physical confrontation either. I always enjoyed a scrap as a kid, and in the Met they'd taught us boxing, as well as self-defence. So when we had to sort out the under-age drinkers in Malton – young girls mostly, very mouthy and backed up by some extremely aggressive young men – we sorted the job out with the minimum of fuss. From there we went across to Kirkbymoorside where the fight outside the takeaway had already died a natural death and we were able to take 20 minutes to have some grub ourselves.

Sitting there looking at a place like Kirkby with its neat rows of stone houses, half of them occupied by artists and writers and retired social workers who've moved out there to be close to the moors, you could easily convince yourself that it's all very cosy and civilized. And so it probably is until the lads get a skinful of beer.

From Kirkby we had to go across to Pickering to sort out a domestic, from there to an off-licence where a burglar alarm had gone off. The problem wasn't so much the alarm as the bloke who lived next door. He had his ladder out and was standing there in his dressing-gown wielding a lump hammer.

'I'll sort the bugger out,' he said; and to tell the truth, I had every sympathy. Just standing there for 15 minutes while we got the key holder out to it had me tearing my hair out. Those alarms never let up, and you have to fight the impulse to rip them off the wall. No wonder matey with the hammer was all but foaming at the mouth. Jayne wanted to have the guy in cuffs, but I told her to relieve him of his hammer and agree with him that it was a bloody nuisance and we were on his side. He'd calm down soon enough; and so he did. Mind you, it would've made life a lot easier if he'd got the job done and gone back to bed before we ever got called out.

So, by the time we arrived back at the station at about four, all I wanted was to sit with a cup of tea, get the paperwork out of the way and slink off home. Then Jayne picked up the phone – and I knew straight away from her tone that there was going to be no peace for us that night.

'And where's this exactly?'

She looked at me and frowned.

'What are they, in the water?'

More furrows on her brow.

'How many of them?'

I could see her scribbling on her pad.

'And you're quite sure they 'aven't got the owner's consent?'

Oh, great. I drained my cup and got up from my seat.

'We'll be right over.'

I already had my hat in my hand. 'Go on, Jayne, tell us the tale,' I said as I opened the office door and let her through.

'More bleeding drunks.'

'As if we haven't had enough of them tonight, eh?'

'Taken a boat out on the river.'

'Oh shit. Whereabouts?'

'Kirkham.'

'Bloody hell, they don't want to be anywhere near that weir.'

We were in the car and I was imagining what we might find when we got to the river. I've had some bad goings-on over the years, pulling bodies out of the water. 'You any good at swimming?' I asked. ''Cos I've got a doctor's note.'

'You're kidding.'

'You're right. I'm kidding. But you do realize it's always down to the probationer to get wet? It's a North Yorkshire tradition.'

'Listen, if they get in the river they can bleeding well get themselves out.'

'Now then, Jayne.'

'Yeah yeah yeah, but if I have one more pisshead breathing in my face tonight . . . I tell you, it's enough to put you off your beer for good.'

It was broad daylight already, and the sky was clear. It wouldn't be long before the sun came up, and when it did it was going to be a beautiful day – and I was going to be sleeping right through it. It didn't take us long to make our way out on to the A64, and barely five minutes to get to Kirkham where we dropped down the steep, narrow lane that takes you across the railway and into one of the prettiest scenes in North Yorkshire. The river is spanned by a beautiful old stone bridge as it broadens out and curves gently past the ruins of the abbey, which are pretty much as Henry VIII's merry men left them in 1530-something before they moved on to demolish Rievaulx and Byland and Fountains and all the rest of them. And we talk about vandalism as if it's something new.

'There they are!' Jayne was out of the car, over the stile and running across the pasture to the water's edge. As I followed her I saw the boat, just emerging from under the bridge.

There were four of them. Two lasses in frocks sitting down, two lads in black suits, white shirts and bow-ties, standing up – just. It was a rowing-boat, and they had hold of the oars okay, but they were using them as poles, punting their way slowly downstream. As the one at the rear end shoved on his oar, the boat tilted up and sent his mate at the front end staggering backwards till he all but fell in.

'I'm gonna bleeding well have this lot.' Jayne was pacing up and down by the nettles that lined the bank.

'Well, let's get them ashore first,' I said.

'They still ain't bleeding seen us.' She put two fingers to her mouth and let out a piercing whistle. That got their attention okay. The girls looked up, mouths open, pointing, and the lads tried to steer the boat away from us, towards the weir and wobbling more than ever.

'Now then!' I shouted. 'Go steady or you'll be in. And stay away from that weir.'

If you've ever seen the weir at Kirkham you'll know how dangerous it is. The water's nice and still until you're right upon it. If you were rowing towards it you'd hardly know it was there. Then it just falls away – 30 or 40 feet at a steep angle, with a nice tangle of willows and broken limbs at the bottom.

'Come on lads,' I shouted, 'let's have her in, nice and steady.' At last they seemed to get the message, and came zigzagging towards us.

They soon got the boat to within a few feet of the bank, where it stuck on the muddy bottom.

'Right,' I said. 'Now you lads are going to have to escort these young ladies to shore. Where've you been anyway, all dressed up like that?'

'We've been to the graduation ball, officer.'

'Oh yeah?' Jayne said. 'And where was that, then?'

'York. We're from York Uni.'

'Yeah? What you studying? Marine law? Common sense?'

'Jayne . . .' I said, 'Let's get 'em ashore first.'

The first lad had the right idea. He just stood up in the middle of the boat, and jumped across the water, making a soft landing on the grass.

'Right now, you want to be next,' I said as one of the girls kicked off her shoes and stood up. 'This young man here'll catch you, and if he doesn't he'll have me to answer too. Tell him how much that dress cost and he'll be ever so careful, I promise you.'

'Come on then.' The lad was leaning forward and reaching out with his hand. The boat tilted, she toppled forward, but just as it looked as though she was gone he grabbed her and she half jumped, half fell on to the grass. Then her mate jumped, leaving just the one lad on board.

'Right,' I said, 'let's have the ladies' shoes, and then give us the rope. We don't want the boat floating off downstream, do we?' He lobbed the shoes on to the grass, then threw me the line. So far so good, but then he decided to take off from the edge of the boat, and rested one foot on the gunwale. As soon as he transferred his weight the thing tilted like crazy and he was in. He landed on his feet okay in the shallow water, but promptly sat down.

'Hire suit, is it?' I said. I was trying hard not to laugh.

'Yeah . . . and the sh—shoes too.'

'Well, at least you're all in one piece. Come on, let's have you.' I reached out and gave him a hand.

'So,' Jayne started, opening her notebook and clicking her pen, 'taking a conveyance without the owner's consent.'

'It was only a bit of fun,' one of the girls said.

'Not for the owner of the boat it wasn't.'

'And not for your parents if you'd got swept down the weir, young lady. You can go down it in one piece and you think you've made it. Then the under-current at the bottom drags you under. And am I right in thinking you've been drinking?'

'Not since we left town.'

'Which was when?'

'About one o'clock.'

'And how did you get out here anyway? Who was driving?'

'No one. We took a taxi.'

'Yeah, right,' Jayne said, looking around to see if there were any cars in the parking spots by the ruins.

'No, we did.'

'What, you stopped a taxi and said we wanna go boating so take us out to Kirkham? I don't think so.'

'It was my idea.' The lad in the wet clothes stepped forward. 'I'd been out here on a f—field trip. I remembered I'd seen a b—boat up there.' He was pointing to the stretch above the bridge where two or three cottages had gardens that ran right down to the water's edge. 'I'm sorry, officer. It's just . . . you know, we've been together three years and this is our f—farewell do.'

'Well,' Jayne said, 'looks like you've landed yourselves in big trouble.'

'Jayne,' I said. I motioned to her and we walked a few yards away towards the stile. 'Look,' I said, 'they're decent enough kids. They seem sorry for what they've done. And where's the harm, apart from getting their fancy clothes wet and muddy?'

'Yeah, but they've broken the law, Mike. They're gonna have to come in for this.'

'The question is, is it in the public interest to arrest them? Is it in our interest? I mean . . .' I looked at my watch. 'Five o'clock, near enough. I dunno about you, but I'd rather wrap it up with a verbal warning and get home. And I'll tell you another thing. What's our custody sergeant going to say when we dump this on him at six o'clock? Y'know, one way or another, nobody's going to gain a lot if we do press charges.'

She got it in the end. I think she was seeing this as a couple of bonus points in her personal criminal conviction record. For me, that isn't what policing's about. God help us if we ever start chasing targets instead of employing a bit of common sense. Four young kids go to a graduation ball, get a bit pissed, have a lark in a boat – and end up with a criminal record? No. This way they'd think twice another time – and walk away with a notion that the police aren't as bad as they're made out to be. That's what I call a result.

'Right, you four. Whose parents are nearest?'

'Er . . . m—mine, I think. They're only at Stockton on Forest.'

'Jayne, fetch the lad a blanket out of the car, will you? Can't have him freezing to death. Okay then,' I said, 'I'll tell you what we're going to do. I'm not happy leaving you to find your own way home. You're still probably under the influence and these country roads aren't safe, especially at this time of day when people are haring off to work. Call your folks and tell 'em to come and get you.'

'Thanks, officer. We're really sorry, honestly we are.'

'I believe you.'

'W—what about the boat?'

'Don't worry about that.'

Of course, I could've made one of the lads row it back and tie it up, but in their state, they could easily come to grief. No, I couldn't risk that. I pulled the boat as close as I could get it to the bank and handed Jayne the rope. 'Hold this while I get in.'

'Where you off to?'

'I'm going to return the conveyance to its rightful owner.' I'm not that keen on swimming, but I am on rowing. Have been ever since I saw the calibre of the women at York Rowing Club and took out a membership.

So there I was as the sun came over the hill and illuminated the tops of the ruined abbey, rowing across the mirror-smooth water, my only companions a couple of swans who circled me curiously. Up at the bridge I eased both oars out of the water and let the boat drift towards the little wooden landing that projected into the river. As I made ready to tie it up I could hear Jayne talking to the students, doubtless telling them all the nasty things that might have happened if Nice Cop hadn't stopped Nasty Cop from putting the boot in. A few minutes later

I was back over the bridge and the lad from Stockton's mother was arriving. Seeing her convinced me we'd come to the right conclusion. She was a decent woman, suitably alarmed at what her son had been up to, and terribly grateful that we'd let them off. 'Not that you're out of the woods yet,' she said to him as she spread a dust-sheet over the seats of her nice new Rover and ushered them inside. 'Your father'll be wanting words with you when you get in.'

•   •   •

We drove back the scenic way, through Langton and over the hill, dropping down towards Norton as the first string of horses were being led out to the gallops. Jayne was pretty quiet until, just as we crossed the railway and made our way into Malton, she said, 'Yeah, I can see where you're coming from.'

'How's that, Jayne?'

'About not coming the heavy hand with those people. I s'pose a verbal warning ought to be enough.'

'Well yes, that's how I see it. I mean, think of them in a few years' time, young professionals, maybe with families. They're the sort of folk we're looking to support us, and when people start slagging us off they'll be able to think back and say yeah, they treated us okay. After all,' I added, 'we do police the country by consent.'

· Seven ·

I used to be a bit of a raver myself. We're going back a while, of course. And we're talking about innocent pleasures like singing along to 'Come On Eileen' down the pub, or belting out a couple of Madness numbers after a few beers on a night out in York. But I did get to see The Police at Wembley – which made me laugh when I showed up there in uniform ten years later for a nice bit of overtime and a grandstand view of the Rugby League Cup Final: Wigan against Leeds, 1994. Memories – they're better than the reality sometimes. One thing I never got into – I was already too old when it came along in the late 1980s – was the rave scene. We all heard about the raves, legal and illegal, that were taking place around the country but it all sounded a bit remote for us lads in North Yorkshire. For one thing, I never had any interest in drugs – and they seemed to be an intrinsic part of that scene; for another, I was starting to get serious about my life around that time, applying to the Metropolitan Police and so on. As for staying up all night, chilling out on a Sunday and going back to a nine-to-five job Monday morning, well, I don't think my body could have stood it even at that age. Besides, the nine-to-five routine was never for me. Perhaps that's one reason why being a copper appealed so much.

Still, you can't avoid things forever, and eventually the rave culture penetrated the rural backwaters of Ryedale. We'd heard about events taking place out at Whitby, which we could understand because it has a bit of a reputation as a music centre, mostly folk, of course, and it's a place where a lot of people move to pursue an alternative lifestyle. But when we heard of one at Escrick – well, that had us baffled. Escrick is just another little commuter village on the southern edge of York, the last place you'd expect to be targeted. But maybe that was what made it a perfect venue, the element of surprise being the organizers' main weapon. What they wanted was to get in, set the gig up, collect the money off the punters and hope that they could give them several hours of loud entertainment before the law got their act together.

It came as no real surprise, then, when our Intelligence Unit announced that they had picked up a whisper – mostly by spending long hours drinking beer in dodgy pubs and claiming it on their expenses – that a rave was due to be held somewhere in Ryedale. And then the whispers were backed up with flyers that were being distributed around the places where young-sters – and the Intelligence Unit – liked to hang out. Malton was mentioned. Hard on the heels of the rumours came the 'Hard Word' from the Almighty – I mean the Chief Constable of North Yorkshire, one of the most fearsome women I'd ever come across. And the Hard Word was that any attempts to organize raves in our part of the county would be resisted. Any raves that got off the ground would be shut down. Any attempt to trespass on private property in order to accommodate such raves would result in prosecutions. As far as She was concerned, there would be no more raves in North Yorkshire. Ever. Had We Got That?

We had, and of course we were, in theory, on Her side. We were against raves for a number of reasons, number one being the nuisance factor. These gigs were likely to generate huge amounts of noise, thus upsetting the locals, whose taxes went to providing a police force – us – whose job was to protect them from such disturbances. They took place through the night, which aggravated the nuisance value; we were told that they

94

often involved mass drunkenness, and the people who attended them were likely to be consuming controlled substances. Well, I knew all this from my time in the Met. I just never expected to encounter the problem in rural North Yorkshire.

The problem up to now had been that we never knew about the raves until they actually got started. This time, it seemed, we had a bit of warning. However – and isn't it amazing the way there always seems to be a 'however' when a cunning plan is being hatched? – it was midweek, Wednesday, possibly even Thursday as I recall, before Intelligence finally penetrated the organizers' website. The good news was that they'd found out where the rave would take place – well, sort of. 'It looks like the woods off the A64, near Sand Hutton,' they told us.

'But there are woods all over the place down there.'

'Ah, but these are right near the MAFF place.'

I didn't like the sound of that at all. The MAFF – the old Ministry of Agriculture, Fisheries and Food – has an important research institute out that way, and the idea of a horde of ravers gathering outside its fences posed a few security issues. I liked it even less when we were told that the gig would take place on the Saturday night. 'But that's York races. John Smith Cup Day,' I said as we sat there in the Super's office with our notepads. 'Hell fire, there's 30,000 race-goers making a bee-line for the city centre, half of them pissed up already. How are they going to spare any men to help us out if we have any trouble?'

'I'll have words,' said the Super. And then he looked at me. 'And you, Mike, had better get your thinking cap on. You'll be the senior PC on duty, and as our Rural Officer this is one for you.'

'Thanks, Super,' I said.

'You will of course show me that my trust in you is not misplaced.'

'Of course, sir.'

• • •

Fair play to the Super, though, he acted quickly and showed that his pronouncements weren't just idle words or posturing. He issued a Prohibition Notice under Sections 63 and 66 of the Criminal Justice and Public Order Act of 1994. And that, for the uninitiated, gave his officers powers to stop large gatherings in certain circumstances, and powers to arrest people attending the same. So much for the theory. In practical terms it was the combined might of the rave organizers and a cast of hundreds against me and Ed, who had the misfortune to be on duty with me, plus whatever back-up we could get from the lads in two cars patrolling Malton town centre. I nudged Ed with my elbow. 'Bloody hell,' I whispered, 'we're going to be stretched,' and Ed covered his face with his clipboard. 'Stretched?' he said. 'Why, by the end of the night you'll know how Bernard Manning's underpant elastic feels.'

On reflection, there was of course our gallant band of Specials to call on. They're volunteers. They receive no pay and have limited training, but they're always willing to turn out and, as they see it, support the community. Good lads and lasses, thoroughly reliable, and at the last count we had a grand total of half a dozen of them in Ryedale. Nah – the ravers didn't stand a chance.

We now had to come up with a strategy, a nice easy-to-follow plan which could be mapped out on a Briefing Sheet and distributed to all concerned. I'd done a few of those, and I always followed what we call the I-IMAC template: I for Information received – in this case that a rave was planned on our patch; another I for our Intention – which was to prevent it happening; M for Method – the big issue, of course: just how were we going to prevent it? A for Admin (well, I was in charge so that was that sorted); and C for Communication, which included such details as issuing radios to any Specials we brought in.

Question one, then, was how did I intend to prevent this thing from taking place? I think the public often imagine that when the police are faced with a problem like this they immediately switch into paramilitary mode and call up the Riot Police with batons and shields and CS gas canisters and horses and all that carry-on. No – it ain't like that. We're talking about much more basic policing here. Far from manoeuvring little plastic figures across a chessboard at Strategic HQ and mapping out a field campaign as if I were some general on manoeuvres, I found myself walking around the edge of the woods one sunny morning, making a general survey of the scene. Back to the basics, in other words.

The first thing I noticed was that the woods, although fenced, were open to anyone to enter. By which I mean that the two vehicular access points, although gated, weren't locked. I walked up one of the tracks and could immediately see the appeal of the place as an unauthorized outdoor venue. It was a mixed woodland, oak and birch predominantly, and quite dense along its borders. But a couple of hundred yards in I came across a delightful clearing where the ground was carpeted with a lush growth of grass. There was even a stack of cut wood, nicely seasoned. Perfect for a barbecue. Alone, surrounded by greenery, with the early summer sun shining in, the noise of the main road no more than a distant murmur, it was wonderfully peaceful. There was plenty of room to park a few cars and accommodate a crowd. Further into the wood I found another clearing, and another. Whoever had come up with this place must have been very pleased with their researches. It got me thinking about the raves I'd had to deal with in the Met, out in Surrey and Kent where thousands of youngsters, many of them drunk and spoiling for a fight, would take over an old warehouse. Those affairs really did need every resource we had, including the Riot Police. Many's the time I've faced a hail of bottles, bricks and lumps of concrete as we tried to close them down. But here, in a sylvan setting like this – well, I have to admit I found myself imagining a summer's night, a nice cold beer, a few mates and some music, far enough from the nearest village so as not to be disturbed . . . Yes, I have to say, I found the idea quite appealing.

However, the Chief Constable had spoken, and, on reflection, she was right. Next day I was back at the woods with a guy from the Forestry Commission, pinning notices to the boundary fence and the gate-posts – 'Any unauthorized person entering these woods is liable to be prosecuted,' that kind of thing. The Forestry man had expressed legitimate concerns of his own. First of all there was the fire risk, which was huge. 'Bad enough with ordinary hikers when they light up a cigarette,' he said, 'but you put alcohol or drugs into the mix and people are going to get very careless. First thing they'll want is to start a fire, then they'll be tearing limbs off the trees . . . No, we can't have it.' He was also concerned about the impact on wildlife, which I had to admit I hadn't considered. 'Well, think about it,' he said. 'There's the basic disturbance to their habitat. Half of them rely on coming out at night to forage for their food. And how are they going to react to amplified music? It'll panic them. Some of them will have young to look after. No, Mike, you don't want owt like that going off in here. It isn't the place for it, not at all.' And he was right, of course. So we padlocked the gates and pinned some more of my notices on tree-trunks where they couldn't be missed. At least no one was going to tell me they hadn't been warned.

I felt we'd made a start there in the woods, but back at base, when I reviewed the manpower situation, my heart sank. We could stretch to one car per entrance: me and Ed in our trusty Puddle-Hopper, the Daihatsu Four-Track – also known as the Bouncy Castle thanks to its over-enthusiastic suspension – and a couple of our Specials in a Peugeot.

We'd been assured that if things got exciting we could whistle up a van-load of coppers from York, but I have to say that that assurance filled me with no confidence whatsoever. As I said to Ed, 'Number one, it's a pound to a pinch of you-know-what they'll be scrapping on the streets. Number two, if they do get the all-clear to come out they'll get lost as soon as they cross the bloody ring-road.'

'You're right, mate. They're as much use as a chocolate fire-guard. I reckon we're on our own here – us and the Specials.'

It was a daunting prospect. But I like a challenge, so what was I complaining about? And, as Ed said, we had our Specials – hand-picked. We had Keith Nicholson: a country lad; solid and reliable and never afraid to get stuck in. I don't mean he was violent or that way inclined – just that when there was trouble you knew you could count on him. He never flinched at wading in, grabbing the ring-leaders and hauling them into the van. The other lad, Will Macdonald, had been a Special Constable for 20 years. He felled trees and burned charcoal up above Howsham and such places, and knew all the woods around our patch. He'd come out with me when we were looking for poachers. I've followed him through the densest woodland at dead of night, not a clue where I was going, and he'd lead me right to our destination – and out again. He was strong as an ox, hands like shovels – which, he liked to say, were just what he needed, the way I kept dumping him in the mire. And the great thing about Will was how calm he was under pressure. Which in itself wasn't surprising for a man who once fell 50 feet out of a tree, and broke just about every bone in his body. He told me he'd woken up in hospital in Middlesbrough just as they were putting him through an MRI scanner. 'I opened my eyes and thought, shit, they've marked me down as dead and now the buggers are cremating me. I tried to shout but I couldn't get me mouth open. They'd wired me jaw up.' It took them two years to get him patched up and fully operative, whereupon he was straight back up a tree with his chainsaw, right as ninepence.

So, not a bad team. Trouble was, we hadn't a clue what the opposition were likely to be.

The night of the supposed rave we came to work early and held a final briefing in Malton. Really, we all knew what was required. We'd all had copies of the Briefing Sheet, so this was more of a last-minute re-cap over a cup of coffee and a round of chocolate biscuits before we set off to see what they would throw at us.

It was getting on for midnight when we turned off the A64 into a dark, apparently empty landscape. It was a warm night and the sky was cloudy, tinged orange by the lights of York, just six or seven miles along the road. There was no wind. Down at the woods my notices were still in place, as were the padlocks. 'Well, that's a good start,' I said, as Ed checked that the Specials had their radios set to the correct channel. If things went to plan we'd only be 200 yards apart in our respective gateways – Ed and Keith in one car, me and Will in the other – and we'd maintain contact on the 'back-to-back' channel, talking directly, with the main channel off. The less general chat we picked up, the better. And so we went to our posts and sat. And sat. And sat.

I think we had one car pass us, a courting couple doubtless looking for a quiet spot for a bit of canoodling. They probably found it too, because by the time they cruised past us in the opposite direction a full hour had elapsed. 'Well, this is no good,' I said to Will, looking at my watch. 'One o'clock. Let's have a word with Ed.' Will handed me the radio. 'What the hell d'you think's going on?' I asked.

'You've got me, bud. Maybe they saw your notices and panicked. Oh no, it's Mike Pannett. Give the punters their money back and get the hell out of town.'

'You could be right, matey. I mean, I have a reputation around here, remember?'

'Aye, Dirty Harry. Anyway, I'll call Control, see what they've got.'

Control had got a complaint – from a resident at Harton. They'd seen a lot of car lights heading past and wondered what was going off. I told Ed to stay put while Will and I investigated. The woods in question were barely a mile or so away. But we'd hardly gone 400 yards when there was another alert. A load of cars down at Bosendale Woods. Maybe, at last, something was about to kick off.

'These cars, Ed – they parked up or travelling?'

'Sort of cruising around, they reckon.'

As soon as we approached the woods we could see what they meant. A car was passing the junction up ahead, making for Howsham, by the look of it. Then another, followed by a third. And as far as we could see, they all had three or four occupants. We crept forward, lights out, crawling along the verge towards the junction as another car approached, driving slowly, the driver hunched forward over the wheel.

'Let's just do a couple of vehicle checks, see where they're coming from.'

Will read out the number plates as they passed and I checked them out on the computer.

'Leeds . . . Bradford . . . Huddersfield . . . Leeds . . .'

'Well, that accounts for them cruising about like this. The buggers haven't a clue where they are.'

'They're playing follow my leader, I reckon.'

'Aye, and using their mobiles. Maybe we should take a wander round.'

It was well past one. If the organizers had got a site in mind they'd surely have it up and running by now. We drove down towards the river at Howsham Bridge. Nothing to be seen. Then I switched off the engine and opened my window. To say the noise was loud would be a laughable understatement. To say it was earth-shattering – well, you could put that down as a bit of mild exaggeration. I could swear I felt the ground shake as I stepped out. The epicentre seemed to be in the woods. As I rested my hand on the open door I felt it vibrating, rhythmically.

'Bloody hell, Will! What in God's name have they got out there?

'You what?'

'I said— oh, never mind . . .'

I got back in the car, wound the windows up and got on the radio. Christ, the racket was going to drive us both nuts. We were surely going to need help, and the sooner the better. Maybe our Duty Inspector had some extra reserves he hadn't told us about.

I soon had that hope dashed. 'We're in the middle of a right old dust-up here, Mike. Day-trippers from York versus locals, Scarborough town centre. And they've thrown the rule-book out the window. Total bloody mayhem. You'll just have to crack on as best you can. But remember what the Chief Constable said: on no account are they to be allowed to get away with this. Got that?'

'Absolutely, sir. Leave it to me.'

I shut the radio off, got out of the car and tapped Will on the shoulder. He was standing facing the woods and shaking his head in disbelief. 'Come on,' I shouted, pointing towards the wood, 'let's join the party.'

My eyes hadn't got used to the dark yet – not that that would have helped me. I had no idea where the entrance to these woods was. But Will knew – as well as the track that led into them. We drove carefully, slung this way and that by the lurching Puddle-Hopper, until we found the way blocked by a VW bus parked all askew.

We got out and walked, him in the lead, me following blind. My eyes still hadn't got used to the dark, and I kept stumbling over the roots and tufts of reedy grass. I hardly cared – all I wanted was to find the noise and put a stop to it. The funny thing about it, loud as it was, was that we couldn't make out any particular tune, just a wall of sound. Tunes, I thought, what are those? I couldn't even hear a regular rhythm, and the way I understood it that's half the point of these all-night jobs, to get hypnotized by the beat. As we stumbled deeper into the woods, though, the reason became clear. These people weren't amateurs: they had three separate sound systems cranking out three different lots of music – each one at a deafening pitch.

Will had led me towards a clearing. We couldn't see anyone yet, just coloured lights shining through the trees, flicking on and off to the pulse of the sounds. But by now the track we'd followed was lined with cars, dozens of them, all over the place. God knows how they thought they'd get out. The epicentre of the noise was still 50 or 100 yards away. I doubt we could've got a vehicle up there if we wanted.

I tapped Will on the shoulder and bellowed down his ear. 'I don't feel like going in with just the two of us.'

'Nor me. There could be a hundreds of the buggers.'

'Right, least we know where they are. We'll rendezvous with the others at Howsham Bridge.'

As we turned around I nudged Will and pointed to a pick-up truck with a generator in the back and a skein of cables that led to the sound systems. He made a sort of switching motion with his right hand. I shook my head. They'd have them back on in no time and what was the point in pissing people off?

Ten minutes later at the bridge, with Ed and Keith in attendance, I called Control. 'Get me the Late Senior, will you.' The Late Senior is the on-call Superintendent, the decision-maker, the guy who can okay your plan of action – and carry the can if you balls it up. 'Yep,' he said, when we finally got him, 'sounds like you'll need help. Let me get on to York and call you back.'

'He's going to see what York can do for us,' I said.

'And what do you think the answer's going to be?'

'Well, Keith, if I was a gambling man . . . Eh oop, here he is.' I pushed the radio to one ear and put my hand over the other.

The Super's reply didn't surprise me. 'Sorry, lads. They're up to their neck in it. Maybe in an hour or so when they've got things under control. Till then I reckon you're going to have to do the best you can.'

'Looks that way, doesn't it?'

'Yes, but don't be doing anything daft.'

'No. Course not.'

'Just remember what the Chief Constable said.'

'Right. No raves on our patch.'

'Correct.'

'Even if we've got a team of four and it's pitch black and they've got a cast of thousands.' – but I'd switched off by the time I said that bit.

'Right, lads.'

'Yeah?'

'Speaking as someone who can never resist a challenge, why don't we go and introduce ourselves to the organizers of this do?'

'Who's we?'

'Well, I think Will and I could go in. A nice, non-confrontational approach, and if things get nasty you two lads storm in and set about them.'

'We have every confidence in you, Pannett.'

'Aye, so has the Super. Have you any idea what it's like to carry that kind of responsibility?'

Ten minutes later we were once more within a stone's throw of the action. 'Ready, Will?'

'Ready as I'll ever be.'

I don't know what we really expected, but I knew what I feared – violence. An angry baying mob fuelled by alcohol and amphetamines. And there was no real defence against that. We walked forward into a blaze of orange and purple lights, instinctively flinching away from the giant speakers which seemed to bulge and teeter this way and that as the music blared out of them, trying to look as casual as we could as we entered the clearing, where people were standing in groups, drinking beer, smoking, shouting into each other's ears or just enjoying the sounds, eyes shut, hands in the air, swaying this way and that. Some were even dancing. The first thing I noticed was that these weren't the kind of young tearaways I'd encountered down south. Many were in their thirties; some were in their forties, perhaps even older. And they looked as if they were enjoying themselves. They seemed completely unfazed by our presence.

'Evening, officer.' I couldn't hear what the bespectacled, shaven-headed man was saying, but I could read his lips well enough as he nodded, smiled pleasantly and walked on by.

A young woman smiled at me and raised her hand in greeting. I dug Will in the ribs. 'They think they're legit,' I bellowed.

'Think they're what?'

'Legal. Authorized. They reckon this is a bona fide gig.'

'I think you're right.'

I tapped a young man on the shoulder. His eyes were closed, and he was frowning, swaying to the sound. I tapped him again. 'Who's in charge?' I shouted as he opened his eyes and turned to face me.

He shrugged, then pointed with his beer bottle at another lad who was bent down at one of the speakers, fiddling with the controls.

'You in charge?' I shouted, as he looked me up and down.

He nodded. 'Can you come out the way where we can hear each other speak?'

We walked back into the woods 50 yards or so. 'Listen,' I said, 'we're under orders to close you lot down. You're here without permission of the landowner, aren't you?'

'Well, yeah,' he said. 'I s'pose we are.'

'And do you realize that you stand to be prosecuted under Sections 63 and 66 of the Criminal Justice and Public Order Act of 1994?'

'Never heard of it.'

'But you'll take my word for it, right?'

'Do I have a choice?'

'Not really, sunshine.'

'So you're telling us we have to pack up?'

'I am. Course, I could decide to bring in my reinforcements and we could organize a search of the premises and all your customers; then we have the right to seize your gear. And the transport you've used to bring it in.'

He was getting the message, loud and clear. 'How long have I got?'

I looked at my watch. 'It's a quarter to two now. Let's say I'll be back here by half past, and I want it quiet, I want it packed away, and I want people to be on their way.'

'Guess I'd better crack on then,' he said.

'Yep. There's a lot of hard-working people around here trying to get a decent night's sleep.'

'I'll do my best.'

'Listen, matey, they look like a decent crowd of people in there, so don't drag 'em into trouble.'

We left the lad to it and went back to the car. Back at the bridge Ed wanted to know whether we needed reinforcements.

'No,' I said. 'Job's sorted.'

'You what?'

'Sorted. Ask Will here.'

''S right, Ed. Everything's under control.'

'The hell it is. What about all that racket?' The music was still blasting out at about 120 decibels.

'That?' I said. 'Oh, it's okay once you get used to it. You have to chill out, lad. Get into the sounds.' I looked at my watch. 'Tell you what, I'll have a little bet with you.'

106

'Go on then . . .'

'That by a quarter past two it'll be all quiet on the western front. In fact, let's drive up to the gate yonder and see that the revellers get safely on their way.'

We didn't have long to wait. By the time we got up there the music had stopped. The sudden silence was indescribably wonderful. Five more minutes and a bus appeared at the entrance, followed by another, and a third.

'Bloody hell, have they bussed 'em in?'

'Oh, these lads are organized, Keith. They're pros.'

Already people were emerging from among the trees on foot. They didn't look happy, but they didn't look threatening. They were a few raised fingers, a couple of muttered insults, but most of all a sort of mute acceptance.

'I feel like a bit a party-pooper,' I said.

'What d'you mean?'

'Well, what harm they doing?'

'Trespass. Probably drugs. Criminal damage, I dare say.'

'Steady on. They're decent-looking people. All they're doing is listening to music out in the open. You stage this in a village hall somewhere or in the Milton Rooms and what are you going to have at chucking-out time?'

'Fair point.'

I got on the radio to Control. 'Ten fifteen,' I said. 'Aye, we've put a stop to it. No, no trouble at all. Everyone's leaving nice and quiet. Listen matey, this is the A Team you're talking to. So tell your reinforcements to go and have a cup of tea and a sandwich. We've got the job sorted.'

●　　●　　●

And so we thought we had. The last of the buses departed, the straggling line of cars bumping their way out of the woods, and then . . . pedestrians. Hundreds of them, pouring out of the woods all along the lane and walking back towards the main road three and four abreast.

'Bloody hell, lads! We could have trouble here.'

Ed was right. We only wanted one daft sod flying home in his car at dead of night, coming round a blind corner into that lot. The last thing the locals would expect is a great snaking crocodile of ravers walking along a narrow lane in the dark.

I drove past the walkers with Will, shouting at them to keep to the verge. It didn't work. As soon as we'd gone by them they spilled back across the width of the road, worse than before.

'What about the other side?' Will shouted, pointing at the woods. 'What if they're coming out from over there too?'

'You're right, buddy.'

I swung the car around, took two left turns, and there on the other side . . . 'Shit! Look at that. It's worse than the first lot.'

They were all over the place – laughing, stumbling, arms around each other, some barefoot, some giving their mates piggy-backs.

'Right,' I said. 'Let's have a word with Control.'

'You won't get any back-up, Mike. You heard what they said.'

'We're not after a van-load of Yorkies this time,' I said. 'Hello. Ten fifteen. Listen, we've got a seriously dangerous situation here. There's hundreds – and I mean hundreds – of people leaving the woods. No, not just on that road. Some are heading to Howsham, some are making for Barton, and I wouldn't be surprised if there's some heading Kirkham way via Crambe. It's pandemonium, mate. Half of them are pissed. I should imagine they're on drugs too. No, no – no trouble, but there will be if we get some mad bugger driving home at 70 miles an hour . . . No, I know you can't spare any men. I don't want men. I want . . . Yeah, I'm hearing you, matey. I want . . . a helicopter.'

I learned when I was very young that if you don't ask you don't get. I'm not saying you always get what you ask for – but you may as well give yourself half a chance, I reckon. And this time it worked.

'Bloody hell, Mike!'

'What?'

'Well, you've got a bloody nerve, haven't you?'

'Listen, mate, we did this regular down south. Crowds like this, they'll obey orders from above.'

'You mean from the sky?'

'Aye, if you like.'

'Well, I got to hand it you. I'd never have thought of it.'

'But you would now,' I said.

'Where's it coming from, anyway?'

'Humberside.'

The helicopter did the trick. While we stationed ourselves along the roads and flagged down any cars heading towards the walkers, the 'copter lads got them into some sort of order with their lights, their loudspeakers – and, I have to say, their sheer presence. When you feel the down-draft of those blades on the back of your neck, and see those dazzling lights, and then they come blaring out their orders at you, you're more or less inclined to do as they say rather than stand and argue.

We got the lot away to their various cars and vans – and another wave of buses – with no trouble at all. By a little after three there was no more than the odd couple sat on the roadside with a can of beer as the dawn spread in from the east. It was at this point that two more buses showed up – crammed full of officers fresh from scrapping on the streets of York.

'Ee, you have to laugh,' Ed said as I went to meet them.

'Now then, lads.'

'Right, where d'you want us?'

'We don't.'

'You don't want us?'

''Fraid not.'

'But they told us there was hell on.'

'There was.'

'So what happened?'

'Me and my team here' – I pointed to Ed and Will and Keith, all sitting on the grass drinking from their flasks – 'we sorted the job. But thanks for showing up, anyway. Fancy a cup of coffee before you go?'

•　　•　　•

I thought we'd done a hell of a job that night. But did I get any praise? No, I got complaints. Who ordered the helicopter? Was it necessary? Did I realize how much it cost? I knew the answer to the first two questions. As to the third, no, I had no idea how much a helicopter cost, but I expected they were about to tell me – £2,500 was the answer. So could I have a full report, explaining why it was needed and what it achieved, on the Chief Constable's desk on Monday morning?

I thanked Keith and Will, sent them back to base in one car while Ed and I drove back in the other. I thought we'd done a good night's work. We'd sorted out a potentially inflammatory situation, handled massive crowds in difficult conditions – and learned that ravers weren't all drug-crazed nutters bent on destruction. Hopefully, we'd done our reputation a bit of good as well. 'You live and learn,' I said to Ed as we got out of the car and went to get changed. 'Well,' he said, 'some of us do.'

· **Eight** ·

Have you ever stood and watched – I mean, left the car and walked through the gateway and stood still on the field's very edge, and taken it all in – as a gentle breeze comes down and caresses a crop of barley, particularly at that time of year when it's beginning to lose its milky-green colour, just before it starts to ripen? When I see those bearded seed-heads sway and dance and send their ripples this way and that before the slightest breath of wind – why, I just want to reach out a giant hand and stroke it. Magic. I was once strolling along the edge of a field like that when I came across a young couple lying down between the rows. I slipped away as quietly as possible. I remember thinking to myself that they'd still be talking about it when they were old and grey.

To me, July is a precious time of year because you know that already, just a few weeks after the explosion of growth that comes with springtime, everything is slowing down and putting its energy into the ripening process. Within a couple of short weeks the velvety fields of wheat and barley turn a pale biscuit colour, and before you know it the harvesters are out and you hear everyone say, 'By heck, it soon comes around, doesn't it?'

I'd parked the car on the roadside and was standing beside just such a field, enjoying a quiet smoke, thinking about the seasons and the passage of time and how my old Grandad used to say they go faster and faster as you get older, and I was remembering how I never really understood him because to me, as a schoolboy, time seemed to drag – especially when the sun was blazing down and there we were, stuck inside, writing in our exercise books, wishing the clock would hurry on and get to our break time. I suppose we all do that – wish the time away, and then as we get older we find ourselves repeating just what the old folk used to say: it's all happening too fast.

But just for a moment that summer evening everything seemed calm and still, as if the clock had stopped. I think it's important to stand still sometimes, and just look at what's in front of you, and take it in. For me, that's the best way of storing up memories that you can look back on when things are difficult, or maybe when you get old and haven't the opportunity to be out experiencing new things. Away beyond the thorn hedge to the west, the sun was lowering itself inch by inch into a bed of puffy, pale grey clouds. Sunset would be a good hour yet, but behind me the avenue of lindens were bathed in the low light, their leaves a vibrant lime-green, their flowers a creamy white. And the air around them was filled with the humming of bees, busy collecting a last load of pollen before they called it a day. They always amaze me, bees, the way they work and work until the last bit of warmth or light has gone. I remembered how I once watched a bumble-bee in a window-box, just as it was getting dusk, die of exhaustion. Just gave up the ghost right there under the marigolds with its little pollen-sac bulging, but lacking the energy to take it home.

●　●　●

There aren't many better places to be than rural North Yorkshire on a summer's evening, and this particular one was about to get better. Not only was I paid to be out there in the Howardian Hills, admiring the view, thinking about this and that, but I stood every chance of being treated to a free concert

112

performance by way of a bonus. They started having open-air musical shows out at Castle Howard some years ago, and with the size of the crowds they attract they have to bring in a few police to monitor the traffic movements and make sure everyone gets in and out without too much fuss.

Mention classical music to most of my colleagues and you won't get much response. 'Boring,' was Jayne's only comment when I tried to tell her about what was now an annual event. As far as I knew, nobody else was that interested, so every year when it came around I cosied up to the sergeant responsible for working out the rotas. 'You can stick us down for the Proms if you like, mate.' I always tried to make it sound as casual as possible, as if I were doing him a favour – and to be honest there wasn't much competition, especially as I made sure I got my request in before he'd even looked at the month in question. 'Aye, go on then,' he'd reply. 'We'll see what we can do for you.'

I'd got myself stationed on one of the approaches, where the cars come up from York direction and then swing off the road into the various parking areas. Once everyone was safely in I'd be free for a couple of hours to take a stroll around the grounds. That was the plan, anyway. I'd been waiting some time before the traffic picked up to any great extent, but now there was a steady trickle of cars, people-carriers, mini-buses and coaches, all slowing down as they approached me, some of the drivers winding down their windows to ask, 'Are we right for the Proms?' as if it wasn't plain enough where they had to go. 'Aye, turn right up yonder and follow the cones.' Patience – I could write a book about it.

The sun had dipped behind the clouds now, and under the shadow of the trees the visibility wasn't so good. The branches of the tall lindens almost met above the road, and around each trunk there was a thicket of brush, so it soon started to get quite gloomy under the canopy of leaves. The cars were still only coming in dribs and drabs, and in the quieter moments I could see a couple of blackbirds darting about in the undergrowth. They always seem to be the last ones to get back to their nests, and they're often first up on a morning. I've often heard them chirping away near a street-light, well before sunrise. I'm always amazed at how they keep going with so little rest. As I was watching them I became aware of another little black creature moving about on the broad verge, but much more slowly. It was almost in the shadow of the squad car, and I couldn't quite make it out. After a while I knew I'd have to have a look, so I walked across to see what it was. Blow me if it wasn't a mole, parting the thick grass with his splayed-out paws and giving every indication of being lost. I say lost; what I mean is, it surely ought to have been underground, especially with night coming on. I wondered whether it had come to the surface and maybe got scared away by some bird of prey, because the only mole-hills I could see were way across the other side of the road, in a grass field.

The traffic was building up now, almost making a solid line. It was interesting to see the different types of people turning up. There were old couples and young ones in suits and dresses, families in casual clothes, even a bloke on a bike wearing khaki shorts and a bush hat, and just about all of them seemed to be equipped for a picnic – even a couple of pedestrians who must have come on the bus and got off at Whitwell on the Hill. As one of them reminded me, in the old days they could have got off at Castle Howard's own private station on the Scarborough line – still there, and now converted into a private dwelling.

Looking into the passing cars I could see cool-bags, hampers, ice-buckets, folding tables and chairs, crates of beer, baskets full of foil-wrapped food, fold-up barbecue sets, balloons, streamers, you name it. It made me laugh to hear what they were playing in their car music systems. There was far more pop than classical, and even a bit of rap. I couldn't see how that would put them in the mood for an evening of Mozart, Verdi and Elgar, but what the heck – there was a real party atmosphere, something most people wouldn't normally associate with a classical concert.

The flow was starting to build up now, and I was at it with the hand signals, urging the slow ones on a bit, answering questions about the length of the queue, the conditions in the parking areas, even the likelihood of it raining. I said to one of them, 'It used to be, "If you want to know the time ask a policeman"; now you expect a blinking weather forecast too!' They liked that. It was that kind of occasion; everyone in good spirits.

Through all the chat I was keeping half an eye on the verge. I was worried about my little friend there, wondering where he'd got to. I soon saw him, still blundering about through the rank grass and now even closer to the roadside. He may be blind, I thought, but he has a sense of direction. I reckon he's trying to get back home.

A few minutes later, with the traffic now building to a peak, and travelling at a snail's pace, I walked down the line of cars and stopped the job.

'What's up, officer? Have we had a mishap?'

'No,' I said, 'I have to escort a little gentleman in black across the road, if you'll just be patient for a moment.' And there was Mr Mole, bumbling along at the edge of the road, pausing every so often to put his snout up and sniff the air, then head down and nosing his way up the camber.

'Oh, look!' By now, one or two of the motorists had spotted him, and out came the cameras.

'Now then, don't be frightening him. He only wants to be across the road, so if you'll just be patient.'

By now of course the good old public had assumed that PC Plod, time-keeper and meteorologist extraordinaire, knew precisely what he was doing. He didn't. He hadn't the faintest idea, just a gut feeling that our mate belonged on the other side of the road and over towards those little dark mounds of freshly dug earth.

'Course, yon buggers are blind, y'know.' That was all I needed, a bloody wildlife expert in a Nissan Micra. Seventy years old, in the traditional flat hat, with his wife beside him backing him up. 'He's right, you know. Can't see a thing.'

'Aye,' I said, 'it's amazing how many people don't know that.'

'You can't get rid of 'em these days, mind. They've outlawed t'old methods.'

I could've kicked myself. Why hadn't I stopped the car after him, or the one before him? I was tempted to move him on, but Sod's Law says he would've run the poor creature over.

'We used to do 'em with arsenic, tha knows.' He was out of the car now, studying the mole's progress. ''Cos you don't want to be shooting 'em. Spoils the skins, y'know.'

As the cars behind me edged forward and opened up a gap in front of my resident expert, one or two more people had got out of their vehicles to get close-up shots of the mole. As he approached the middle of the road there was a chorus of 'oohs' and 'aahs'. I needed to catch hold of him, but how?

Mr Flat Hat was reading my thoughts. 'Tell, you what, mister. You catch hold of him. Then I can deal with 'im if you like.'

His wife chimed in from the car, 'He used to do a bit of game-keeping. For the Willoughbys out at Birdsall, y'know.'

'Aye, but I say – you'll 'ave to grab 'im. I aren't so quick on me feet nowadays, like. Used to catch no end of these buggers on t'old estate.'

'He did that,' the wife continued. 'And my old dad used to line the skins up to dry and Mam would sew 'em together, wouldn't she? That's what moleskin trousers are, d'you see?'

'Fascinating,' I said – and in other circumstances I might have prompted them to go on, because I was actually interested

116

in what they were saying. But right now I had a problem. The little fellow might be lacking in the eyesight department, but he was well aware of my presence. Soon as I approached him he shifted back a couple of feet, whereas I wanted him to keep going the way he was.

'He'll tek some catching, will yon bugger,' Mr Flat Hat said. Now that I'd had a good look at the little fellow I wasn't so sure that I wanted to catch him. If you've ever seen a mole close up you'll notice the size of his paws. They're made for tunnelling, and the claws at the end of them are strong, and sharp. There was only one thing for it. I took off my helmet, moved stealthily forward and dropped it smartly over the mole.

'There. Gotcha.'

'Aye, but now what you gonna do?'

I reminded myself that the law doesn't permit the wanton throttling of pensioners. It's a shame, because sometimes you think it'd be justifiable. But there you are. You're here to uphold the law, not to dole out summary justice. Anyway, I'd long ago learned that the best way to deal with a busy-body is to recruit him.

'Right,' I said, 'if you'll stand watch over him for me I'll go and get some more equipment.'

He liked that. He even adjusted his tie – which he wore outside his dark green v-necked pullover. 'You leave it to me, officer. He won't get far with me in charge.' As I walked to the car I could hear him address the gathering crowd on his game-keeping days on the Birdsall estate. 'Aye,' he was saying, 'them Willoughbys, they always treated us right. Goose every Christmas. Dropped it off at your door. You can say what you like about your aristocracy, but them lot were true gents.'

I pulled my clipboard off the front seat. That should do it. As I walked back I heard some smart-ass call out, 'Hey up, he's gonna interrogate the poor bugger now!' Nice one, I thought, but I kept a straight face. No point encouraging them. Not that

Mr Flat Hat needed any encouraging. 'You'll not kill him with that,' he said.

'I'm not aiming to kill him,' I said. 'I'm aiming to take him home. Now, thanks for your help. You've done a fantastic job. If you'll just step aside . . .'

I lifted the helmet a half inch or so, slid the clipboard underneath, and hey presto – one mole, trapped.

'Ooh, he's taken him into custody, do you see?'

'Won't be a moment, ladies and gents,' I said as I lifted the clipboard with one hand and placed the other over the helmet. Across the road I straddled the wooden fence, popped over the other side and walked towards the mole-hills. God knows what any passing farmer would have said, but what was I supposed to do? Sure, to a landowner a mole is a pest, digging great holes and tunnelling through his pasture; and believe me, if I found them tearing up my lawn I'd be round to Walt asking him how to do away with them, because he had some very effective methods; but there's something very vulnerable about a creature that's got away from its natural habitat. This thing – pest or not – looked harmless and frightened. Who wouldn't take pity on it? Who's to say he hadn't a family of young ones under one of those little hills? I dropped him out in the grass and he stood there, sniffing the air, then shambled off towards the mounds of bare earth.

Back on the road I was treated to a ripple of polite applause before Mr Flat Hat got back in his car and the back-log of traffic filtered into the car park.

●　　●　　●

Half an hour later they were all in, and I was patrolling the grounds of the great house ready to enjoy the evening's entertainment. This was one of those times when the phrase 'perks of the job' really does mean something. All the time I was in the Met, I never quite made it to a Cup Final, nor a Test Match. At least, not until I signed up for the TSG – we were on stand-by for any event that threatened trouble or wanted crowd control, and it was one of the best moves I ever made. Rugby matches at Twickenham, football derbies, even a couple of Wimbledon finals, believe it or not – although why they wanted riot police there I was never quite sure. Still, I wasn't complaining. But if I think back I have to say I've never been present at such a marvellous spectacle as that night at Castle Howard. To stand amongst the crowd, some of them in evening dress and drinking champagne out of long-stemmed glasses, others seated on canvas chairs drinking beer from cans, kids eating ice-creams or playing ball on the grass with the floodlit stone façade of one of England's greatest country houses as a backdrop, all reflected in the still waters of the lake – well, it simply took my breath away. I was spell-bound. Above us the stars started to appear in a clearing sky, and from the stage across the water came the exquisite tones of an operatic tenor belting out arias from *La Bohème* and *The Marriage of Figaro*. It sent a shiver right down my spine – although that was nothing to what I'd felt earlier as a flight of Second World War Spitfires swooped in from the west and roared over our heads. The crowd loved that, and when the orchestra broke into the *The Dam Busters* theme they climbed on to their chairs, spread their arms wide, and waved white scarves, Union Jack flags and paper napkins before bellowing for an encore. The climax of the evening, when darkness had fallen and the moon had come up, was a magnificent display of fireworks, with great bursts of red, white and blue stars exploding over the house as the orchestra cranked up the volume and gave us the *1812 Overture*. The crowd were in raptures. They loved every minute of it.

I felt good as I drove back to the station, some time after midnight. I was aware that it was a rare thing to experience genuine joy in pursuance of your duties, but that was how I'd sum that evening up – joyous. As far as I was aware, there hadn't been a single policing incident of note. Nobody had stepped out of line. It was one of those wonderfully well-tempered events where everyone was happy, nobody felt left out of it, and they all had the satisfaction of celebrating a few things of which we as a nation can be proud: our cultural heritage, our landscape and the ability of the various social groups to mix in good humour. It was one of those occasions when you felt really good about being a Brit.

· Nine ·

I was feeling well settled in my new patch. I was really starting to get to know the country – the highways and by-ways, the short-cuts beloved of Transit vans in the night, the little pull-ins up secluded lanes where you'd see a couple of cars parked up on a lunchtime, one empty, the other one with the tell-tale steamed-up windows.

I was loving it. People were starting to get to know who I was, and of course I now had what I called my 'regional HQs' set up around the county. I mean my tea-stops. In fact, I now had contacts calling me up in the middle of the shift, even when I was off duty. 'Mike, when are you going to pop by? Haven't seen you for a week or two. You haven't forgotten about us, have you? The wife's just been baking, and we thought of you.' If I'd taken up every offer I was getting I could have spent a couple of full days a week just supping tea and eating home-made cakes. Still, I wasn't complaining. My efforts to get to know the local farmers, game-keepers and the like were about to start paying dividends.

The thing that kicked it all off was when one of my new friends rang in early one morning to report an outlandish theft from right outside his own front door – well, let's say his front gate, which was about 100 yards away down his drive. I was getting ready to go out on patrol when Jayne took the call.

'Gawd, got a right one here,' she said, her hand barely covering the mouth-piece.

'Plenty of 'em about, lass,' I said. Jayne was still getting used to what we Yorkshire folk call 'characters' but she referred to as 'bleeding nutters'.

'Oh, 'ang about,' she said. 'It's you he wants.'

I took the phone from her. 'Hello,' I said, 'Mike Pannett speaking.'

'Ah, Mike.'

'Colonel Enderby,' I recognized the voice right away. 'How nice to hear from you.' I knew the Colonel through his game-keeper. The Enderbys, to put it crudely, were loaded. They had thousands of acres of Wold land to the south and east of Malton, all centred around their country estate near Rillington, and all of it tenanted. 'And how are you this fine morning?'

'Personally I'm in fine fettle, Mike, but I have to report that I've suffered a grievous personal loss.'

There was a pause. The Colonel had a bit of a reputation as a raconteur and he knew how to wind an audience up, even if he was reporting a crime.

'Oh, I'm sorry to hear that. Are we talking about lost live-stock, or goods and chattels?'

'I'm talking about me balls, old chap.'

'Your balls, you say?' I raised my voice quite deliberately, knowing that Jayne would be all ears. The Colonel wasn't the only one who liked to wind an audience up. 'That sounds . . . well, frightfully unpleasant.' I couldn't help it. I get chatting to a bloke like Colonel Enderby and I start imitating him. It's the language these toffs use – cracks me up.

'Well, it is,' he said. 'I mean how would you feel?'

'I'd find it very painful, Colonel. But perhaps you'd better explain exactly what the problem is with your . . . balls.' I flapped a hand at Jayne, trying to shut her up, but she couldn't control herself now. The poor lass was wiping the tears from her cheek and stuffing tissues into her mouth.

'Well, I woke up this morning and they'd gone.'

'You quite sure?'

'Positive, old bean.'

'No sign of 'em?'

'Nope. Disappeared. Vanished. Nothing left but a nasty dent in my drive . . . oh, and a cold chisel.'

'I see. And they used a cold chisel, you say. That's a bit savage.' I put my hand over the mouth-piece. 'For God's sake, Jayne, stop laughing will you?' Mind you, I was having a job keeping a straight face myself. Except that by now I knew very well what the old boy was on about.

The Colonel's house – well, it was a mansion really – lay at the end of a long, snaking drive which ran through an avenue of lindens planted by his grandfather about the time of the First World War. At the end of the driveway, just off the road that led into the village and overshadowed by a couple of venerable yews, was a pair of wrought-iron gates hung on two massive stone pillars all wrapped in ivy. And those pillars were topped with two stone spheres. Or rather they were until that morning. Whoever had shifted them must have had a job on, because they were big ones. Huge, in fact – bigger than a football, more like those medicine balls we used to have in PE when I was at school, but made out of solid millstone grit. Must've weighed half a ton apiece.

'Just let me get finished here in town,' I said, 'and I'll be on the job right away.'

'I bet you don't get many retired Colonels calling you in Peterborough,' I said to Jayne as I put the phone down. But she didn't answer. She was scuttling off to the washroom – to wipe the mascara off her cheeks.

• • •

I started getting my gear together. It can be a bit of a going-on, getting organized for a shift, but I always make a point of

123

travelling light. And this was a day turn, so I wouldn't need my Dragon light, for one thing. That still left me with quite a pile to get together – although nothing like you see some of these new recruits carting about. Makes me laugh sometimes when I watch them staggering across the car park, all kitted out in their body armour, stab-proof vest, their belt-pouches packed with rubber gloves, oxygen mask, ASP baton, plus a pile of paperwork. With a hold-all full of other bits and pieces they look less like Action Man, more like Michelin Man going on his holidays. And you wonder why the majority of British police are against carrying firearms. They'd have nowhere to put them, that's the fact of the matter. God knows how these younger PCs ever fit in the car – or how they bend in the middle when they try to sit down. Me, I couldn't be doing with it. Against the rules, yes, but my anti-stab vest stays on the back seat unless I'm sure I'm going into a potentially violent situation. Otherwise I manage with a few bare essentials. The pocket-book, a spare re-chargeable battery for the radio, the handcuffs, a can of CS gas, the good old trusty ASP. That's an import from the States, a sort of expanding metal night-stick. Light, and very effective; and when you're carrying it about, you collapse it like a telescope, barely six inches long. As the Yanks would say, you hit someone with that and they stay hit.

I also carry a briefcase with a few bits and pieces in it, but nowhere near as much as most of my colleagues. I'll carry a few statement forms, the latest crime reports and the like, plus a couple of blank tickets – although if ever I had to write one of them on the beat I make a special note of it in my diary. I think I've done that once in all my years in Ryedale. You can do a lot with a verbal warning – and save yourself a stack of paperwork. Finally, of course, there were my maps. I never went out without them.

'Jayne?' She was back from the ladies now. She'd re-arranged her face and was at her desk, tapping away at the keyboard.

'Yeah?'

'Seen my maps, have you?'

'Maps? I thought you'd know your patch backwards, the time you've been on the job.'

'Excuse me, there's 600 square miles of country out there.'

'Yeah, but you were brought up here. You're a local.'

'Listen, you go out there in the fog and try to find some bugger who's come off the road halfway across the moors and all he can tell you is there's a sort of a track going into a wood and he thinks he was heading south . . .'

'All right, all right. Don't stress.' She shuffled her seat back and pulled a drawer open. 'So they're really important, are they? That what you're saying?'

'I think that's what I'm trying to say, aye. If you listen carefully.'

'In that case then . . .' She reached into the drawer and pulled out my pile of red and yellow OS maps.

'What the hell were they doing there?'

'You left 'em on the counter yesterday when you went home.'

'Oh, cheers.'

'Don't I even get a smile?'

Women. Sometimes I can't fathom them. She'd been what my old grandmother used to call 'tart' with me the last week or two. Tart meaning acid, that is. And now here she was looking all coy as she handed the maps across the desk. I hate it when people try to make me smile to order. Mind you, if I'd fancied her it would've been different. But she wasn't my type.

'Cheers,' I said, baring my teeth.

'That's not a smile. That's a grimace.'

'Sorry, Jayne. I'll practise.'

I grabbed my flask and sandwiches and headed out the door with the maps shoved under my arm. I had four of what we used to call one-inch maps. I mean 1:50,000. They covered Ryedale.

Then there was a couple of the two-and-a-half-inch jobs for the North York Moors: 1:25,000. They give you a fantastic amount of detail: every contour, every little building, whether the fields are fenced or hedged – brilliant. The covers were beaten about a bit, but the maps themselves were laminated. What a wonderful idea that was, making them waterproof. Must've been a Yorkshireman.

In the car I checked the list I'd made in my notebook. I had a couple of calls to make in town before I went over to see the Colonel. Routine stuff, nothing to get excited about. There was a complaint about a dog that had been barking all night – nowhere to be seen now, of course, and probably sleeping it off. Then someone had called in to report a bunch of kids hanging about by the river after dark. Likewise disappeared, naturally, and only a collection of empty beer cans, a broken pint mug and a regurgitated chicken tikka masala to mark their progress. And then there was someone who claimed to have seen a monster cat on the prowl. As big as a lion, he said; well, maybe a cheetah. Anyway, it was big and black and it had knocked a dustbin over. And where was that? Right outside the pub. Which said it all, in my book. It wasn't the first time I'd heard about the 'Ryedale Panther', but I've always made a point of never letting those words escape my lips. No point encouraging people to come up with 'sightings'. Show me some tracks and an animal expert who can identify them and I might start believing. Or bring me a body. Until then I'll continue to report it as 'one cat, large, black, probably feral'.

When I finally got over to Westdale Hall the Colonel was at the gates, prodding at the moist black earth under the yews with his shooting-stick, his handle-bar moustache a vivid white against his ruddy face. His faithful bulldog, Winnie, was at his side.

'Ah, there you are,' he said. 'Was about to send out a search party.'

126

'Well, you know how it is, Colonel. Patrolling the mean streets of Norton and Malton.'

'Ah, quite so. Keeping you on your toes, are they?'

'No, I'm keeping them on their toes.'

'Splendid, splendid.' He raised his stick and rapped it on the top the gate-pillar where tentacles of loose ivy waved to and fro in the breeze. 'Well then, what d'you make of this? Been there over 100 years, y'know.'

'That may be the problem, Colonel.'

'Easy to dislodge, that what you mean?'

'I was thinking more of their antique value.'

'Don't make 'em like that anymore, I suppose?'

'Aye, and there's plenty of people about these days with lots of money and no scruples. If someone offers them a bit of antique masonry they aren't going to ask where it came from. You put the word out that you've got a pair of antique stone—' I didn't want to say it, and fortunately the Colonel let me off the hook.

'Orbs, m'boy. Orbs.'

'Aye, a pair of orbs that size . . . well, what would they fetch?'

'Hundreds of pounds.'

'And the rest of it,' I said.

He was prodding at the ground again. There was a neat circular depression in the earth. 'You can see where the blighters dropped them – and rolled them towards the getaway vehicle. There's one either side of the drive, see?'

'Nobody seen anything suspicious?'

'No, we've had hordes of people up and down. The post, the milk, the vicar. Gardener too – he didn't even notice they were missing. Too busy texting that woman of his, I shouldn't be surprised.'

We were still there, batting around a few ideas as to how the thieves might have manhandled the balls off the grass and into their vehicle when the Colonel's game-keeper arrived in his Land Rover.

'Morning, Nick.'

'Now then.'

'Bad show, this. Frightful.' The Colonel was tapping at the pillars with his stick.

'Why, it's to be expected,' Nick muttered, kicking the mud off his welly against the step of the vehicle.

'I don't know. It took me by surprise when I came out this morning, I can tell you,' said the Colonel.

'Bloody thieves.' Nick seemed to have a point to make. 'They have the upper hand, that's the trouble. There's things going missing all over the place. You ask around. Diesel, machinery, livestock, game birds, quad-bikes. My mate had all his Christmas poultry nabbed last year. And no bugger ever gets prosecuted.' He kicked at the step once more. He was clearly fed up.

'Listen,' I said, 'I've every sympathy. I'm as keen as you are to put a stop to it. But I'm working on my Jack Jones most of the time. Six hundred square miles of countryside takes some covering, let me tell you.'

'Reinforcements,' said the Colonel. That's what you need, old chap. Manpower.'

'Tell me about it,' I said. 'Or try telling the Chief Constable. Or the government.'

'You know, I'm sure if we asked for help you'd have plenty of volunteers. Dad's Army sort of set-up, don't you think?'

And that, in a nutshell, was how Country Watch came to be born. We may have drawn a blank with the Colonel's balls, but the old man had planted the seed of an idea in my head. What if I could get together a network of country people, farmers, landowners, game-keepers and the like, people who were out and about and knew what was going on, people who would keep their eyes and ears open, have some sort of hot-line to me, and agree to turn out on watch at night, on a rota basis?

128

We went into the house and batted the idea around over a cup of tea. We were sitting at the Colonel's enormous old kitchen table, under a beamed ceiling with Winnie sprawled out in front of a four-oven Aga, right under the watchful gaze of his namesake, whose portrait hung on the stone wall. The Colonel worshipped the old fellow – Winston Churchill, that is.

'Sounds a splendid idea,' he said. 'Tell you what, old chap, why not let me draw up a list of likely suspects and make a few calls, see if we can't arrange a meeting to chew it over?'

* * *

I like to think of Country Watch as my baby. But credit where it's due – it would never have got off the ground had it not been for the Colonel. I suspect that, like Winston when the nation turned to him in 1940, he'd been waiting all his life for a challenge like this. This was to be his finest hour, and once he spotted the opportunity he was at it like – well, like a bulldog. I agreed with him that it would be a good idea to meet up one evening and talk it over with whoever he could round up. I had in mind a handful of neighbours getting together over a quiet pint, and a lot of bluster about running the bad guys off their land. To be honest, I wasn't overflowing with confidence. Back at the station that afternoon when I mentioned to Ed that I was planning a meeting with a bunch of farmers who wanted to join the fight against crime he laughed out loud.

'Hell,' he said, 'I can just see 'em, all dressed up in smocks and carrying burning brands . . . storming the castle and looking for witches to kill.'

'I tell you what,' I said, 'if they do get the bit between their teeth, there'll be no stopping them. And there won't be any worries over equipment. Four-wheel drive, two-way radios, sat-nav . . . they've got the lot.'

'How about pitch-forks?'

I wasn't going to let on, but when I thought about it I was no more hopeful than he was. I fully expected a turn-out of three men and a dog when I made my way along the A64 towards West Heslerton one evening a week or two later. But when I got to the Dawnay Arms I had a job getting parked, there were that many vehicles, most of them four-wheel drives, splattered with mud up the back.

There must have been 40 of them in the pub. I had to fight my way to the bar. I knew some of them, but not all, not by any stretch of the imagination. The Colonel had certainly done a job, rousting them out. There were landowners, tenant farmers, game-keepers and one or two local business people. There was a retired pilot. The local hunt was represented, as were a couple of racehorse trainers. They'd all suffered from thefts from their yards and outbuildings. One or two had had their houses burgled. They were champing at the bit.

Sadly, there wasn't a pitch-fork in sight – although as I walked in the Colonel was brandishing his shooting-stick this way and that to make a point. 'Ah, there you are, Mike old boy!' he called across as he caught sight of me. 'Look at this. The grass roots response to crime!' I ducked as his shooting-stick swished past my head. 'The oppressed minority fight back, eh? Once more into the breach, dear friends!' I was half expecting him to twirl his moustache.

It was an impressive turn-out. More impressive was the willingness of all concerned to agree to what I suggested. 'What I'd like to organize,' I told them, after the Colonel had called them to order and introduced me, and after I'd explained that I was a humble beat copper, not the North Yorkshire's new Crime-Busting Tsar, 'What I'm after is quite simple. Most of my night's work consists of patrolling the countryside, keeping my eyes and ears open. But, despite the impressive build-up I've been given, even I can't be in two places at once. Now, if you could agree to mount patrols in your cars on a night, in pairs, maybe once or twice a month on a rota basis, we could do two things. One, we'd increase our surveillance capacity. By that I mean just sitting and watching. Believe it or not, that's what I spend a lot of my time doing on a night when I'm out and about, and you'd be surprised what I see. And two, we'd stand much more chance of nabbing the odd villain. You can imagine how frustrating it is when I see something suspicious and can't follow it up because my back-up is too far away.'

'Ah, I get it,' the Colonel interrupted. 'You want us to wade in and collar the villain. Road-blocks, car chases, that sort of thing.'

'Er, regrettably no. We have to tread very carefully where that's concerned. I'm going to have to ask any of you who volunteer for this to abide by a very strict set of rules. What I want from you more than anything else is vigilance. That, and information – about late-night vehicle movements, and of course about any patterns of crime in the area. I know you'd like to join in the chase, but you have to leave that to us. Apart from the obvious risks – to yourselves and others – you'll all be well aware of the Health and Safety issues.'

'That's all very well but how are we going to communicate? A mobile phone isn't much use out on the Wolds.'

'Good point. Leave that with me. I'll have a word with my Superintendent at Malton and see whether we can't get a few police radios out to you. Because that's the other vital aspect of all this, that we can communicate rapidly and effectively.'

I left the pub feeling I might just possibly have got things rolling. The question was, would it add up to anything? I didn't have to wait long to find out.

●　　　●　　　●

The countryside is governed by the seasons. Not quite in the same way as it was when our grandfathers worked the fields with horses, when the kids' school year was built around the harvest – and interrupted every autumn when the potatoes had to be dug up – but there is still a tide in rural affairs, and it's ruled by the turning of the earth. The fact is that if you're up to no good, travelling about the land looking for things to steal, you're generally going to wait until the days shorten and the nights lengthen before you set out with your Transit and your crow-bar. Firstly, once autumn comes you're that much less visible. Secondly, you'll know that most country people will be indoors with the fire blazing and the curtains drawn. When we get to midwinter you've got anything up to 16 hours of darkness in which to operate, but even in November and December, when it's dark from four in the afternoon through to eight o'clock next morning, most thieves will wait until the small hours. Up until midnight there are far too many people travelling to and from town, or coming back from the pub. And it's easy to forget that criminals, like anyone else, are creatures of habit. From the reports we get, you could say that most break-ins and thefts take place between about one o'clock and three-thirty in the morning. Professional criminals know full well that around half past two to three most people are in their deepest sleep and least likely to be aroused. I once had an argument with a fellow copper about this, and I remember saying to him, how often do you wake up in the night and see the clock showing three? It's nearly always earlier or later.

So we decided that our Country Watch patrols would operate from about midnight. There was little point turning out any earlier. And if the volunteer force were to get back to their jobs next morning, and if my theories about the criminal pattern were right, we agreed four o'clock was just about the right time to wind things up.

My biggest worry, when we got started, was that people would get disillusioned. They were motivated to get into this because they were fed up with having their equipment nicked.

And they came into it with what I thought were unrealistic expectations. It's pretty rare, even for an experienced copper, to actually apprehend a burglar as he goes about his business. We come back to that 600 square miles again. What are the odds, realistically, that you'll be right there when Bill the Burglar is jemmying open a door or a window? Or that you'll just happen to stop a suspect vehicle in the small hours and find it full of loot? It doesn't happen that often, and I could well see the average amateur sleuth getting fed up with sitting in his car, parked up in a gateway, clutching a flask full of cocoa and trying to stay awake in the freezing cold. Time drags when you're out in the middle of nowhere under a blanket of cloud with nothing to look at but the clock on the dashboard. Add a bit of fog or a touch of frost into the equation, and it's enough to sap anyone's enthusiasm. So the question was, would we get an early result to keep their spirits up?

As luck would have it, the chance for a concerted operation came up much sooner than I'd hoped. One after another my contacts around the patch started calling in with reports of break-ins and thefts. Diesel was being siphoned off from outside storage tanks, quad-bikes were disappearing, tools were going missing – anything from post-hole drillers, pumps, chainsaws and mobile generators, right down to basic garden tools. Someone even reported the loss of an antique pitch-fork, much to Ed's amusement. The noticeable thing was that there was a pattern. The burglaries were first in one village, then another nearby. And all were taking place within reasonable range of what was to be our centre of operations, the Colonel's estate.

For Operation Bulldog – it was the Colonel's idea, and who was I to argue with him? – we agreed to meet up in the big house. I'd never been further than the kitchen, so when he took my coat and led me through into the hallway I was all eyes. I particularly noticed a huge grandfather clock with a pastoral scene painted on its face, huntsmen chasing a fox across a wintry field. We entered what the Colonel called the gun-room. What a set-up. The first thing that struck me was the smell: it smelled . . . old, if you know what I mean. I don't mean old as in musty, not like a cellar or outhouse. I mean more a kind of historical smell. Maybe it was the wax polish on the oak table – a huge thing that that could seat 40, he told me. Or perhaps it was the varnish on the oil paintings that hung on the wood-panelled walls, portraits of the ancestors in military uniform and various coats of arms. I wondered whether they were all in the family or whether some represented enemies dispatched on the field of battle. I'd have to ask him some time. But that smell – it reminded me of a smell I'd come across in the National Gallery one time when I lived in London, and every time I smell it, it seems to me it's the authentic odour of antiquity. But of course, it could equally well have had something to do with the preservatives used by taxidermists, because there on the walls were the stuffed heads of a red deer with a huge set of antlers, a prize bull staring at us with its beady glass eyes, a couple of foxes, teeth bared and nostrils flared, the odd deer – and any number of birds in glass cases. There were pheasants, ducks, an owl, snipe, even a peacock. 'And in here,' said the Colonel, rapping his knuckles against a set of tall wooden doors, 'here's the jolly old arsenal. All under lock and key, of course.'

'And licensed,' I added.

'Oh, naturally, old chap.'

We'd rounded up about a dozen volunteers that night. The aim was to work in pairs, two per vehicle. We had Nick the game-keeper and his son, a husband and wife who were in the agricultural machinery business and had had a tractor stolen from right outside their yard, a retired pilot, all dressed up in a leather flying-jacket and a woolly hat. We had a neighbouring farmer and his son, a couple of former Special Constables and another farming couple from over West Lutton way who'd got up one morning and found their wrought-iron gates had been lifted off their hinges and spirited away. After the Colonel had served us all coffee and biscuits I outlined the plan for the night's operation.

'Right,' I said, 'as you know, we've had a spate of break-ins these last few weeks.' I unfolded one of my OS maps and spread it on the dining-table. 'And I've circled in red the villages that have been hit. As you'll see there is a pattern. Mostly, they're all within easy reach of the A64. I've made you all a copy of the eastern Ryedale area – if someone'll pass them around, so you can follow what I'm saying.'

'I get it – so's they can be off to Leeds or wherever as soon as they're done.'

'Precisely, Nick. They'll be trying to get in quick, grab what they want, and off down the road within minutes. Easy-peasy. It's a pattern, but with just a little bit of luck it may be their undoing. Anyway, I've had a bit of a think, and I've spoken to the Crime Analysis girl at Malton and between us we've mapped out six or seven villages where we think they might hit next.'

The villages I was focusing on were all within a mile or two of the main road, and none of them had yet experienced the kind of crime-wave that my volunteers had had to put up with over the past couple of months. They ranged from Barton-le-Willows, which has a railway crossing and a pub, to Sand Hutton, with a school and maybe 70 or 80 houses, right down to Horton, which has barely a dozen houses to its name.

'Now then,' I said. 'Gather round.' To tell the truth I was rather enjoying this. Here we were in this fabulous wood-panelled room, hundreds of years old, the clock in the hall striking midnight, with all of the Colonel's ancestors looking down at us, planning a military-style campaign. Shades of Churchill's War Planning Council at work in the bunker under Downing Street – or was it Captain Mainwaring at Walmington on Sea? To tell the truth, for just a moment I felt more like Father Christmas as I handed out the police radios, all tuned to our dedicated channel, and explained how to use them.

'Right,' I said, 'you all know which village you've been allocated to. And here you are on my map, look.' I had a packet of fluorescent adhesive labels to mark their positions; post-it notes – nice and easy to move around if there was a change of plan. 'I want you to park up, discreetly, lights off, engines off, where you can watch the road. Farm drives, gateways, that sort of location. I don't want you to react to anything. What I'm hoping for – and it's a bit of a shot in the dark – is that our friends will be out and about reconnoitring. As far as we can we'll leave them to it, and hopefully grab them as they leave for the main road with the loot. Now, you all know the kind of vehicle you're looking for?'

'Aye, vans, small trucks, that kind of thing.'

'That's it. We're not particularly interested in private cars. But remember, we are interested in anything travelling slowly, like they would if they were weighing the job up. Okay, is everybody ready? You've all got your call signs, yes? You've all got your maps. Torches, everyone? Flasks? Blankets – because it's another cold one forecast. Anybody feel the need to synchronize watches?'

But they were already on their way to their various observation points. As well as half a dozen pairs of Country Watch volunteers, I'd got back-up from three other PCs in two cars; so all told we had ten vehicles staking out the area. As well as the police radios we all had mobiles and we all had each other's numbers. I was starting to get a good feeling about this.

We'd agreed that we would be on watch until about four, so by the time we'd gone our separate ways there was barely three and a half hours to go. Even so, the night dragged. The roads were deserted, and the moon, shining high above Bossall Woods, silhouetted the bare branches against a clear sky, picking out an owl as it swooped into a hedge bottom in pursuit of its supper. I gave everyone 20 minutes or so to get settled in, then called them one after another – Alpha 1, Alpha 2, Alpha 3 – to see that everything was okay and to make quite sure that we had radio contact. Fine, fine, fine. Everything was fine. All quiet on the western front.

After a while I left the woods and drove over to Claxton, parking out of the way beside someone's nice tall leylandii hedge. We hadn't deployed anyone out there, so I thought I may as well cover it. It was nice and handy for the main road and, hopefully, I could get to any of the team within seven or eight minutes if things came to life. In fact, after I'd had my sandwiches I decided to drive around the patch and just see whether there was any action. Not a thing. Everyone was wrapped up against the cold, sipping hot drinks and whiling away the night the best they could. Some were bored already, and I was starting to worry that they'd nod off. It was all right for me: this was a Thursday; I'd been on nights all week. But as the lady from West Lutton said, 'I haven't been out this late since I were young and foolish. Not since we were courting.'

'Aye, but you weren't wearing so many layers of clothing in those days,' her husband added.

Around two I did get one or two calls, but they were both false alarms. The first turned out to be a newspaper van, but the second, a Transit coming out of Flaxton and on to the main road, sounded interesting. I trailed it and checked the registration – but there was nothing untoward on the record. Even so, I pulled it over. You never know. All I found was a bemused greengrocer and his lad on their way to Leeds market.

As the night wore on, and with nothing happening, I was starting to worry that my volunteers would be getting disheartened. I knew full well that nine times out of ten when I'd tried to set a trap I'd drawn a blank. Still, having this many pairs of eyes shifted the balance in our favour, I told myself.

Then my mobile rang.

'Hello.'

'Mike, Mike.' I recognized Nick the game-keeper's voice straight away.

'What is it, mate?'

'Hell, I've been trying to call you for long enough. Bloody radio ain't working.' He was talking ever so quietly, almost whispering, and the sound was muffled as if he was sunk down in his seat. He actually sounded frightened – which was unlike him. 'We saw two blokes but we couldn't get hold of you. They walked right by us. Not 15 yards off.'

'How long ago was this?'

''Bout five minutes.'

'Well, why didn't you tell me?'

'I said, bloody radio's died on us.'

I knew what he'd done. I'd done it myself more than once. He'd been that excited he'd grabbed it in his hand and knocked it off channel.

'Okay Nick, calm down mate.'

'And then we saw a van, like, crawling along right slowly.'

'A van. That's interesting.' I started up the engine.

'Aye, a red 'un.'

Christ, if he hadn't been so eager. 'Can you describe the people you saw, Nick?'

'Not really, but it wasn't a couple, like. It was two men, definitely.'

There was no way that two blokes would be innocently strolling through a village like that at 2.30 a.m. 'Stay where you are. I'll be along in a minute.'

'Hang on, Mike. There's the van now, heading out of the village.'

'Which way?'

'Main road direction.'

'Got a registration number?'

'No, it's all covered in muck. Out of sight now.'

'Right. Stand by.'

I drove out of village towards the A64, contacted the other two police cars and put out a call for any available help. We needed to blank off every exit from the village. I radioed the details of the van we were after, such as they were. It's standard procedure, the idea being to allow any other police vehicle in the vicinity to respond. I couldn't believe our luck – there was an Armed Response Vehicle just our side of Malton, York lads on patrol. No reason why they shouldn't join in the fun.

There's no getting away from the fact then once the chase is on, your blood gets up. And I for one get excited. I know I do. The prospect of getting a result, actually collaring someone on the job – there's nothing like it. So there I was, geeing everyone up over the radio. 'Get your foot down, lads. We may have lost the buggers,' I shouted. 'They've got five minutes on us – bloody idiots back there knocked the radio off channel. Can you believe it?'

It was only after the words had escaped my lips that I realized I was so excited I'd been speaking on an open channel – and every one of my Country Watch volunteers was listening in. But I had other things on my mind now, like making the five miles to the A64 exit before the red van did.

I maintained radio contact as I sped on to the main road at Barton Hill and headed east. I was torn between my eagerness to get there as fast as possible and the real possibility of hitting an icy patch on the frosty roads. It's a balancing act, and you know that your judgement is on the line every time. Over the radio I could hear the other two cars on their way towards the roads that led to Howsham and Sand Hutton. The idea was to cover every possible escape route, but what if the blokes in the van – always assuming the two men on foot were in it – had sneaked off across the little track that led to Crambe, or did a crafty shuffle via Braithwaites Wood? If they were local, they

139

might be familiar with any number of the minor roads and farm tracks. It's like a bloody rabbit warren out there.

Back on the radio I organized the volunteers to cover every avenue of escape. 'But do not – repeat, do not – intercept,' I told them. 'Don't even follow them, or my neck'll be on the block. We have every exit covered.' And all our fingers crossed, I said to myself as I clicked off.

I really was confident now. The more I thought about it, the more certain I was: two men on foot, a van cruising slowly through the village – that was no coincidence.

Just as I was about to pull out on to the main road I heard the ARV boys. 'Yeah, red van, Transit. We have contact.' At that point it's normal for all radio chat to stop so that we have an uninterrupted commentary, for want of a better word. 'They just shot past us heading east.'

I could hear them rev their engine as they turned around on the empty road.

'Heading towards Barton Hill. Not hanging about either. We'll have the bugger for speeding if nowt else. And he's got a rear light out.' At this point I could hear their siren going in the background as they carried out the vehicle check, spelling out the licence number for the Police National Computer. 'Right, we've got him. About half a mile ahead. Just passing Claxton Hall doing 85.'

I caught up with them a few minutes later, just as they were pulling up behind the van. They'd got it parked on the roadside, orange lights winking and illuminating the dense woodland that borders the road just past the Little Chef. I remember thinking that if these were professional robbers they'd be clenching their buttocks at this point. ARV boys are easily recognized by those in the know. They drive the same car as the traffic cops, Volvo V70s, and although they might not be wearing their Berghaus fleeces and body armour – that's supposed to be for when they go into action – their combat boots and gun holsters would have been all the evidence a serious criminal needed that they weren't dealing with a couple of village bobbies here.

One of the boys was at the driver's-side door with his lamp shining in – it's amazing how effective a bright light is in immobilizing a suspect. They've no way of knowing what you've got in your hand. Not that these lads normally carry guns on patrol – they'd be stashed in the back of the car.

'Now then, mate. Looks like we've got a result.' I was standing there, my breath coming in clouds, anxious to see what kind of treasures were hidden behind the battered, mud-coated doors. 'What did the PNC say?' I asked, as me-laddo put the key into the lock.

'Dodgy as hell. Pops up in half a dozen cases.'

His mate had got the driver out of the cab now, and had him standing against the side of the van while he pointed the flashlight at the other occupants. There were two of them, same age as the driver, mid-forties, shaven heads.

The rear doors were twisted somehow. They opened with a creak that set my teeth on edge. And there inside was what I was hoping for, a heap of garden and farmyard tools and machinery. There were three lawnmowers, a strimmer or two, an antique stone bird-bath, a trail-bike, a couple of electric drills, two separate locked tool-boxes, several other bits and pieces and a solitary bag of spuds. I walked round to the front of the van and shouted out, nice and loud, as per regulations, 'Right, I'm placing you all under arrest on suspicion of burglary.' Then came the formal caution. 'You do not have to say anything, but if you do . . .'

Actually catching or apprehending criminals is the fun part of an operation like that, the deep satisfaction you hope for when you first sit down and map it all out. But then comes all the procedural stuff, and that can seem like a real anti-climax. As soon as the other two patrol cars arrived we were able to arrange for the three suspects to be taken to York Police Station in separate vehicles. The last thing we wanted was for them to start concocting stories. But first we had to preserve the evidence – and in this case that meant the van and its contents. Our friendly vehicle-hire people in town weren't overjoyed about being woken at three in the morning, but they were contracted to take such vehicles into their secure compound. Two officers had to go with it to take formal possession of the stolen property and log it. Next day the scene of crime officer had to come out and fingerprint both the van and the stolen goods inside. It's a lengthy old procedure, but it has to be done by the book.

Once all that was under way I was able to thank all the Country Watch volunteers personally for their efforts, congratulate them on a job well done, and send them home in time for a few hours' sleep before they got back to their day jobs. I made a point of apologizing for the way I'd gone off over the radio. Put it down to the adrenalin, I said. They were fine about it. 'We were a bit worked up ourselves,' Nick said. After I left them it was time to get into the car and drive to York with all the officers involved. We weren't going home until we'd written our statements of the night's events. A couple of hours later, back in Malton, after a bite of grub and a cuppa, we handed over to the early shift CID and called it a night. Next day I would learn that the interrogations had led to all three being charged with a list of break-ins that night as well as a whole raft of motoring offences.

•   •   •

A week or two later I was on the night shift again when the Colonel asked me to pop in – partly to fill him in on the outcome, partly to offer me a little farmhouse hospitality. It was a typical autumn night, clear and frosty, and as I drove in through the open gates just before midnight I noticed that the Colonel had got himself a new pair of . . . spheres. Not millstone grit this time, by the look of them, but some sort of light stone. A three-quarter moon was just rising and as it shone through the lower branches of his yew trees, they almost glowed, a beautiful soft pale colour, a bit like York Minster if you ever catch it after the floodlights have been switched off and the moon strikes the façade. Honey – that's the colour I mean.

'Colonel,' I said when he opened the door to me. 'I see you've got a new set of balls.'

'Indeed I have,' he beamed.

'Bet they set you back a few bob, didn't they?'

'Ah, but that's where you're wrong old chap. The Volunteers . . . no, I mean the Country Watch chappies, don't I? Anyway, "the lads", if you like, were so pleased to get their mowers and what-not returned that they passed the jolly old hat and got me a new set.'

'Well, I hope you've got them bolted on this time,' I said.

'Oh good grief no. Can't go drilling beautiful stone like that. No, I've got 'em wired up to the cable that runs the security lights. Anyone messes with them they're in for a shock, what?'

· Ten ·

Of course I was loving every minute of my new job as a Rural Community Beat Officer. It was great to be back on my home territory, patrolling the countryside I loved so well – and, I have to say, getting to know it in a way I never did as a kid. I was also getting acquainted with some of the characters who make North Yorkshire such a great place to live. On the home front, though, things weren't all sweetness and light. Being a copper's wife has its perks: security and a decent wage, for one thing, but there are drawbacks too. Goodness knows I've seen enough in the way of break-ups, and they're not all caused by unsocial hours and on-the-job affairs. Even coppers who think they're doing well, getting promoted and moved on to fresh pastures, find that sometimes there's a price to pay. Wives and children who find it hard to settle in a new home can soon start to resent being uprooted and shifted halfway across the country. And the last thing you want after an eight-hour shift grappling with the criminal fraternity is to come home and be told that you're the cause of someone else's unhappiness.

I don't really want to say much about my marriage. The way I look at it, yes, by all means tell the world when you're happy. They say all the world loves a lover, and a woman in love just radiates beauty. As for a man, well, even the dullest fellow, when he's smitten, seems to smarten up his dress, wear a smile, whistle a happy tune – although there's a thin line between being a little ray of sunshine and a total pain in the rear end. So by all means spread a bit of joy around, I say – God knows we can do with it.

But when things aren't going so well I think the less you say about it the better, because the temptation is to try to get people to take your side and agree with you that it's the other person's fault. It's never that straightforward.

The fact is that as the year went on I could see the sun setting on my marriage once and for all. I hope I didn't point the finger at anyone. To tell the truth, when I look back I can see that I must have been hard to live with. In some ways I suppose I could blame my new job. I was enjoying it so much – it was a little bit like being in love, and I was full of it. Too full, I wouldn't be surprised. Always talking about what I was up to on my beat and how great the countryside was and all the amazing characters I was bumping into. It's obvious looking back – I simply wasn't taking as much notice of things at home as I should have done. It was just two people who weren't getting on any more, and in the end one of them decided that we'd both be better off if one of us moved on. My decision, my move. Trouble was, where to go?

Perhaps I should have given it more thought. Instead, like most men, I decided I could figure it out for myself. I couldn't see me waltzing into work and telling everyone my problems. I once knew a man who did, and he got short shrift. 'This is the cop shop, not marriage bloody guidance, pal!'

But of course things start to build up, and in the end I spilled the beans to Walter when I called by for a cup of tea and a little treat.

'It's a bit early for mince pies, isn't it?' I said, as he pulled a tray out of the oven.

'Aye well, I'm having to clear a space in the freezer, like. Soon be getting ready to put a few game birds in. Anyway, you'll like these. Me sister makes 'em, and she can't half bake, I'm telling you.'

146

'Why, I've never eaten a mince pie in the middle of summer,' I said.

'Well, they want eating up, so stop chittering and get 'em down you.'

But, pies or no pies, schedule or no schedule, I'd no sooner dropped my cap and radio on the kitchen table than I slumped into the wooden captain's chair at the head of his kitchen table. I wasn't feeling good, and Walt knew it.

'What's up with you, lad?' He slammed the oven door shut, lifted the lid on the fire-box and gave the coals a good riddling. 'Is the job getting you down?'

'No, Walt. It's me and the missus. We're both of us miserable as sin. Hardly talking now.'

'Why, they do reckon it's hard work, this marriage caper.' He lifted the kettle, poured a few drops of boiling water into the teapot and swirled it around. 'That's one reason I never went in for it.' He set the warm pot down and started spooning tea into it. One, two, three – he made a strong brew did Walter. 'My Dad used to say, why give half your food away just to get the other half cooked.' He gave a little chuckle, then he must have seen the look on my face. 'Aye, well . . . That were him being funny.'

'Thing is, Walt, I'm at the end of my rope. I've made me mind up.'

'What do you mean by that?'

'I reckon it's time to be packing my bags.'

'That bad is it?'

'Aye, that bad. We don't want to end up hating each other, but that's where we'll be if we stay as we are.'

He set the pot on the table and got my blue mug down from the shelf. Funny to think that this time last year I didn't even know Walt existed and now here I was sitting in 'my' seat and supping tea out of 'my' mug while he listened to me talking about my marital problems.

'Thing is, matey . . .' He fetched the pot over and poured us our tea. 'Thing is, where you going to go? Have you thought about that?'

'I've had a look in the *Gazette*, see what there is to rent.'

Walt shook his head. 'You don't want to be renting, lad. It's like chucking your money down t'drain.'

'Aye, but I can't buy another place – leastways not until we can get ours sold and divvy up the proceeds. Even then I'm going to be looking at shoe-boxes. And so's she. I s'pose that's why we've kept shelving it this last year or two. Don't want to face the realities of breaking up.'

'Aye well, price of houses these days, you need to tread careful.' Walt was sliding two more hot pies on to my plate. 'Here,' he said, 'and mind you don't burn your tongue.'

Walt's sister made the most divine pastry I'd tasted since I left home, and her mincemeat – home-made, of course – was that perfect blend of the sweet and the sharp, not like the stuff you get from a shop. For a moment we sat there in silence, just the ticking of the clock in the hallway, the occasional shifting of coals in the stove, the whistling sound as Walt blew on his pie to cool it down. Then the door from the living-room squeaked open and the black Lab came waddling in.

'Ah, smelled the food, did you?' Walt pushed his old cap back on his head and had a little scratch. I found myself wondering what he looked like without it. I realized I'd never seen him take it off. He took a bite out of his pie and set the rest of it on the floor for Tess.

'Steady on, mate. She's carrying enough weight as it is.'

'Aye well, I look after her, don't I, Tess old pal?' He patted the dog's ample rear end. 'You can say what you like about this place, but no bugger ever goes hungry.'

Then he looked me right in the eye. 'I shan't want any rent, mind, but I shall ask you to help with t'groceries now and again.'

'I beg your pardon?'

'When you move in, like. I've no mortgage to pay so it's cheap enough to run. Just so long as I get a bit of help with the extra grub.' He sat there and nodded toward my empty mug. 'Now then, shall you have a refill?'

I moved into Walt's spare bedroom at the end of the week. I'd no idea how long I would be staying there, and I tried not to worry about it. Walt made me welcome and he fed me well. I'd no complaints there. It was traditional country grub, and plenty of it. That first night I got back from work to find him pulling three roast pheasants and a stack of golden brown spuds out of the oven. Sometimes it'd be a haunch of venison, a couple of rabbits he'd shot or some spring lamb from one of his freezers. And then there were his game pies. God knows what was in those. I didn't ask, but they weren't half tasty – his sister's pastry, and gravy to die for.

And after we'd eaten we'd sit in his front room and have a natter over a cup of tea, or maybe a can of beer if it was the weekend. He hadn't got a TV, and he wouldn't have electric light in there, but unless it was proper hot weather he'd always burn a few logs in the grate, even if it was just for an hour before bedtime, so we spent many an evening chatting away as the fire cast its red glow on the ceiling.

The thing with Walter was that as much as he believed in being well fed he was a true Yorkshireman with deep pockets. Very deep pockets. He regarded money with great caution. 'Runs in my family,' he said. ''Cos years ago we had nowt. Every penny had to be accounted for. Old habits die hard, y'know.' I wouldn't call him penny-pinching, but he certainly took caution to a new level. One evening – I hadn't been there long – I was rummaging about for a new light-bulb to take upstairs. There was no light fitting in the spare room, but there was one on the landing, and when I tried to switch that on I realized that the bulb was defunct. 'Walter,' I said, 'where are your spares?'

'Oh, I don't keep spares,' he said. 'I reckon what I've got ought to last me. If you don't over-use 'em they'll keep going for years.'

'Bloody hell, Walt. You can make 'em last forever if you never use 'em, you know.'

'Tell you the truth,' he said, 'I was thinking about getting one of them energy-efficient jobs, save a bit on me bills like, but I was in Yates' in town, and have you seen the price of them?'

'Well, aye, they are a bit dear, but the point is you'll save on electricity in the long run.'

'Aye, but what if they last too long – I mean, will I be around long enough to benefit? You have to weigh these things up, you know.'

I looked at him. He was into his seventieth year, but he still had the fresh-faced look of a schoolboy – with a fair amount of mischief in his eyes. Take that flat hat off and replace it with a peaked school cap and you'd have an older version of Just William.

In the end I suggested running an extension cable to my bedroom, because I like to read when I go up, something to take my mind off the day's work. But when I saw the way he pursed his lips at the thought of it, I decided to let it pass. I'd manage with a candle. To his way of thinking, illuminating the night by running a light-bulb was unnatural. No different from burning money. 'Why,' he'd say, leaning toward the fire with a week-old *Evening Press* I'd brought in from the back of my car, 'if God had wanted us to stop up all hours he'd have . . . he'd have . . .'

'Given us a full moon every night?' I suggested, throwing a few dry birch twigs on the dying embers to give him a bit of extra light.

'Maybe so.'

'Or how about infra-red vision?'

'No,' he said, getting out of his chair and yawning. 'Once it gets dark you're as well getting yourself off to bed.'

● ● ●

They say that trying times can drive you to drink, and it was when I was living up the hill there that I first started going down to the Jolly Farmers from time to time on an evening. I had my doubts at first – not about the pub, which I knew from way back before I was ever in the police – but rather because it was now my local. In the Met you had to be very wary about your social life – who you mixed with, and who you confided in. You had to feel you'd really got to know someone before you'd tell them what you did for a living, because to a lot of people the police were the enemy. Simple as that. But that was in the Smoke. I knew it would be different in my new patch – as the Super had told me on my first day.

The Farmers is a bit of a rabbit warren once you get in, with a sort of locals' bar to the front, a back lounge where there's an open fire, another room beyond that where people can go for a more private conversation, a dining-room even further back, and then off to one side a games room with darts, pool and the like. It was a wet, cold evening – cold for August – but I'd walked down the hill all the same; I never use the car if I'm having a drink, unless it's a quick half on the way home. I went to get served at the bar nearest the door. There were quite a few in considering the weather, but none of them even looked at me, let alone spoke. I didn't like it. It didn't feel right. Even when I ordered a glass of Timothy Taylors there was still a sort of eerie silence about the place. The girl behind the bar pulled my pint. I looked around and smiled. Suddenly everyone was peering into their beer glasses. I paid for my drink and tipped about a third of it straight down my neck, not a thing I generally do – but I have to admit it, I was nervous. Still not a word. It was almost like being in London, where you can walk into a pub, sit down for an hour and never pass the time of day with anyone. But this was North Yorkshire, my home.

151

Then, finally, someone spoke. Nice and clear – a refined sort of voice, almost plummy – and louder than I would have liked. 'Pannett, isn't it?' It seemed to echo round the place. I swear if there'd been a piano playing it would have stopped there and then.

He was a tall man, younger than me, 30, maybe 35, and he looked for all the world as if he'd stepped out of one of those TV series set in rural England 40 or 50 years ago. He wore a tweed jacket, a green and white check shirt, a dark green tie with some sort of insignia on the front, and he was drinking from a pewter mug. The only thing missing was the pipe.

'Our new bobby, am I right?'

Oh shit. In front of all those people. In my new local. Back in London, the minute someone calls you 'copper' you're ready for trouble – unless you can get out the door first. 'That's right,' I said, 'and the name's Mike.' I held out a hand, which he shook, firmly and warmly. 'Miles,' he said, 'Miles Waring. But call me Algy. Everyone else does. And this is Soapy – or Terry to give him his correct name. You have to watch him. He's a slippery customer.' And so it went on – the chap next to him shook hands with me, and then his mate did – and his mate's girlfriend, and before I knew where I was, I was in the centre of a crowd of beaming locals, all wanting to press the flesh and welcome me to the neighbourhood.

'Frightfully sorry that we gave you the hard stare when you came in, old chap.' We were in the back room now, and Algy was standing by the little serving-hatch ordering another round. 'But one or two of us were pretty sure we knew who you were. Just weren't sure whether you'd be the sort of chap who'd come in and have a drink with us.'

'Why wouldn't I?'

'Well, one always worries. I mean, you might be the kind who comes in and wants to talk shop with mine host. You know, never off duty sort of thing, always trying to follow up a lead.'

152

'No, I just popped out because I fancied a drink,' I said as Algy handed me another pint and passed one over to Soapy. I glanced up at the clock. It was half past ten. 'A little night-cap, like.'

The beer was going down a treat, the company was convivial, and the log fire drew me like a magnet. I edged a little closer to the hearth and soon saw the steam start to rise from my trouser legs.

It wasn't long before Algy was draining his glass – and Soapy wasn't far behind him. I was trying to weigh the pair of them up. Algy boy was obviously one of your upper classes. He kept talking about 'my land' and 'up at the hall', whereas Soapy – well, at first glance he was a weasely looking fellow, the sort who, if you saw him get into a car, you'd automatically check its registration. Like Algy he was a typical countryman, except that whereas his boss looked every inch the toff, Soapy was wearing a pair of grubby jeans held up by a broad leather belt, a Def Leppard T-shirt, a red bandanna tied around his neck, and one of those quilted body-warmers, blue with an orange lining. And he had a roll-up in his mouth that he kept re-lighting. If they'd told me he was the village rat-catcher – yep, that would've made sense.

As I was taking this all in, they both drained their glasses. 'My shout,' I said, knocking back what was left of my pint and edging towards to counter.

'Oh, that's frightfully decent of you, old chap.' Algy thrust his glass into my hand.

'Cheers, me old cockbird,' said Soapy. 'I'll try a drop o' that Bomber or Bombardier or whatever they call her.'

I ordered the drinks and leaned on the counter, watching the landlord fill the glasses. Then, just as I felt in my pocket, I remembered. I'd only brought a fiver out with me, and I'd spent over £2 on that first pint.

'Landlord,' I started. No, it was too late and he hadn't heard me. Besides, what I had left in my pocket wouldn't even have covered the two pints he'd already pulled. I looked around for Algy. He was down on his knees shoving another log on the fire. As he stood up I took my courage in both hands.

'Give us a hand here, will you?' I shouted out. As he came up to the bar I lowered my voice. 'Look, I'm ever so sorry, but I only came out for a quick one and I've nowt left but a couple of quid.'

'Ah,' he said, 'well, that puts us both in a spot, doesn't it, because I'm a trifle short myself.' He leaned closer. 'Only ever bring out enough for the one round. But I tell you what, we'll ask Soapy here.'

I hadn't seen Soapy lurking behind him, but here he was at the bar unfastening his belt and undoing the top button of his jeans. I looked at Algy but Algy just winked at me as Soapy shoved his hand down inside his trousers and pulled out a great fat wad of £20 notes. 'Peel off what you need, cockbird,' he said as he dropped the warm bundle in my hand. There must've been £700 or £800. I couldn't remember when I'd last handled so much.

'Hell,' I said, peeling of a single note, 'that's a lot of cash to be carrying about. But thanks, I'll pay you back tomorrow if you tell me where—'

Soapy shook his head and jerked his thumb at Algy. 'No, you pay him, cockbird. It's his money.'

I passed the note across to the landlord and looked at Algy. He was grinning like a naughty schoolboy. 'The thing is I don't always trust myself. Couple of drinks and I tend to get carried away. Champers all round, that kind of thing. So I leave the old wallet with Soapy here. He's what you might call my social manager. Makes sure I get home all right. Manages the finances when I'm out on the town so to speak.'

That third pint went down very nicely. Very quickly too. When Soapy called for another round I checked the time, but

154

it was only a quarter to eleven. I knew I ought to be on my way before long, but it was still raining out there and I was enjoying a bit of company.

'You'll have to pop into my place when you're out on your rounds,' Algy was saying.

'I will. Where d'you live exactly?'

He waved towards the door. 'Just across that way. Half a mile max. Take the Malton road and there's a handy little track leads right to the old front door.'

'You'll find her easy enough,' said Soapy. 'Can't bloody miss it.'

'Why's that?'

'Great big white rose flag flying over it.' Soapy re-lit the remains of his roll-up. 'See it for miles.'

'Well, we're all proud of living in God's Own Country, aren't we?' Algy said.

'Oh aye.' I held up the last of my pint to the firelight. 'Well, I need to be on my way. They'll be chucking us out soon.'

'Why, he won't sling us out yet a while, me old cockbird.'

I glanced at the clock. 'Is that all it is? Ten to?'

'Soapy, old boy, where's that change Mister Pannett gave you?'

'Right here in my pocket.'

'Well, get another round in. You can surely stay for just one more, can't you, old chap?'

I looked at the clock once more. Perhaps it had stopped – but no, there was the big hand, jerking forward another half a minute.

'Aye, go on then.'

The clock showed five past the hour when I left, and I was ready for some fresh air. I said goodnight to Algy and his mate, and turned to walk through the village. There was a real back-endish feel to the night. The rain had stopped but the wind had freshened from the north-west. As I climbed the hill towards Walt's place a few raggedy leaves were being blown off the sycamores.

I was looking forward to having a cup of tea with Walter if he was still up but when I got in the fire was dead in the hearth and the place was in silence. I lifted the kettle from beside the stove, hoping it might have some hot water in, but it was empty. Never mind, I could do with getting to bed. I made my way up the stairs. I wasn't on till lunchtime next day but I needed to be in town early for a dentist's appointment. I'd maybe set the alarm for seven. What was it now? I picked up my clock off the floor and turned it so that it faced the light from the landing.

'A quarter to two?' I pressed it to my ear, but it was ticking away like a good 'un. 'A quarter to bloody two? Hell, I must have had more fun than I realized.'

· **Eleven** ·

Walt had been good to me. He'd taken me in when I was at the end of my tether, but I couldn't see myself staying at his place up the hill for too long. It wasn't a matter of being uncomfortable. In many ways it was very nice set-up there, very cosy in fact – but that was the problem. I reckon that once you start feeling cosy, that's the time to think about moving on. It's one reason why I'd left the Met after nine years. It wasn't just that I was wanting to get back to God's Own Country, but the job was becoming routine, predictable, safe – and, dare I say it, easy. Similar thing with Walt's place. He'd even cleared me a little spot beside the fire for my slippers, right next to his log basket. And that really bothered me. Next thing I'd be buying a cardigan and wearing my cap around the place like he did, and putting my loose change in a jam-jar at night till I'd saved up enough for a day at York races.

No, it was definitely time I found a place of my own. I valued Walt's friendship, and I wanted to remain on good terms with him, but it was obvious to me that he was happier living alone. Always had been, and probably always would be. 'Aye,' he told me one warm night towards the end of the month, as we sat out the back on a couple of fold-up chairs enjoying a glass of beer and a bag of crisps, watching the rooks in the sycamore trees, 'I'm best off on me own. Never wanted to get tangled up with no woman.'

'But what about the lass you're seeing now?' I said. Not that he'd ever let me meet her, but I'd had a look through the window when she came by and honked her horn for him. She was a handsome-looking old girl, from what I'd seen of her over the top of the front hedge, and she drove a super big car. She wasn't short of a bob or two – but then neither was Walter. The only difference was that he hated to part with his money.

'Ah well,' he said, screwing up his face and waving his hand in front his nose. He'd just had a load of cow muck dropped off for his vegetable patch. And of course Sod's Law said the wind had to turn around to south-east and blow waves of ammonia-scented steam right across where we were sitting. 'Thing is, I'm not tangled up with her, am I?'

'I don't know,' I said. 'You're seeing her two three times a week. I'd say she's maybe spinning a web for you, mate.'

'Don't be daft, Mike. I see her when it suits me. When I want to go out for a pint and suchlike.'

'So you treat her as your chauffeur, do you? She won't settle for that, you know. Modern women, matey, they demand more than that out of a relationship.'

'At your age, aye, they do want attention. They want a home, an income, young 'uns.' He shook his head. 'Couldn't be doing with all that. That's why I took the old man's advice.'

'Oh, about not giving half your food away?'

'That's it.' He tipped his head back and emptied the last crumbs of his salt and vinegar crisps.

'He really say that?'

'Aye, many's the time – and in front of Mam too. Not that she minded. Used to laugh at him. By 'eck, he was a rum fellow was my Dad. He had a few quaint old sayings. Used to tell Mam a woman's place was in the bed, and she should only be allowed out to get the coal in.' He shoved his hat back and scratched his forehead. 'You see, Mike, when you get to my age you want . . .' He got up and shuffled his seat a few feet back from the steam rolling off the muck-heap.

158

'Companionship?'

'No, not that so much. I'd say you just want a bit of an interest, and no commitments, and the same goes for her. You want someone you can rely on for a bit of company, but not getting under your feet all the time. I reckon she likes it that way too. She values me, y'know.'

I looked at him, sat there in his scruffy old cardigan, bottle clasped between his knees while he pulled his dental plate out and picked at the bits of crisp that had got stuck on it. 'It'd be no fun for her to go to the pub on her own, would it now?'

'Fair point,' I said, as he gave his denture a good lick and popped it back in. I was going to ask him whether he did that sort of thing in the pub, but I was distracted by the sound of a couple of shots which seemed to come from the woods at the top of the brow.

'I see missen as a sort of escort, like.'

'An escort?' I laughed aloud at that. 'You want to be careful, Walt. You'll be getting into deep water at that game.'

He looked puzzled for a moment.

'Personal services,' I said.

'Gerraway with you, lad. I ain't gonna her charge her for that!'

I let it drop. I was wondering who was out shooting, and I was straining my ears for another crack. We sat there for a while in silence as the rooks squabbled and jumped clumsily from branch to branch. As often as I've watched them, I've never worked out whether they're playing some mating game, establishing territorial rights, or just larking around before bed time.

Walt gestured towards the birds with his bottle. 'You see, that's what happens once you get tangled up in relationships. Look at 'em. A lot of arguing and shouting and never a quiet moment for yourself. No, you're better off on your own, I reckon. Why, if I was cooped up with a woman, I'd soon get fretful.'

There it went again, the shooting. 'Who's out there popping away?' I asked, pointing a thumb over my shoulder towards the hill-top.

'Could be old Thommo, he has a bit of woodland out that way. Or one of his keepers. Bit early for poachers, with t'sun still up.'

'Is there much activity out this way?'

Walt laughed. 'Just get yourself out and about on the stubble-fields on a night . . . well, more like three or four in t'morning.'

'We talking about locals or outsiders?'

He shrugged and didn't answer. I suppose I shouldn't have been putting the question. I'd always steered clear of asking where he got his game from – although I knew he had shooting rights on a few farms nearby. It was the same with quite a few of my contacts. Soapy, for example. I was pretty sure he did a bit on the side, but why not? His father had been a poacher all his life, and a clever one at that. He'd never been in trouble, but he'd never gone short of meat either, and as a good father he would've taught Soapy all he knew. The thing was, chaps like Soapy's old man only ever set out to furnish his family's needs. He was what you'd call a traditional countryman. Not out to make money at the game, nor to rip anyone off. And so his activities were more or less accepted. Or shall we say overlooked. And if I popped round and he offered me a slice of game pie I knew better than to ask where the filling came from. It's not as if the roads out there aren't just about paved with dead pheasants in the early autumn when they've been released from their breeding pens and are scurrying about the hedge bottoms without a care for the cars and vans speeding by. People call them stupid – the fact is, they never have the chance to learn.

'I'm not talking about the odd local nabbing a pheasant or a rabbit for his personal use, Walt. It's these bloody gangs that come in from Middlesbrough and Leeds – them places. Even from Liverpool, they reckon. Ones that come lamping. Those are the ones that bother me.'

I looked at him, but he just sat there watching the rooks for a moment. Then he said, 'Like I say, try going out about three o'clock time, where t'fields have been harvested.'

I knew what he was on about. Like every countryman he was outraged about what went on. But like many a game-keeper, he was powerless to do anything about it. And for the moment, I wasn't sure what I could do – until I took his advice and went out on a dawn patrol.

I decided to go out on a Monday morning. Or was it Sunday night? It was about two – which, this being late August, meant it wouldn't be getting light for a couple of hours. But there was a three-quarter moon, so visibility was good. I'd had a suspicion for some time that a gang was working in this area. Firstly, I'd had a word from my game-keeper mate – Nick, the lad who worked for the Colonel down Rillington way. He'd been a bit more talkative now that he'd seen what I was about – I mean Operation Bulldog. He'd realized I was on his side, serious about sorting out the local villains – and the incomers. He'd been out this way seeing a woman who lived in a cottage on the Birdsall estate – not that he knew I knew that. He thought it was a well-kept secret; and since they were both divorced it was nobody's business except theirs, but I guess they were trying to stop the local tongues wagging. They may as well have tried to send water uphill. Anyway, according to Nick he'd been coming home late one night when he'd been passed by a van with unfamiliar plates. 'I wouldn't have thought too much about it, Mike, but as it went by me I saw a dog jumping up at t'back window. Lurcher, I reckoned it were, cross-bred. In fact I'm positive. Had stripes on its head, as if it had a bit of bull terrier in it, and I thought to myself aye-aye, what they up to at three in t'morning miles from home?'

Eyes and ears. I've said it before and I'll say it again. You can't patrol a rural beat successfully without them. I've been accused by people who don't know any better of socializing too much on my rounds. Fair enough, I like a cup of tea and a bun – especially if it's on the house; and I have been known to have a drink with some of my contacts after hours. But that's where you learn what's happening. It's how you establish trust. Word even got back to the station one time that I was mowing Algy's grass when I was on duty and he was away in South Africa. Better still, it was true – but as I said at the time I'm entitled to a meal-break, same as anyone else. And if I care to give up my 20 minutes to help a mate out, that's my affair. If I listed all the coppers I've known who conducted their personal affairs while 'on the job' so to speak – well, perhaps we'd best not go there. But without personal contacts – who in many cases become friends – you can't do the job properly.

Anyway, not only had I had a tip from Nick but I'd also been called out to look at a gruesome sight that Jim Cockerill, one of my farmer contacts, came across a few days earlier when he went out to feed some pheasants he was rearing in a pen. It was a dead deer. Hadn't been hit by a car. Hadn't been shot. Hadn't died of natural causes either – unless being mauled to death by dogs comes under the heading of Mother Nature's population control.

'Reckoned I might as well preserve the evidence for you,' Jim said as we trudged through the rain, following a path that had been freshly trodden through a tangle of nettles and into the beechwood. ''Cos I know bloody well what this is about.' He'd covered the evidence with a tarp and weighed it down with a couple of logs from a stack on the edge of the copse.

Under the tarp was the body of a full-grown roe deer, female. 'Hadn't been dead long when I got here. Hardly a fly on her – and I don't think anything else has been at it. Too bloody wet.' As he stood up he brushed against a low-hanging branch and showered us both with big fat drops. I looked at the dead animal. All along its side were a series of vicious cuts. No, not cuts so much as ragged tears. Whatever had attacked it had torn at it, again and again, exposing the ribs. And underneath where its belly had been ripped a great loop of gut had burst out, blue and sticky. One of its hind legs was mangled and twisted as well, and soaked in dark blood. The head had been chewed up pretty badly too. The white patch at its rear end was matted with blood and faeces.

Jim poked at the gut with his stick. 'And the buggers call this sport.' It was a bloody mess all right. Like Jim, I found it sickening. Not the gore, the spilled guts – that's just a fact of life, or death. If you eat meat you should be able to cope with that. I mean the dreadful waste of a fine animal. Mauled to death and left for the crows.

That little find out at Howsham, and Walt's remarks, had convinced me that it was worth my while digging around. What I was hoping for, as I waited there on the edge of the woods between Duggleby and Grimston Brow, supping coffee from my flask and watching the sky start to lighten ever so slightly in the east, was to see any suspicious-looking vehicles on the road that led to Beverley and Hull. There's a surprising amount of traffic at that time of day. Newspaper delivery vans, milk wagons, retailers heading for the markets, and by about half four you start to see a few commuters off to Saltend refinery or the food factories in north and east Hull. I even know three or four nurses who make the journey. Out in the sticks people will travel a long way for a decent wage – or a reliable one. What it means, when you're looking for a van-load of ne'er-do-wells with dogs, is that you have to make quick decisions. Is this a dodgy one or just a gang of builders on their way to a job? And of course Sod's Law says that as soon as you see one van coming there'll be another right behind it. What do you do then? Which one do you stop?

As it happened, I was never faced with such a dilemma. I

sat there under my tree for the best part of an hour and never saw a single van that looked the tiniest bit suspect, and by this time a band of blue had opened up above the eastern horizon. I weighed my options. Sit around for another half hour hoping that something would drive by flying the 'search me' flag? Or scout around, in the vague hope of spotting something or someone along the back roads? I started the car up, put her in gear and eased my way out from my hiding-place.

A few moments later as I turned off the Beverley road and dipped down a narrow lane I switched off my lights. There's no rule anywhere that says a copper is allowed to break the law that way, and I'm not recommending it. But if there was anyone about I certainly wasn't going to advertise my presence. In country as empty as the Yorkshire Wolds a single vehicle with its lights blazing will be visible from miles away. I was cruising nice and slowly, working on the reasonable assumption that anyone else on the road would have their lights on, giving me plenty of time to see them and get out of their way. The road I'd taken narrows as it dips down across the old Malton to Driffield railway. There's only room for a single vehicle and there's often a nice puddle at the bottom. It skirts the site of a deserted medieval village before climbing steeply to a farm track which in turn brings you over the top and back towards Leavening Brow. Why an entire village should have been abandoned all those hundred of years ago has never been fully explained as far as I'm aware, although it used to be said the plague was to blame. The thought of an entire settlement being wiped out lends a wonderfully mysterious atmosphere to the place, especially when you're looking down on the ruins of the church and the outlines of abandoned houses late at night with the moon illuminating the crumbling stonework.

When I reached the top of the wold I cast an eye around. The sky was lightening all the time, the moon slowly fading. I turned off the road and took the winding track towards

Wharram Percy Farm. There was little to see across the bare, unfenced fields but a scattering of large, rectangular straw-bales, each casting its dark shadow over the shaved barley-stubble. I didn't like being out in the open there. If anyone were watching they'd soon see me, lights or no lights. I headed towards a straggly clump of trees, just past a pull-in where the farmer regularly dumped a small mountain of muck and straw from his cattle-sheds. And there, behind the steaming heap, was a Range Rover. It could have been anyone's, of course, but it wasn't. Not just anyone's, I mean. Behind the metal grille that divided the back section from the seats, was the loose straw bedding, the food bowls, even a spare leash – and not an ordinary one either. This was the slip-leash, the kind that will allow a hunting dog's handler to let the dog loose after its prey the minute he sees it.

It was looking very much as though I'd happened upon something quite sinister, and I needed to get out of the way, quickly. If I had stumbled across a gang they'd be winding things up any time now, anxious to be on the road before it got properly light. The question was, where would they have been working? It had to be in the trees that topped Birdsall Brow to the north-west of where I was, or possibly just below that, where the woods sweep down the hillside towards Picksharp Farm. Less than 50 yards from me to the east was a stack of bales the size of a small house. Perfect. I parked the car around the back, cut the engine and got on the radio to call for back-up. It was a calculated gamble. If there were no gang, okay, I'd look pretty silly. But if there was one, I could be in real danger.

I got hold of a couple of Scarborough lads but they were way out at Ganton. They were on their way, but they'd need a good 20 minutes from there. Fingers crossed that they'd find me in time. Now it was a matter of waiting. I had my Dragon light and CS gas at the ready, and a pair of thick leather gauntlets

Walt had lent me. He used them when he went ferreting. The last thing I needed was a set of lurcher teeth embedded in my wrist.

Funny how it always seems to get extra chilly as the dawn breaks. I couldn't stop myself shivering as I leaned against the straw stack, taking regular peeks around the corner. One part of me was geared up for action, another was half hoping it was a false alarm. You never know quite what to expect in these situations, and the uncertainty makes it worse. I tried to push the doubts out of my mind. At least I had the element of surprise.

I didn't have long to wait. From out of the woods on the ridge, barely 400 yards away, three men with dogs came loping towards me. One of them was carrying what looked like a lantern, the sort that weighs four or five pounds and casts a beam 200 yards. They were walking in a straggly line, with their dogs on leashes.

'You bastards,' I shuddered, the image of that mutilated deer fresh in my mind. I ducked back out of their sight, the clean sweet smell of the straw in my nostrils. I wasn't going to expose myself until they were at their vehicle, preferably with the dogs locked away.

It took them three or four minutes to make it up the rise to their Range Rover. I waited till I heard the door creak open, then started up the car, shot out from my hiding-place and drove the 50 yards towards them, low gear, high revs, lights on full beam, a quick flash of the blue lights to let them know who I was. They'd just closed the tailgate on the dogs, but they were in no position to make a run. One was leaning into the driver's cab, and seemed to be fiddling about under the dashboard. A second was sitting against the rear passenger door pulling his boots off, and the third, with his back to me, was urinating against the straw-bale.

'Now then lads,' I was out of the car and walking across the stubble towards them, car lights still blazing, the Dragon light fixed on the face of the man at the driver's door as he turned, mouth open. My left hand was clutching the CS gas canister. If there was going to be trouble, I was ready for it.

Two of them were young, mid-twenties. The third, the one with his boots off, was more like 45. He was broad shouldered, with a thick neck. He wore a heavy khaki sweater with shoulder-patches, and a pair of dark combat trousers. His head was covered with a black beanie hat, and his brow was deeply furrowed, as if the scowl he wore was habitual. He was much calmer than I would've been in the circumstances. He was putting a pair of trainers on, and he was taking his time about it.

'You talking to me, pal?' He had a pronounced Liverpool accent, and he was chewing gum.

I avoided the obvious answer. 'Just wondering what you're doing out here,' I said. My aim at this point was to stall them, act a bit country copperish if I had to, and pray that the lads from Scarborough hadn't got lost. 'Are you out early, or up late?'

The man by the straw-bale zipped up his trousers. 'We're exercising our dogs, officer.' He was perfectly calm. He seemed very sure of his ground.

'Oh . . . seems an odd time of day. Are you not from around here?'

'How'd you focking guess, Einstein?'

'Ah, so you've come a fair way then.'

'Aye well, you know how it is, pal. Bit cramped for space in Liverpool, know what I mean?'

'You must be keen.'

'We like a bit of fresh air and a drive out.'

I walked towards the rear of the vehicle, the light still shining in the older man's face. I looked in through the window. The dogs were sniffing and pawing at it, steaming it up. From

167

a distance I'd thought they might be lurchers, but these were some kind of cross-breed. Lurchers are a gentle enough type of dog, like a greyhound, but the sort of people I was dealing with here will breed them with a collie to give them a bit of hunting nous. These ones had me puzzled with their powerful jaws and striped marking on their heads. Staffordshire bull terrier maybe. Wasn't that what Walt said?

'Interesting dogs. What breed are they?'

'No idea.'

'They look like hunters. D'you ever do a bit of hunting with them?' It was blatantly obvious that that's what they did. The slip-leads were the giveaway.

'No. I'm a vegetarian. Any more questions?'

I looked at the lamp, lying in the ground. 'Nice bit of kit that.'

'Aye well, we like to see where we're going. So as we don't, you know, trespass.'

The older man was on his feet. He stepped forward, close enough to me that I could smell his breath. Spearmint.

'What we do is our business, copper. And unless you wanna charge us with something, we don't need to tell you fock all.'

The best way to deal with people like that is to stay perfectly calm and not react. I was playing for time, but the longer I stayed my ground the sooner he would realize what he was dealing with. He would've met plenty of coppers before, and I could well believe he would've seen them off, because a lot of policemen, particularly young ones, on their own, will be intimidated by a fellow like him. They'll fudge it, take a blatant lie as an answer and back off. I'm not saying I'm any braver than any other copper, but I am stubborn. In this case I was angry too. I really, really detest what people like these do, and here, maybe, was a chance to collar them.

'We've had reports of deer-hunters operating illegally around here,' I said.

168

'Well, why aren't you out chasing them, 'stead of harassing innocent dog-walkers?'

'No, I was just wondering whether you'd seen any suspicious types. Blokes with guns, for example? Could've sworn I heard shots being fired a bit back.' Where the hell had my back-up got to?

'Excuse me, copper, but do you see any guns on us? Or any dead meat?'

'Listen,' I said, 'you're not dealing with a thick country copper here. I know very well what you've been up to. It's as plain as the nose on your face.'

'Well, you can just fock off, you four-eyed bastard.' As he stepped towards me again, the two young lads were at his side, squinting against the light of my lamp. I could be in trouble here, I was thinking, but as I mentioned earlier, the Good Lord blessed me with more than my fair share of luck. Just when I was wondering whether it was time to give them a sample of CS gas I heard the familiar sound of a Volvo V70.

'Well, isn't that an amazing coincidence,' I said, as my Scarborough lads appeared over the brow of the hill and swung towards us across the stubble. 'You travel all night and never see a cop car, and now look. Two show up at once. Dear oh dear, what would the odds be on that? Now, keys please. I think it's time to have a look in your wagon.'

I soon found what I wanted, tucked away under the front passenger seat with the jack. The hand-held camcorder would probably contain evidence which would convict all three of them under the Wildlife and Countryside Act of – now, when the hell was that Act? – one of these days I'd have to go on a proper wildlife course and get myself up to scratch. The trouble was – and I knew this very well – that in a straight poaching case we only had powers to summon a suspect to appear in court, not to make an arrest. Unless – and here's where the video could clinch it for us – unless we could bring a charge of cruelty to animals. By now my colleagues from Scarborough had run a check on the vehicle. It had been reported several times as out and about in the small hours, and was suspected of being involved in illegal field activities. The video – distressing as it was to watch it – gave us what we needed. It revealed in ugly detail precisely what these self-styled 'sportsmen' had been up to. Just as cock-fighting in some countries generates a huge amount of betting, so illegal hare-coursing or, in this case deer-hunting, is backed by big-money stakes. Huge bets are laid on which dog will make the first kill, or which one will be the first to attack a running deer. A filmed record of the gruesome spectacle, such as I had to view, serves two purposes. One, it provides entertainment for certain perverse individuals. But more importantly it provides the evidence that gamblers require to see. As innocent creatures in the wilds of North Yorkshire are literally hounded to their death, certain individuals in bars in cities far away are rubbing their hands, anticipating a big pay-out if their favourite dog comes up with a result. When the job is done, the prey is left to rot, the dog handlers drive home, and sooner or later the film ends up on the Internet for the amusement of like-minded individuals. Well, here was one that wouldn't.

The suspects thus had a nasty shock in store. Not only were we able to arrest them for cruelty to animals, but we were empowered to seize their vehicle, and their dogs, which we did.

Illegal coursing is a nasty, evil business, and very hard to police – although recent changes in the law have given us wider powers. I'd got lucky up there above Wharram Percy, no doubt about that. Lucky to stumble across the gang and extremely fortunate that my relief didn't show up any later. If they'd been delayed another five or ten minutes I could've been up the creek without the proverbial paddle, because we later found out that all three men had records of violent assault.

· Twelve ·

I've said it before – I hate death. I hate having to cope with dead bodies. I can cope with violent confrontation with a cool head. No problem at all. A lot of coppers dread that, and when chucking-out time came and I was in town I knew which of my colleagues I could rely on to be there with me, and which ones would suddenly find they had a call to make out in the villages. But that's one of the things I'm trained for, and I'm good at it. In my days in the Met I kicked down doors in the full knowledge that the men on the other side were desperate, and probably armed. I've stared down the barrel of a gun, I've been threatened with knives, with baseball bats, with bricks, and on one occasion with a vicious curved sword. And I dealt with it. The lad in question told me afterwards it was called a scimitar. But put me face to face with a dead body and my first instinct is to back away. It's a dread that's been with me since I was a boy, and I can't seem to push the thought out of my mind that one day, some day, that'll be me. I always say that it's the one thing you can absolutely count on, that from the moment you're born you're on this conveyor belt that's heading one way and one way only.

Don't get me wrong: I'm not a Jeremiah; I'm just a realist. The knowledge that we're all going to die some day keeps me concentrated on what I think is important – the preservation and enjoyment of life. To the full. While it lasts. But when I see a corpse, cold, grey, naked, lifeless, it makes me shudder and want to shut my eyes to the awful reality. Maybe it's immature; maybe it's something I need to sort out; but I'd prefer never having to think about it, and therefore I manage not to. Most of the time.

The trouble is, though, that being a country copper you encounter more dead bodies than you'll ever have to face in the big cities. That surprises a lot of people, not least new recruits to rural forces. It's about the nature of policing in an area like ours. Out here we're scattered pretty thinly, whereas in London we were confined to a much tighter area, maybe a couple of square miles. As a new copper, yes, it's part of your training; it's considered good for you to deal with dead bodies – toughens you up. Whenever there was a sudden death to investigate on our patch it was always, 'Where's that probationer?' Out here in Ryedale, though, you're often on your Jack Jones, and one of your duties is to act as the coroner's officer. So, not only are we often first on the scene when a death takes place, but it falls to us to check for signs of life and see whether there's any indication of foul play. And, as obvious as it sometimes is that a person's died, you can't perform your official duty just by looking at the body. You have to run the checks – and that means that as much as your instincts are telling you to shrink away from a body, your duty is to lean over it and unbutton the clothing to make quite sure there's no breath left. Then you'll reach out and probe with your fingers between the tendons under the wrist to make quite sure there's no faint pulse buried away beneath the skin – not the easiest procedure if *rigor mortis* has set in.

The funny thing is that it's not so much sudden, accidental deaths I'm talking about here. Because to me they're not the worst. Some of the injuries you see in road traffic accidents are horrific, sure they are, and I hate those too, but at least at a roadside scene, or – God forbid – a murder, you have a whole stack of things to get done, and the adrenalin kicks in as you tape the site off, create a crime scene, take witness statements, liaise with the traffic police and all of that. No, forget crash scenes. Not nice, but you do to some extent switch to auto-pilot. Think instead of some poor old fellow popping his clogs in an old folks' home – because we cover those deaths too, just as we cover any sudden fatality. In a case like that there's not much to set your pulse racing, just the unpleasant business, nice and methodical and by the book, of making sure that there is no sign of life.

I could probably sit down and list on my fingers every sudden death I had to deal with in my Battersea days, but in Ryedale, in the winter, when the death rate goes up, especially amongst older people in the rural communities, it's a pretty regular occurrence. That rainy November afternoon, when I was informed that someone had died at home in a tiny village at the foot of the Wolds, it was my third such call of the week – and this was only Thursday.

•　　•　　•

I turned off the A64 above Kirkham Abbey and down past Crambe. Through the murk I could see the grey shadow of the hill across the river, the bare trees of Howsham Woods almost obliterated by the driving rain. As I dropped down and crossed the bridge I could see the swollen Derwent swirling angrily over a tangle of branches, spilling over the alder-lined banks and into the pasture, dissolving the dark mole-hills one by one. I was heading for a place out towards Leppington, a little row of cottages. I wondered, as you always do when you're called out like this, what I would find. All I had so far was that it was an elderly man named Willoughby, and that his family was with him. But how long had he been dead? A day? A few hours? Surely he wasn't one of those poor people whose neighbours realize they haven't seen him for several days and you find him wedged in a toilet with flies crawling all over him? Or might he have died in the bath? That's not uncommon. Or was he lying in a pool of blood after an accident? A fall, perhaps? I've been to one or two of those and they aren't pleasant.

The longer the drive, the more chance your memory has to replay all the worst cases you've had to deal with, a grisly montage of scenes you'd like to forget. There was that decapitation by the railway line just outside Clapham Junction, a drunk who'd somehow managed to clamber over the wall and fallen down the embankment. We spent 20 minutes in freezing fog searching for the missing part, until a railway inspector pointed out that the train had thrown it down an embankment. I had to go and pick it up – and I remember my relief when I found that the victim had long hair. It makes it easier to carry – especially when you're scrambling up a slope like that, because a human head is surprisingly heavy. There was the *Marchioness* disaster, when I was involved in pulling bodies – and survivors – out of the river. That's always haunted me, the way you could let a victim slip from your grasp and watch them go under, not to re-appear until they were half a mile or so downstream. I always remember one young female, expensively dressed, good-looking too – if you can say that about a corpse. That was what stayed with me – that she would've been drop-dead gorgeous if she'd been alive.

I nosed the car along the bumpy lane, steering my way round the puddles. You never know quite how deep they are on these single-lane roads. I was consciously steeling myself, even as I found the cottages, tucked away up a pot-holed track behind a stand of larches. You just never know what you might find. Three or four cars were parked outside the end cottage, and a young man standing in the porch, shoulders hunched against the rain as he puffed on a cig.

'Oh, Mike. I'm glad it's you, mate.' I recognized him as soon as he spoke. I knew him from the Jolly Farmers. Peter, his name was. We'd played pool together a time or two. Never knew his surname till now. I was about to ask him who had died – and when you think about it, that's not an easy question to frame – but he spared me the trouble. 'It's me Grandad, Jackie. Did you know him?'

'Can't say I did, Pete.'

'Only went a couple of hours since.' He threw his cigarette into the road. 'Come on, me Grandma's inside.'

She was at the door when we stepped into the porch. Her name was Eva, she told me – a nice old-fashioned name. 'I'm sorry,' I said. 'I wish I wasn't seeing you under these circumstances.'

'Oh, you have it to do,' she said. 'Come and meet the family.'

There was a round of hand-shaking. Her brother, a squat man in a chequered shirt and one of those quilted body-warmers. Then her and Jack's daughter and husband, Pete's parents, a couple in their late to mid-fifties by the look of them. They were all sitting there at the table in the living-kitchen. There was a teapot, a vase full of chrysanths, and a clutter of empty cups and saucers. Willow pattern, very traditional. There was a matching plate in the middle with a few ginger biscuits on it, and a sugar-bowl. I was wondering whether to set about the business, but Eva was already filling the kettle. 'You'll be wanting a cup of tea,' she said. 'You look frozen half to death.' She must've noticed me shuddering.

'Aye, it isn't very nice out there,' I said. Then I took a breath. 'I'm afraid I'll have to ask you what happened,' I added.

'Well,' she said, 'when we got up this morning he said he wasn't feeling too bright.' She paused at the work-top and flicked on a switch. She had a ring on her finger that sparkled as a fluorescent strip-light came on. 'Tired, he said. But not ill. He was never ill.'

175

'Do you know, he hadn't seen the doctor for 20 years and more,' her brother said.

'Oh, more than that, and then it was only a check-up for the insurance.'

It seemed they'd had an early lunch and then he'd taken the dog out for its walk. 'He always took him down the lane after lunch.' She smiled.

'Liked his walk, did Jackie.'

'Aye, and that old collie thought the world of him.'

I looked around for the dog, but I couldn't see it.

'Anyway,' the old lady continued, 'he was back within five minutes. Said he just didn't feel he had the energy, and besides it was coming on to rain. So we made up the fire' – she nodded towards the door that led to the sitting-room – 'in there. Sat ourselves down for a little nap.'

She broke off to fetch a cup and saucer from the dresser. When she'd set them on the table she continued, 'I must have woken up after an hour or so. Come on Jack, I said, let's see about some tea and a biscuit, but as soon as I looked at him I . . . well, I could see.'

Peter put arm around his grandmother. 'Now then, Gran, sit yourself down while the tea mashes.'

You have to read people at times like this. You're there in an official capacity and you have things to do, but you have to operate at their pace. No good forcing it. That'll only add to their difficulties. Luckily Peter was on the ball. 'You'll be wanting to see him, I suppose,' he said.

'Aye.'

'I'll come in with you, mate.'

The doctor, he told me, had actually been by and pronounced life extinct an hour ago. 'Said he'd had Grandad on his register for over 20 years, and never set eyes on him.'

We entered the sitting-room. It was warm, almost too warm, the fire blazing away. And there he was. He made a strange sight, sitting in his big armchair next to the hearth. They'd not covered him or anything. He was wearing a thick, snug cardigan and a pair of dark green corduroy trousers. He must have nodded off looking at the newspaper, because there it was on the floor beside him, open at the TV guide, and his glasses still perched on the end of his nose, his hands clasped in his lap. He might have been asleep, at a casual glance, just a paleness about his face to make you wonder. And there beside his chair was the dog – an elderly, overweight border collie, looking up at me almost questioningly as I set about my business.

I explained to young Pete what I was doing. 'Have to check his pockets to make a note of any valuables,' I said. 'It's a formality.'

'Oh aye,' he said. 'You have your job to do.'

It was strange, this, because as I moved his hands to one side to check his hip pocket he was still warm. It'd be the fire, of course, but it did feel peculiar. I noted his watch, a wallet containing a couple of tenners, a few loose coins in his pockets, the plain gold band on his left hand. Otherwise that was it.

As I made my notes I saw that Eva and the family had followed me in and were sitting down as if this was a normal social get-together over a cup of tea. Her son was petting the dog, and his wife was handing me my cup with a couple of biscuits in the saucer. She bent down and picked up the paper from the floor, folding it carefully. It didn't seem to strike anyone else as odd, that we should be sitting around the fire, with the head of the family there in his favourite chair, dead. It reminded me of films I'd seen of Irish wakes. For a moment I was worried I might start laughing. The old lady seemed quite up-beat as her daughter perked up and started to reminisce about the old fellow.

'Well,' she said, 'he's been such a lovely man, hasn't he? Been loving, caring . . .'

'Been a grafter too,' her uncle added. 'By golly he could work,

177

back in the days when we had to. Horse days, I'm talking about. Never had no machinery back then, you know. You should've seen him when he had those five-stone sacks of grain. He could lift 'em all day.'

'Aye, and then play cricket on a night.'

'He's had a good innings has t'old lad. Eighty-three and never a day's illness since he fell off that tractor.'

'Oh aye, that. When would that be now?'

'Has to be 30-odd years since.'

I'd never experienced anything like this. Where was the distress? The tears? The sense of awkwardness you usually get when you're the official taking charge of the scene and everyone's going to pieces? It was actually a very peaceful scene. And as I thought about it I could see why. Here was a man who'd had a good life, a family who loved him, and he'd slipped quietly away, no fuss, in his own home. It was as if he'd known when the time was right. And I could see they were all glad for him. No months and months in hospital, drugged, fading away, his memory failing; no crying out in pain that nobody could help him with; no mental disintegration. That's what it was, I realized: they were happy for him. And me? I was envious. I realized that that's how I want to go. There's no escaping death, so why not have it that way?

I filled out my forms, jotting down the old man's date and place of birth and suchlike. And they were quite happy to answer my questions. Was he on any medication? No – never needed any. Fit as a flea. Did they know when he'd last visited the doctor? Ah, they'd figured it out now. It was 1969 when he fell off a tractor and did his ankle. Summertime, it was, because they remembered now how he stopped home for a week with his leg on a stool and watched the moon landings on TV. Liked to tell everyone it was an ill wind and all that.

I now had to organize an undertaker. Had they anyone in mind? Of course they had. They knew the form. It was only

15 years since they'd buried Jackie's mother. She'd lived to 94 – and there they were, off again, reminiscing, until Peter reminded them that I'd asked a question. There were two firms in town and of course they chose the old established one.

I popped into the kitchen and got on my radio. It didn't take long to get an answer. The undertakers would be along in 20 minutes, maybe half an hour. I sat and filled in my report for the coroner's officer, then went back to tell the family that Jack would be taken to Scarborough. 'That's the nearest mortuary,' I said. 'They'll let you know if they think a post-mortem's called for.'

I decided I'd stay until the undertaker arrived. He might need a hand. Couldn't really ask the bereaved relatives to help shift the body. While I waited Eva showed me around the place. I hadn't really noticed before, but she had photographs everywhere – in frames on the sideboard, or hung on the walls in the kitchen, living-room, hallway. There was their wedding, just towards the end of the war, one of those black-and-white pictures that had been colour-tinted to show off her rosy cheeks and blue dress, his bronzed handsome face. There were pictures of the children, at school, on their holidays, playing with pets in the garden. There was the silver wedding, and the golden, and a whole series of Jackie in his whites holding a cricket bat or ball. 'Oh, he played for all these villages,' Eva said, and her face was glowing with pride. 'Burythorpe, Acklam, Leavening. They all had teams and he turned out for anyone who'd give him a game.'

As I followed her round the house and listened to her stories of the life they'd shared I realized this was more of a celebration than a mourning. When the undertaker arrived at the door it was as if he was just another visitor popping in. He knew the family. He'd buried Jack's mother, and Eva's sister. He'd brought his wife with him. She was soon sat down with the family, explaining that they'd be back next day to talk about

179

what kind of service they wanted. I looked at Eva. It seemed to me she might be in shock now. Being busy had helped her, but now she realized we were going to remove the body from the house. Again, Peter was on the ball. 'Here, Grandma,' he said, 'let's you and me go into kitchen and get them pots washed, shall we?'

Jackie may have been 83, but he was still a big man. It took three of us – me, Ted the undertaker, and his wife – to lift him carefully from his seat and lay him on the mat in front of the fire. There's a very particular quality to the weight of a dead body. You get no help, not like when you're shifting someone who's injured, for example. You can soon pull their clothes half off if you aren't careful. But we managed. I remember looking at his face, calm and peaceful, as we eased him on to the stretcher, and thinking once more, I hope I live that long and die that way. Then we spread a blanket over him and, with Ted one end and me the other, we carried him out through the kitchen. I did glance at his wife, and I saw the tears in her eyes. But her daughter was there at her side, comforting her.

They were good people. They thanked me as I got into the car. I told them I'd come back in a week or so just to see whether everything was okay. I like to say that, and I always make a note in my diary and follow up. I call that good community policing – especially when people are alone, as Eva now would be.

●   ●   ●

What light there had been was fading fast as I drove back down the lane towards Howsham Bridge, and the countryside was still dripping wet. All the traces of colour that normally hang on through November seemed to have been washed away by 24 hours of continuous rain. Usually you'll see a few yellow ash-leaves clinging on in a sheltered corner, or a cluster of rose-hips, but all I could see that evening was blackened trees,

180

the dark earth of ploughed fields, and a grey sky flushed with orange as the lights of Malton came on.

It's always a bit of a jolt getting back on to the main road after an episode like that. There's everyone driving home from work, gripping the wheel and snarling because the traffic's so slow again on Golden Hill. And there you are, straight from helping a family come to terms with the loss of a mainstay, a rock, removing his body from the house that's been his only home these last 60 years, and suddenly the radio's going. Somebody's rear-ended a car right by the level crossing in town. Nobody hurt, but you're nearest so will you go and sort it out.

They talk about stress. I don't think it's the actual situations you deal with as such, just the fact that you never have time to sit down and think them through afterwards. There's always another situation to deal with. And living on my own, as I was then . . . I swung down through town, lights flashing, and went to see what all the fuss was about.

· **Thirteen** ·

Things change fast when you're out on patrol, faster than the North Yorkshire weather. One minute you can be sitting in the car eating a sandwich, watching the silhouette of a combine as it rolls along a sunlit horizon in a cloud of golden dust, the old harvest hymns drifting through your memory . . . the next minute you're haring off to a bust-up outside a pub, the air thick with foul language, combustible breath and dire threats. The one thing seems to drive the other out of your mind. But as much as you imagine that one day's excitement is buried under the weight of the next, you soon learn that that's all it is – buried. Or should I say smothered? Because it's still down there, as vivid as ever, and the one certainty is that all those memories, serene, violent, tragic, uplifting, haunting, will re-emerge from time to time like so much acid reflux.

Take something like the beheading I mentioned. You never really kill off a memory like that. We tried, back at the station over a cup of tea. We made light of it. Someone cracked a couple of feeble jokes about 'no point losing your head', 'running around like headless chickens' and so on, and we tried to convince ourselves we'd put it to bed. And in any case, within the hour we were preoccupied with some new drama; but in the end I had to face the fact that it would live with me. Sometimes these things'll come back and haunt you weeks, months, even years later. Sure, you think you've dealt with them, but you haven't killed them off. They're there. All the time. The trick – well, it works for me – is to try and summon up a happier memory in its place. Special days. Special people. Special events. I do that when I have to go to the dentist and they want to shove a needle into my gum. I used to think about falling in love – but then my gorgeous female dentist moved on and was replaced by a chap with a beard and a baritone voice. So now I lie there and think about the time I went to Old Trafford and watched York City beat Man U 3–0. That takes my mind off things for a few moments – even his hairy forearms. It still makes me grin, ten years after.

Strange as it may sound, though, that sudden death out there at Leppington had actually been an uplifting experience. It must have made a big impression on me, because I remember I told Walt about it that night when I got back to the house. I think it was the first time I'd really understood that death was a natural part of living – especially if you've lived well and had your full share of happiness, and are able to pass peacefully away with your loved ones close by like old Jackie did. But it was those very circumstances that started to eat away at me that night as I lay in my bed in Walter's spare room, huddled under a pile of blankets with the rain lashing at the window. Here I was, 38 years old, and on my own. What if I were to die now? Who would be there for me? Who would come and sit by me until the police or the undertaker came along? Who would be there to tell them what a great fellow I'd been?

I'd been on my own for a few months now. And in a way I suppose it suited me. I'd been on one or two dates, but that's all they were – dates. I never really followed them up. I told people I wasn't ready, or that I didn't want to get involved. I said I was okay on my own, being the single man again. My time was my own to do as I pleased. And since most of my colleagues were married, they all agreed with me that I was a lucky fellow. I could come and go as I pleased, never had to report back to anyone or explain where I'd been. Most married men want to believe that about you, because from where they stand the grass generally looks greener. Half of them, I came to realize, feel trapped.

After a while, though, I started to have my doubts. Then I started wondering what, if anything, I might be looking for. It was Ed who got me thinking. We were sitting in the Jolly Farmers one night enjoying a steak dinner. It was the end of the month and you always feel a bit flush then.

'You're a lucky man,' he said. 'There's never been a better time to be single.'

'You reckon?'

'Well, take a look around. There's so many women on the loose these days. Single, divorced . . .' He winked at me over the top of his pint. 'Otherwise available.'

'I'm not looking for a loose woman, mate.'

'Okay then, what about a respectable girl, never been married, steady job?'

'Mm . . . could be interested.'

''Cos I can tell you one, and I have a feeling you could be just her type.'

'Tell me she's not a copper first.'

'Why, something wrong with that?'

'Ed, mate, I have a horrible suspicion I know who you're gonna say.'

'Who?'

'Our cockney friend.'

'She's keen on you, you know.'

'I've had a strange feeling about that. But she's just not my type, Ed. She's too . . .'

'Too what?'

'Well, her accent for a start. Does my bloody head in.'

'You could send her for elocution lessons.'

'Very funny.'

'Staple her lips together?'

'Now you're talking.'

'Problem solved, then.'

'No. There's . . . well . . .' I was struggling for words, gesturing with my hands. 'I mean, would I want to be going out with a copper?'

'How about if she was really, really fit?'

'Aye well, that always helps.'

Ed attacked his sirloin, and chewed thoughtfully. ''Cos I did see one the other day.'

'Oh aye, and where was that?'

'In the Wendy House.'

We called it the Wendy House not because it looked like one – although personally I never had one when I was a kid, and I still haven't the faintest idea what they were supposed to look like, but I'm sure they don't resemble our Super's lair out the back of the station. No, the reason we call it the Wendy House is that we never really give anyone in authority a great deal of respect. And, of course, we fancy ourselves as comic geniuses.

'Anyway, what was she doing in there? Or, more to the point, what were *you* doing in there?'

'Ah, you see, you're interested already. You're hooked, mate.' Ed was grinning from ear to ear, prodding his fork at me as he spoke. 'And what do you *think* I might have been doing in there?'

'Well, speaking for myself, mate, I only go over there when I've filled in another of those report sheets he gives me.'

'What report sheets?'

'You mean he doesn't send them out to you?'

'What you on about?'

'The ones where I have to make an assessment of all my fellow officers. Tell him what you've all been up to, your sexual proclivities and drinking habits and suchlike.'

'Yeah yeah yeah. Very funny. Now look, do you want to hear about this WPC or not?'

'Aye, but not until you've got your round in.'

What Ed told me was that he was in the Wendy House one morning when they were interviewing for the vacant post. 'They had four candidates, all in their smartest outfits. Shoes polished, trousers all pressed, buttons nice and shiny, hands by their sides. Stood there like a bunch of startled rabbits.'

'Four WPCs? You're kidding.'

'No, three of them were lads. There was just the one lass.'

'Lads? Lasses? How old are we talking about?'

'Oh, pretty young. Well, the lads were. Mid-twenties I'd say.'

'And the lass?'

'Well, I'm a married man, so I didn't look. But if you were to ask me, I'd have to say she was fairly young. And very fit . . . outstanding in fact.'

'Outstanding? Is that one of your smutty innuendos, PC Cowan?'

'I mean . . . outstandingly good looking.'

'Great, but she was one of four, right?'

He nodded, and stirred his leftover spuds around to gather up the gravy on his plate.

'Well, there you are,' I said.

'There you are what?'

'Why are you trying to get me excited about a fit young WPC who's one of four candidates for a vacant post – bearing in mind that half the time we've a budgetary squeeze on and they never bloody fill them anyway?'

'Because, you four-eyed pillock, I have heard a whisper.'

'Ed, this could go on all night. Spit it out, will you? No, no, no – please, not your steak in red-wine sauce.'

He closed his mouth, somehow managed to chew and grin at the same time. He was loving this. 'Well,' he said, pausing to wipe his mouth on a paper napkin, 'I've been told, by a reliable source, that the vacant post has indeed been filled. By a WPC.'

'Oh, has it? Well . . . watch this space, as they say.'

'I've also heard that she's from your neck of the woods.'

'What, out here at Leavening?'

'No no no – London. From the Met.'

•   •   •

It's funny looking back, the way little things stick in your mind. I distinctly remember that night when I got back home having a night-cap with Walt, and saying to him, 'There's a rumour going round they've appointed a new WPC, and she's from the Met as well.' And Walt said, 'Ah, that's just what you need, young fellow-me-lad. Get yourself settled down with a good woman.'

'Steady on, Walt,' I said. 'It's a rumour. She hasn't even arrived yet. And whoever said I was ready to settle down?'

And Walt just sat there, reaching out with his slippered foot to kick a log towards the back of the fire. 'Aye,' he said, 'but you must be hopeful, otherwise you wouldn't have told me, would you now?'

I thought about what Walt had said when I went off to bed that night. Maybe he was right. Maybe I really had had enough of being single. Perhaps it was time for a change. In any case, I thought, it was surely time I moved on from Walt's, time I made a serious effort to find a place of my own. I should be able to find somewhere now that I was properly established in the area. As well as my 'Regional HQ' at Walt's place I had any number of places where I could stop off, have a natter and get some refreshment. It wouldn't be an exaggeration to say that I was rarely more than five minutes from a cup of tea – except out on the moors, maybe. There were all the people involved in Country Watch, for a start. And then there were people like Algy. Correction – there was actually nobody quite like Algy, and probably never has been. I'd already met Algy in the pub that time when I'd touched him for a tenner, but it wasn't until his name came up in relation to a house that might be available in the village that I realized I hadn't paid him back yet.

It all kicked off when I was told to investigate a spot of illegal flag-flying.

'Illegal flag-flying? You're having me on, of course.' Chris Cocks, our desk sergeant, loved a good wind-up. He'd once sent a young probationer out to search the banks of Pickering Beck and look for ducks. Told him the local takeaways were suspected of stealing them and serving them up to unsuspecting punters in a curry sauce, so would he do a stock-take and report back. It was all very elaborate. He even gave the lad a little camera and told him to gather evidence. And he made sure he called him in when we were having fish and chips on a Saturday teatime, and grilled him about his findings while we all sat there trying to keep a straight face. But he wasn't taking the mick this time.

'Nope,' he insisted. 'There are certain flags you are not allowed to fly in the public view.'

'What, the skull and crossbones? Swastikas?'

'Interesting point. Tell you what, I might look it up when I get a moment. However,' he said, leaning back in his chair with his hands behind his head and a smug grin on his face, 'I think you should go and explain to one country landowner that in furtherance of certain complaints received he can no longer display his Yorkshire flag in view of the public highway. It's all in here.' He picked up a copy of the *Yorkshire Post* and ran his finger down the page. 'Here we are – Ryedale farmer told, quote, "it was illegal to display the Yorkshire flag without formal planning consent and payment of a £60 charge."'

I'm not often lost for words, but I know I stood there with my mouth open until Jayne squeezed past me carrying the sergeant's morning coffee on a tray.

'Stand there like that you'll catch a fly.' She put the tray on the desk and squeezed past me again, rubbing her hips against mine.

189

'Thank you, Jayne, and— oi!'

'Wassup, doncha like 'aving your bottom pinched?'

'No, I do not.'

'Well, now you know how we women feel, eh?'

'Listen, I'm very selective about whose arse I pinch.'

'Get you. Mr Choosy.'

'I bloody well am, Jayne. And I think I'll choose not to hear what our desk sergeant is saying.'

'Oh, you mean that nutter with the Yorkshire flag?' She grinned at Chris. 'Told ya he wouldn't like it.'

'What is this? You two been cooking sommat up?'

Chris leaned forward and brought the front feet of his chair thudding to the ground. 'Look, given a choice of you and our Cockney friend here, I thought you could handle it more tactfully,' he said, 'you being a fellow Yorkshireman. Anyway, it seems our friend has a huge pole and he's threatened to ram it up—'

'Aye, go on then, it's a man's job. That what you're saying?'

''Fraid so, old buddy. Anyway, joking aside, I just think you might want to have a word. He's on your patch, after all, and he seems to have got himself in a spot of bother.'

'You mean, you want me to make sure we haven't got a madman on our hands?'

'Look, it's the Super. He read this thing in the paper. Said we should check the guy out. Tell the truth, I think he's just curious about him.'

'Go on,' I said, 'give us the details.' I looked out through the window. After a frosty start the sun was getting up and it was turning into a lovely late autumn morning. 'I can handle anything on a day like this.'

'Name's a bit of a gob-full.' Chris picked up a yellow report sheet. 'Hubert Miles Fortescue Bigby-Waring. Lives out at—'

'Hang about. Miles? Waring? I know that name. Lives out my way, just outside Leavening?'

'Aye, he does. Big country house sort of place. They reckon he's loaded.'

'He is. Stinking.'

'How d'you know?'

'He happens to be one of my drinking buddies,' I laughed. 'We call him Algy. In fact . . . hell, you've just reminded me. I owe the bugger a tenner from way back.'

• • •

Miles' full name was indeed a bit of a mouthful, but it was soon tripping off my tongue as if I'd known him all my life. Only someone rich and eccentric – and trust me, his family were exceedingly rich – would saddle their eldest son with a name like that. It's a thing the aristocracy do, same as the royals. They do it so as to name-check a few ancestors, and any well-heeled relatives, keeping them sweet in case they're ever stuck for someone to leave their fortunes to. And then after the christening they give the lad a proper name, just to confuse everyone. Well, I say a proper name: in this case, they came up with Algernon, poor bugger – Algy for short. I have no idea why they chose that, but then, as someone once said of the rich – they're different from us. And as someone else rightly replied, yes, they have more money. Algy probably had more money than I will ever see. He had land, here and abroad, he had property in the shape of a huge Georgian farmhouse with cottages and outbuildings, a super collection of old vehicles, a share in a gold mine in southern Africa, and he loved to splash his money around.

As I drove up the gravelled drive I checked my wallet. I'd got in the habit of never taking much money out of the house with me. I was saving up. Not sure what for, exactly. Perhaps it was Walt's frugal ways getting to me. Or the realization that some-where down the line I needed to find my own gaff and move out. Anyway, I was okay – I had a couple of notes, and a few pound coins. First thing I'd do was pay back what I owed him.

The house stood on a slight rise, a large, solid, pale stone affair with tall windows, deep eaves, roses growing up over a dark blue front door, and all overshadowed by a huge copper beech. I got out of the car and was about to tug the brass bell-pull when I heard him call out to me.

'Ah, Pannett. Thought you must've joined the Foreign Legion. So you've come to wipe the old slate clean, have we?' He was standing 30 yards away on the lawn, right beside his flag-pole with a paint-brush in his hand. Beside him lay an aluminium extension ladder. The pole must have been 20 feet high, glistening with a new coat of Dulux and topped by a huge silky pennant. Pale blue background with a Yorkshire rose: five white petals and a yellow centre.

'Aye,' I said. 'I'm ever so sorry about that. Tell you the truth, I forgot all about it. Woke up with such a hangover the next morning.'

'Ah yes. Well, you can thank young Soapy for that.'

I didn't get what he meant, but I let it pass. 'Anyway, it wasn't until my Sergeant told me to come out and see you that I remembered.'

'Come out and see me? You're not here on official business, are you?'

'Well, it's a bit embarrassing really, but it's about this.' I pointed up at the flag, fluttering gently in the breeze, its colours sharp against the bright morning sun.

Algy groaned. 'I knew they wouldn't listen to reason. Blasted planners. So they've set the law on me, have they?'

'Well,' I said, opening the notebook and clicking my pen, 'it's a serious matter. You're allowed to fly the Union Jack, the Cross of St George on appropriate days, as you know; but a regional or sectarian standard could be construed as a traitorous act. Tantamount to sedition, they tell me.'

As his jaw dropped lower and lower, I could feel my face cracking. 'And you know what the penalty for that is.' I drew a finger across my throat, at which point the penny dropped.

He put down his brush as I took the tenner from my pocket and handed it over. 'Good God, Mike, you nearly stopped the old ticker. You know the planning bods have been on to me, don't you?'

'Aye, it was all over the *Yorkshire Post*. What are you going to do?'

'Fight 'em on the beaches, old chap.' He set down his brush on the paint-pot and sighed. 'It's a bloody farce. According to them, flying the flag is advertising and for that I need planning permission. You ever heard of anything so patently daft?'

'I'll give you my candid personal opinion on that when I'm out of uniform,' I said.

'Listen, won't you come inside and have a cup of tea?'

'Result,' I murmured under my breath.

I was sitting in the kitchen waiting for the kettle to boil when the door opened and in walked a couple of bedraggled Patterdale terriers followed by Soapy.

'Now then,' he said. 'How are you, me old cockbird?'

One of the terriers had come straight across to me and put his head on my knee. 'Better than the morning after I last saw you,' I said.

Soapy loosened the red bandanna around his neck. 'Why, were you badly?'

'No, I was bloody hungover, that's what I was. Christ, it was half past one by the time I got home.'

For a moment there was silence as I started pulling sticky burrs out of the dog's coat. When I looked up I saw Soapy glance at Algy, who then beamed at me.

'You knew that bloody clock had stopped, didn't you?' I said.

'Soapy, old chap, put him out of his misery.'

Soapy took three china mugs off the dresser and sat down. 'Well, fact is, matey . . .'

'Go on,' I said.

'Best get it off your chest, old fellow.' Algy was grinning like a bloody hyena.

'Aye well, it weren't stopped as such.'

'No, but it had slowed to a crawl.'

'Well, it weren't that neither.' He was almost wincing as he spoke, lining the mugs up with the crack that ran along the centre of the old oak table. 'It were . . . it were getting turned back, do you see? That's what were happening like.'

'How d'you mean?'

'Why, every time your back was turned someone was up on a chair fiddling with the hands, like.'

'But you can't . . . that's against the law, that is!'

'That's what I said,' Algy put in. 'But you know what some people are like once they get an idea into their head – and a few pints of best bitter inside them.'

'You mean there's no stopping them.'

'Yes, rather like me and my flag out there.'

'Oh well, at least it makes sense now. The . . . why, the crafty buggers. Couldn't have a lock-in with me there, I suppose, so . . . No wonder I was . . . But who was doing it then? Who was turning the hands back?'

Soapy was back at the dresser. He pulled the lid off a big square cake tin and held it out to me. 'Here, cockbird, have a biscuit with your tea.'

'Aye, I don't mind if I do. But you haven't answered my question yet. Mm . . . chocolate Leibnitz. Ve—ry nice. You lads live well up here.'

Algy grabbed a couple for himself. 'Come on, Soapy, get it out, m'boy.'

Soapy put the tin on the table. 'Why, the lads put me up to it, like. Every time you turned around they was digging me in

194

t'ribs, like. "Go on, quick." Or when you went outside to t'toilet, so I just shuffled her back a quarter of an hour or so.'

'Why you cheeky . . . So that's what was going on.'

'You're not peeved, are you?' Algy asked as he poured the tea.

'Well, I might have been if I'd known what was happening at the time.' I nibbled on my biscuit. 'But no . . . at least you've put me mind at rest. Thought I was losing the plot when I got home.'

'How's that, cockbird?'

'Well, I went down the pub for a quiet pint and ended up drinking about five . . . and all in three-quarters of an hour. I never drank that fast even when I was young and foolish. I couldn't imagine how I'd done it. Now I know the answer, don't I?'

'Aye, because you was there about three bloody hours and more.'

'Yes,' said Algy as he poured the tea into my mug, 'and to compound your sins, it was after hours – so you're in no position to press charges, are you constable? Now then, one lump or two?'

· Fourteen ·

It was a gorgeous day in early November – a bright sun, a pure blue sky, the fields of winter wheat a sparkling emerald green, and as I drove into the station for my late turn a light breeze was sending down showers of copper and gold beech-leaves. As if that wasn't enough to raise my spirits, I had on the seat beside me a letter telling me that I'd been selected to go on a course. Now, the police offer all kinds of courses for personal and professional development, and because someone, somewhere – usually in London – is being paid a fat salary to dream them up, they get kind of miffed if nobody applies. And very often, nobody does. The reason is that amongst us foot-soldiers, these courses are viewed with grave suspicion. At a local level we have what we think of as an ongoing manpower problem – namely that there are hardly ever enough officers to cover our patch. And of course we're deeply suspicious of anyone with pretensions. So the usual assumption when someone announces that they're off on a course is that (a) they're a lazy bugger looking for a week or two's lozicking, or that (b) they think they're destined for better things than patrolling the streets and dealing with the public face to face. There's also the usual 'haven't our supposed superiors got anything better to do than dream up ways of depleting our resources and lumbering us with overtime?' – except of course from those people who lap up all the overtime they can get. I wouldn't say that necessarily makes them money-grabbing pillocks, because we've all welcomed a bit of extra now and then, but nobody in their right mind wants it foisted on them – which is what's likely to happen when your colleagues swan off on a course in stress management, or team-building, or familiarization with yet another piece of computer software, or the one on lifting heavy objects which comes around every so often. Bend your *knees*, ladies and gentlemen!

However, I had been approached by our Inspector – which in itself would be guaranteed to get some of my colleagues whispering behind my back. Most coppers assume that any contact with the Almighty is instant grounds for suspicion, but in this case what he said to me made sense. He said that since I was getting on so well on my rural beat I ought to be appointed Wildlife Officer, which would mean taking responsibility for cases involving hunting, fishing – and poaching, of course – as well as some broader environmental issues. And to that end, would I fancy a week's course at the delightful old Warwickshire Police HQ in Leek Wootton?

Would I fancy . . .? Hah! Does the Pope wear a funny hat, I was thinking to myself as I drove towards my usual parking spot right under the silver birch tree – only to find a red Mercedes A170 parked there. And then, just as I was shoving my faithful old Astra into reverse and looking around for an alternative spot, a lovely-looking woman in a long winter coat walked across my field of vision, flashed a warm smile at me, and got into the Merc. About five four . . . dark hair . . . maybe eight stone . . . I'd remember her if we ever ran across each other again. Unfortunately she was wearing gloves, so no chance to check on the ring situation.

The fact is I'm no different from any other man. I accept that from about the age of 12 we blokes are fated to be distracted from our work by any good-looking woman who happens by. Of course, it wears off as you get older, so that by the age of about 79, which I believe is the average man's life expectancy, you don't worry about it quite as much as you used to. You have other things on your mind, such as your failing organs, the whereabouts of your false teeth, the hereafter and so on. But until then, show us a pretty face or a shapely figure and we're inclined to lose the power of reason. However plain we may be, however overweight, however old, however married, as soon as a good-looking woman smiles at us we still think, 'aye aye, we might be on to something here.' We can't help it. We're programmed to do it – and all because Mother Nature is worried that the species might die out. You have to wonder whether Mother Nature has done her sums recently. Anyway, while I constantly blame her for making the opposite sex so attractive, at the same time I thank her. Like this glorious afternoon, like the yellow leaves and gleaming white bark of the birch tree that shaded my parking spot, the young woman with the ready smile who had parked her fancy car right where I wanted to be had raised my spirits.

●   ●   ●

I think I first started getting interested in the opposite sex – I mean seriously interested – when I was 14. I remember asking my big brother if his girlfriends could bring their sisters round to our house. He was having none of that. 'When you get to my age,' he used to say – he was a full two years older than me – 'you can't be doing with little sisters around the place.'

'Why not?' I asked. As far as I was concerned, the more the merrier. His answer, to a lad of my tender years, may have been dismissive, but it seemed the height of sophistication at the time. I was, remember, a simple country lad. 'They cramp your style,' he said, as he kick-started his moped and puttered off for a night of table-tennis, orange squash and groping down at the youth club in Easingwold. Style, I remember thinking. Aye, maybe that's what I need.

Twenty-five years on – and leaving aside the question of whether I would ever acquire this elusive thing they called style – life was pretty good. I was back in North Yorkshire. I had a well-paid job which I loved. And, according to everyone else, the world was full of women with nothing on their mind but having a good time. Trouble was, I never saw anyone I really, seriously fancied. Somebody who made my heart stop and my jaw drop. Unrealistic perhaps, but, looking back, I now see that that's what I was after. Trouble was, as time went by it seemed ever less likely.

We men are inclined to spend a lot of time talking about our ideal of feminine beauty. We'll argue for hours about blondes versus brunettes, slim ones against cuddly ones, and whether you should go for youth or experience. It's a favourite pastime of unattached fellows. After all, they have a lot of time on their hands. It's all speculation, and it's all pure, unadulterated cobblers. Because when it comes right down to it, the minute a halfway presentable woman shows the slightest sign of interest in us, we're done for. Putty in their hand, slaves to their every whim. And I was no different from any other man – except for one thing. I actually did have some sort of picture in my head, a vague fantasy of the kind of woman I was looking for. You see, I reckoned I'd met her, many years before.

When my brother turned 17 he bought a car. It was a Mark 1 Viva in brick red, probably the ugliest car ever produced by the British motor industry: it looked as though it was designed by a zombie, cobbled together from a collection of old sardine-tins and given a quick paint-job in a kids' nursery. It was horrible, a real blot on the roadscape, but that car raised my brother's profile. The village girls soon formed an orderly queue at our door asking him if he'd take them for a ride, or run them into town – or, better still, would he come to the party on Friday and act as chauffeur for a whole gaggle of them? The bad news was that he actually believed it was him they were after rather

200

than his wheels, but the good news was that his sudden popularity brought out an expansive streak I'd never seen before. When he saw me looking wistfully at his redundant moped he waved a dismissive hand in its direction and said, 'Go on with you, tek it. I've got me passion-wagon now. Here, you may as well have the helmet too.' Of course, I had to wait a full year – the longest year of my life – before the law allowed me to take it out on the open road, but by the time my sixteenth birthday came around I was an accomplished rider, having put in long hours of practice on the bare autumn fields, along deserted farm tracks, and – I think it's safe to admit it now – up and down the lane at the end of the village when nobody was about.

So there I was, 16 years old and full of myself, with 49 cc of brute power throbbing away between my legs. There was one particular stretch of road just outside the village that I loved to race along. I'd crouch down over the handle-bars, twist the throttle round as far as it would go and watch the speedo nudge its way up to and past the 30 mark, and I'd lean into the sharp bends with one knee grazing the tarmac. Which is what I was doing one fine autumn afternoon when I came hurtling through the woods just outside Huby and saw in front of me a chestnut mare rearing up on her hind legs in the middle of the road. I slammed the brakes on, went into a rear-wheel skid, and ended up on the verge, knee-deep in fallen leaves and facing the wrong way. Looking up, I saw this elegant young girl all dressed up in hard hat and jodhpurs with a white silk scarf around her neck, and looking down at me from the saddle.

'Are you all right?' she asked, her brow furrowed, her red-painted lips pursed in an expression of deep concern.

'I'm fine,' I gasped. 'Fine.' In fact, I'd twisted my knee and lost a shoe; my helmet strap was round my neck and strangling the life out of me; and the foot-rest was bent down at 90 degrees so that it now acted as an impromptu stand.

'I'm ever so sorry,' she said, patting the horse's neck. 'She's a little nervous.'

'No, no, I'm fine,' I repeated.

'You quite sure?'

'Aye, fine. I'll be . . . fine.'

As I said, putty in their hands – and my vocabulary suddenly reduced to that single four-letter word. I reassured her with one more 'fine' and she rode off. My eyes followed her, and so did my heart. I stood there gazing at her slim figure, silhouetted against the low sun as she jogged up and down in the saddle and disappeared down the lane. Then I grovelled around in the leaves and mud for my missing shoe, clambered aboard my own trusty steed and hobbled home as well as the bent foot-rest would allow me, fantasizing about her having an older sister who could go out with my brother, and . . .

My knee stopped hurting after a week or so, but as for my heart – well, my heart kept on aching until about 18 months later when I got a date with a girl from Stillington. I still saw the lass on the horse now and then, although only fleetingly, and always from a distance. It was probably a good job I never had the chance to speak to her, because I knew I'd be lost for words. Unless she happened to ask me how I was doing, of course. In that case I knew very well what the answer would be.

• • •

'We had a visitor?' I asked the desk sergeant as I walked into the office.

'What d'you mean?'

'Saw a super-looking lass in the car park. Long beige coat, red Merc, London plates.'

'Ah, you mean Ann.'

'Oh, aren't you the dark horse! On first-name terms already?'

'Course I am, she's been working here since Monday.'

'Working?'

'Well, they aren't gonna pay her to sit on her pert little arse for 40 hours a week, are they?' He looked at me, and I just gaped. 'They've had her on the early turn,' he said, 'with Jayne.'

It was slowly dawning on me. 'She's not . . .'

'The new WPC? That what you mean? Go to the cupboard and get yourself a gold star, Pannett.'

'Ri—ight.'

'Name's Ann Barker. Been out and about looking over the beat.'

'She'll be the lass Ed was going on about.'

'Well Ed can dream on. Married with two kids?' He shook his head disapprovingly. 'I think not, matey.'

'No no no, he wasn't planning a . . . he just mentioned her a few weeks ago. Said he saw her in the Wendy House.'

'Oh, when she came up for interview, you mean?'

'Aye, that'd be it. By, I tell you what though, she ain't half—'

He held up a forefinger and wagged it from side to side. 'No, Mike. Don't even think about it. She's out of your league. Way out.'

'Tell you what, Chris.' I shudder when I look back, but I've always been a bit of a cocky sod. 'I'll have a little bet with you.'

'On what?'

'On me getting a date with her.'

'You're on. Tenner?'

'No, I'm confident on this one, mate. Call it 20, and don't say you can't afford it on a sergeant's pay.'

'Question is, can you afford it? 'Cos you've no bloody chance. You know it and I know it.'

'We'll see.'

And that, for the time being, was that. Or so I thought, until the next day, which was a Friday. I drove into the car park and saw my parking spot, unoccupied. 'Aha, I see someone's had a

203

word,' I said to myself. But just as I shaped to back into it a red blur crossed my field of vision and there was the bloody Merc nipping in behind me.

'What the—?' My hand hovered over the horn, and my lips were shaping up for a volley of abuse – and then I saw that dazzling smile again.

'Nice car,' I said, as I walked towards the door with her.

'Aye, it's nippy enough,' she said.

I held out my hand. 'Mike Pannett,' I said.

'Ann Barker.'

Did I say I was born lucky? We were at the desk, and Chris Cocks was looking down his duty sheet. 'Ah, Mike, I see you've met Ann.'

'I have.'

'Could you take her out with you this aft, show her around your patch? She's been with Jayne on the early turn all week. I think they could both do with a change.'

'Well . . .' There it was, that instant nerviness. The power of a good-looking woman scrambling the line between my brain and my tongue.

'Right then.' Chris turned to Ann. 'I hope you like supping tea with crusty old farmers, 'cos that's all this bugger does all day, y'know.'

'Intelligence,' I said, rapping my hand on the desk. 'That's the name of the game. Gathering information. Remember how I cracked The Great Lawnmower Theft?'

'You got lucky, Pannett. Anyway, I'm not sending WPC Barker out with you to pick up your bad habits. I'm hoping she can refresh your memory on a few elements of modern policing.'

'What did he mean by that, teaching me about modern policing?' I asked a few minutes later as we got into the squad-car.

'Oh, just about me coming from the Met. He has a bit of a complex about it.'

'Is that right? You were in the Met?'

'Oh yes. More years than I care to remember.'

'Get away – but you're a Yorkshire lass.'

'I am that.'

We were driving through town, but I wasn't really thinking about where we were heading. I only had one call down for the early part of the shift, and that was out towards the Moors.

'Bit of a coincidence, that,' I said as we swung out on to the A64.

'What is?'

'You being a Yorkshire lass and working in the Met.'

'Why, are you a Yorkshire lass too?'

'Ah well, that's for me to know and you to find out.' Smart-ass, I was thinking as I negotiated the roundabout and got out on to the A169. 'No, I did my time in the Met too. They let me out after ten years.'

'Whereabouts were you?'

'Whisky Alpha.'

'Oh, Battersea – you'll have tangled with the bikers on Chelsea Bridge then.'

'Ha, those buggers!' It was a regular thing, the last Friday of the month. Hundreds of motorcyclists from all over London and the Home Counties, congregating on the bridge to parade up and down, showing off their machines, their leather gear, their women – and then roaring off in convoy through Battersea and up Lavender Hill, doing wheelies and weaving round bollards, riding four abreast and slowing it right down till they all but stopped the traffic, and generally making a bloody nuisance of themselves.

'Regularly,' I said. 'Spent many a happy night at the south end. Why d'you ask, anyway?'

'I was on the other side. Chelsea was my home station.'

'Ah, Bravo Charlie. So we could have met in the middle.'

Ann didn't answer. We were out past Eden Camp now, heading north. 'Where we going?' she asked.

205

'Village called Cropton. You know it?'

'Do I know it? Ha. Edge of the moors, Pickering way.'

'That's it.'

'They still have that brewery there, in the pub?'

'They do. You ever been there?'

'It's been a while, but . . . yes.' She seemed reticent, and I was going to let it pass, but she went on, 'It was one of the ex's favourites.'

'Ah. Okay.' So – married and divorced, and an ex-Met officer. Interesting, as Barry Davies famously said, very interesting.

We were soon through Pickering, and out on to the A170 which links Scarborough in the east with Thirsk, some 50 miles west in the Vale of York. It's a big county, ours. As we turned off at Wrelton and made our way up towards Cropton village I glanced across at my passenger. She had small hands, slender wrists, and her hair was cut to a perfect length, short enough to leave her elegant neck exposed, but long enough to be brushed over her rather delectable ears. I must have let my gaze linger a little too long.

'Whoa, what you up to!'

I was lucky – I'd misjudged the bends coming out of Cropton, but my nearside wheel only clipped the edge of the grassy bank. 'Sorry,' I said. 'I got distracted by the . . . er, the outlook.' I nodded towards the moors, their sombre winter colours streaked by the rays of a sun which was already dipping towards the horizon. 'Beautiful, isn't it?'

'You wanna bloody concentrate, you do.' But next time I stole a sideways glance I could've sworn she was smiling.

We didn't stop long at the forestry place. The lad up there made it plain he was busy – so no tea today for a couple of wandering coppers. But he had time to tell us about all the trees he'd had nicked the previous year. 'The buggers were driving in with lorries,' he said. 'I reckon they're shipping them out to Leeds market. I mean, they were fetching £2.50 a foot last year. Bloody scores of them I lost, and that's not including the chancers who nip in and stick them on the roof-rack when I'm not looking.'

'D'you get a lot of that?' Ann asked.

'Hell aye. And they're not riff-raff from Norton and suchlike. I saw a couple of brand new Volvo estates last year—'

'Not white with a blue badge on the side were they?'

'It ain't funny, Mike. I mean these locals, far more money than we'll ever have, but I reckon they think the bloody things grow wild, so they can just help 'emselves. Same with poultry. My mate raises free-range birds for Christmas-time. Wiped out last year – and people think it's a laugh.'

'Well, mate, you know what to do. If you see any suspect vehicles just give us a bell. And I'll do me best to swing round this way on a night as we get into the season.'

'Aye, it won't be long now. Another few weeks and we'll be there.'

It was a quiet shift, which suited me fine. The longer I spent with this particular WPC the better.

'So, what part of Yorkshire are you from,' I asked as I dawdled back towards Pickering.

'I was born a Yorkie.'

'Oh aye?'

'Yep, the old Fulford Maternity Hospital.'

I was born there too, but I thought it would sound daft if I told her that. 'Now a Designer Outlet or something,' I said.

'Something like that.'

'And you lived in York?'

'No, I was a country girl. Still am at heart.'

'Whereabouts?'

'Huby. You know it?'

I laughed aloud. 'That's amazing.'

'Well, someone has to live there.'

'No, I mean . . . I'm from Crayke.'

Ann slapped the dashboard. 'I knew I recognized your name! Didn't you use to come and buy cabbages off my Dad?'

'Now that does takes me back. No, that wasn't me. It'd be my brother. He was starting out in fruit and veg deliveries. Traded in the old Viva and got a Bedford van. Right old rattle-trap. And you say he bought stuff off your Dad?'

'Aye, spuds, caulis, all that. We had a small farm.'

'Oh, landed gentry, eh?'

'Oh yes indeed. We had a paddock too.'

'And a horse, I suppose?' We were through Pickering, heading south again and I was wondering whether to turn off towards Flamingoland and track through the villages on the river Rye – Habton, Brawby, Butterwick and so on. I don't often get out that way.

'Oh yes, I had my horse. And my schoolgirl dreams. Was going to take her to Badminton and everything.'

We fell silent for a minutes. We were heading west and as we crossed the river Seven at Barugh the sun was almost on the horizon, dazzling us across the flat empty fields. I was deep in thought, remembering. A mile or so later as we went over the hump-backed bridge at Brawby I asked her, 'Wasn't a chestnut, was it?'

'My horse?'

'Aye.'

'As a matter of fact she was. Why?'

'Oh, nothing. I like a nice chestnut mare.'

· · ·

I was away on my course the next week, down in rural Warwickshire. It wasn't quite what I'd expected. I imagined we'd be concentrating exclusively on how traps are set, or how to deal with injured animals, that kind of thing – and fair enough, we did look at police powers regarding poaching; and we had a butcher come in and cut up a dead deer before lunch one day, so that we'd be able to recognize bits of a carcass if we came across any suspects. I seem to remember lunch that day was beef, sadly. We also covered a lot of legal aspects I'd never really thought about. We learned that there's a lot of illegal importation into this country – not just of exotic pets, but of products taken from protected species, things like ground tigers' teeth which are used in Chinese medicine; rhino horn – a well-known aphrodisiac, apparently; and ivory, of course, plus snake skins and alligator-hide as used for shoes and handbags, and authentic caviar, which finds its way into restaurants all over the UK despite being illegal. Traffic in these commodities is often controlled by gangs connected with Triads or the Russian mafia. There are some very unpleasant people involved, we were told. More astonishing to my ears was the fact that the illicit trade in plant and animal products is second only to drugs in its monetary value. So, an interesting course, but I have to admit that my mind was never fully engaged with what we were doing. I was elsewhere, dreaming of Ann Barker. I was planning a campaign: short-term objective, a date; long-term aim, a life together. I hadn't a clue how I was going to achieve the first, let alone the second, but as I lay there in my room at night, wide awake and staring at the ceiling, I reminded myself that once my mind is set on something, I take a bit of shaking off – as Ann was to find out over the next few months.

· Fifteen ·

There are advantages and disadvantages to the rural beat. On the plus side – well, they're almost too many to list. When it comes to actual perks, the most welcome on a day-to-day basis has been the odd bit of fresh meat. I never turn down a brace of pheasants, even if it does mean plucking and cleaning them when I get home at night and spending the next few days hunting down stray feathers – believe me, they get everywhere. You spread half an acre of newspaper on the floor, you pour a kettle full of boiling water over the birds so that they'll pluck nice and easy, you sweep up carefully after you've done, and days later you're still picking little bits of grey down off your cushions or opening the fridge to find a fluffy brown feather floating out. How they get there – or upstairs and into your wardrobe – I'll never know. Some people say you should just skin the birds, peel the lot off. But you'd be throwing all that lovely crisp skin and a layer of fat, on the hen birds at least.

Anyway, messy they may be, but free grub is free grub, and wild meat always beats the domesticated variety in my book. Occasionally in the winter I'll come across a piece of venison. Slap that in a slow cooker with some shallots and half bottle of red wine, and you can't whack it – especially if you drink the other half while it's simmering.

So there are perks to the job – as well as the gifts of meat, garden produce and the odd day's shooting, there's also the daily joy of setting off to drive through some of the most beautiful countryside in England.

As for the downside, well, there I'm struggling. I suppose the only thing that bothers me from time to time is that business the Super warned me about on my first day – that everyone can get hold of you anytime they want. Once someone gets to know you, they'll ask for you by name whenever they've got a problem – and you don't always want that. With some of them it's fine. Old folk living alone, farmers out on the moors: you know they're not going to call you out on some trivial matter, and you welcome the chance to help them out in an emergency, if someone's taken sick or they're stranded by the weather, for example. But some people can be a blooming nuisance, always ringing you and expecting you to drop everything for them. I think they imagine we're a part of the Social Services. I once had a woman ringing me on my day off because her cat had gone missing. She couldn't seem to understand why I was 'unavailable' thereafter. But, to be fair, that sort of thing doesn't happen too often. Once in a while, though, a friendship can lead to embarrassment – which is what almost happened with Algy and the bicycle.

I'd come to know Algy pretty well since I'd paid him back his tenner. We got along well, and we'd often have a natter over a pint in the Jolly Farmers. He'd even suggested to me that I move into one of the several houses he rented out. He had property all over the place, and I'd been to see a cottage in Leavening that was going to fall vacant early in the New Year. He also invited me out to one of his parties – and what a do that was. He got a live band in, not that I like trad jazz, but at least they played a few numbers you could dance to. He bought a couple of barrels of beer from that pub out at Cropton, just on the edge of the moors, where they serve their own brew. Two Pints they call it, and after a couple of glasses you know why. He invited a great bunch of lads, and some very interesting women, one of whom

I almost got entangled with – until Algy had a quiet word in my ear and told me who her husband was. So one way or another we considered ourselves chums. His word, not mine, I should add. Like I say, you get chatting with some of these toffs and it's inclined to rub off on you. Anyway, it was my chum Algy who put me in a tight spot one grey November morning.

It was a Tuesday, market day in town, and I'd been looking forward to it. I liked hanging around there, partly to maintain my contacts among the local cattle farmers, but also for the crack. There's something special about the livestock market, and the people who attend it. And we always start the day off with a cup of tea and a sandwich at the hospital canteen. They give us a discount. No idea why, but it's not something you question.

I'd actually been in the office some time, tidying up my paperwork, and was just about to set off into town when I heard Chris Cocks the desk sergeant shout my name. 'Call for you, mate!'

'Is that you Mike?' I recognized Algy's voice – but only just. Not many people talk like he does, not in North Yorkshire at least, but he sounded strangely hesitant that morning, not at all his usual self, and he seemed to be breathing heavily.

'Now then, Algy, what can I do for you?'

'I'm . . . turning myself in,' he panted. 'Just . . . wanted to know whether you'll . . . whether you'll be around.'

'Turning yourself in? What are you talking about?'

'It's a . . . it's a delicate matter,' he panted. 'Tell you when I get there. I'm just coming up Old Maltongate now.'

I wasn't sure what to make of it, but I didn't push him for an explanation. I just hoped it was nothing serious, because I wanted to be on my way. In fact, I was already putting my gear into the car when he rode into the yard – not in his Range Rover, but pedalling a fancy red mountain-bike and looking very hot and bothered.

213

'I'm afraid I've dropped myself in the mire,' he said as he dismounted, unzipped his shooting jacket, took off his fore-and-aft hat, and propped the bike against the wall by the side door. With his striped rugby club tie, his dark blue blazer, one side of his shirt collar standing up, and his hair all sticking out over his ears, he looked like a schoolboy who'd been sent to the headmaster's study. All he needed was a catapult sticking out of his pocket to complete the picture.

'Now come on, Algy, what've you done? You haven't fallen out with officialdom over that Yorkshire flag, have you? And what are you doing riding that thing on a damp old morning like this? You on a keep-fit kick, or what?'

He was rubbing the knuckles of his right hand as if they'd got chilled – hardly surprising considering the cold mist that had settled over the area the last few days. 'No, I'm afraid I've ballsed it up good and proper this time,' he said.

I could see now that he really was worried. This wasn't one of his wind-ups. 'Come inside,' I said, 'and tell us the tale.'

'Can we go somewhere with a bit of privacy?' he asked.

'Sure we can.' I sat him down in an interview room and closed the door.

'You know I have a couple of houses in town that I let out,' he said.

'Aye, you've one at the back of the cattle market, haven't you?'

'Yes, yes, that's the one. Have you heard?'

'Heard what?'

'Oh, so you haven't. Well, that's a relief.'

'Algy, what is this all about?'

He seemed to be calming down now, and he clearly had a tale to tell. 'It's like this,' he started. 'I have a chap in there, bit of a tearaway.'

'You mean a tenant?'

'Yes. He's only young. I really shouldn't have let him have

the place, but his mother used to work for me, and she'd been pestering me. Said it was time he had a place of his own – him and his girlfriend, I might add.'

'You mean she couldn't stand living with the pair of them any more?'

'It wouldn't surprise me in the least. I mean, he behaved himself the first few months, paid up more or less on time, but then he lost his job, and . . .'

'And fell behind. That what you're saying?'

'I played it by the book, Mike. But it's nine months now since I received a penny in rent, they've upset the neighbours with all-night parties, broken two windows, and they had a bonfire out the back that nearly sent my shed up in flames.'

'Yes, I think I get your point.'

'I mean, they're getting away with murder, and I'm going to have to pay for the clean-up when they finally move on.'

'Well, it sounds as though you've got a problem, Algy, but where's this all leading?' I was looking at my watch. I'd sat and listened to Algy's stories before, and he had a way of beating around the bush before he homed in on the main point.

'I know I shouldn't have done, but I—' He sighed wearily, leaned back in his seat and looked out of the window. It was drizzling now, one of those November days when you know it'll never get properly light. 'I just decided to take the law into my own hands.'

'All right, Algy, you'd better tell me what happened,' I said. 'Shall I get you a cup of tea?'

'No, I'll be all right.' He straightened himself up and carried on. 'For a start,' he said, 'there's that bike out there.'

'What about it?'

'Well, it's not mine. Haven't owned a bike since I was at school. I was in the Spotted Cow last night with some of my rugby chums.' He looked up at me and grimaced. 'Well, you've met 'em. You know what they're like.'

'Aye. Lively crowd.'

'And I was telling them about this character. I mean, dash it all, he owes me nine months' rent. They were outraged. Said they wouldn't stand for it and neither should I.'

'I'd probably have said the same, if it's any compensation to you.'

'Well, that's what got me started, I'm afraid. When it came to chucking-out time I decided I'd jolly well have it out with him there and then. Stormed out of the pub, over the road and banged on his door.'

'And what did he have to say for himself?'

'Ah, well, that's the point you see. He wasn't in. Or he wasn't answering, and that made me even madder, so I banged again.' He was rubbing his hand again, and I could see it was red and swollen. 'Put the jolly old fist through it,' he said.

'You mean through the actual door?'

'It's only single glazed.'

'Hell, you're lucky you didn't cut yourself to bits.' I winced as he showed me his middle knuckle. It was twice the size it ought to be, but by some miracle he'd only bruised it. 'Well, go on then, what happened next?'

'The thing is, it didn't feel as if I was breaking and entering or anything like that. I mean, it's my house, and once the glass was broken all I had to do was slip my hand through the hole, flip the latch and I was inside. And that was a shock, I can tell you. I mean, the place was simply littered with rubbish. Cigarette ends on the floor, carpets covered in crumbs, empty beer cans, leftover pizza on the settee. And the kitchen – well, you just wouldn't believe the mess. Or the smell. I didn't dare look upstairs. Who knows what I might have found. It'll cost a fortune to make it right, if I ever get rid of the blighter.'

'But you have a deposit from him, surely?'

'Yes, £400. And how far will that go? Anyway, I haven't got to the worst bit yet. When I saw the bike in the hall, I looked at it and thought, I've had a skinful, shouldn't be driving home . . .'

'I should bloody well think not.'

'No. So I thought, right, I'll have you for a start. Has to be worth a few hundred.'

'And that's the bike you've just brought in?'

'Yes. Rode it all the way to Leavening at one o'clock in the morning. No lights, I'm afraid. But I did leave the fellow a note. Said I'd borrowed it and I'd be fetching it back today.'

'So why didn't you just take it back this morning?'

'Wiser counsel prevailed, and all that. I realized I'd done wrong and decided to turn myself in. That's the trouble when you've been brought up to have a conscience. "Your sins will find you out" and all that.'

Algy had left me no choice, and he knew it. 'Listen,' I said, 'I don't like to say this, because you've done the right thing coming in here, and that'll go in your favour, but you're basically confessing to me that you've committed an act of breaking and entering. You do understand that, don't you?'

'Yes, of course I do.' His voice was fainter now. He looked very subdued indeed.

'So my unpleasant duty, I'm afraid, is to place you in custody.'

'Not in a cell, surely?' He didn't exactly go white as he said that, but his eyebrows arched up and he had a sort of pleading look in his eyes.

'Er . . . no. The cell is occupied. One of last night's drunks. Placing you in custody is a formal way of saying we're detaining you here while you are interviewed and the matter is investigated. Then we'll decide what's to be done with you.'

So there we had it. My chum Algy was handing himself over to me in my official capacity, and I was having to explain to him that he could call his solicitor to be present if he so wished. But he wasn't having any of that. 'Good God,' he said, 'I can't have old MacMasters see me in a scrape like this, can I?' I could see his point. 'Can you imagine it?' he said. 'In a small town like Malton?' He shook his head. 'No no no. Wouldn't do at all. I'll place myself at the tender mercies of North Yorkshire's finest and take my punishment like a man.'

'I wish they all took that attitude,' I said, before handing him over to the custody sergeant. It would be his job to decide what course of action to take, but first of all we would conduct a formal interview. That would be recorded, as they all are these days. We make three tapes: one for whichever court is to hear the case, always assuming charges are pressed; one to be kept at the police station; a third to be handed to the offender. On the basis of Algy's interview and the complainant's statement, the sergeant would make a decision – either to press charges and send the case on to court, or to issue a formal caution, meaning that he would be verbally admonished, the caution would remain on his record for use if he got in trouble again and could be cited in court if he were convicted in the future. A third option would be an NFA – No Further Action – which we use if there's insufficient evidence to charge or caution, or where the complainant refuses to make a statement or refuses to support a prosecution. With people like Algy – first-timers, as you might say – a caution was the most likely outcome.

But whatever the decision, it didn't look as though I was going to be around when it was made. A call had come in for me to get myself across to the cattle market, sharpish.

'What's the big rush?' I asked. 'I haven't had my breakfast yet.'

'Seems the cattle are stampeding.'

'Very funny.'

'No, seriously, they've a pair of bullocks on the loose.'

'Sounds painful. Is there a doctor in the house?'

'Just get yourself down there, will you?'

'Why me?'

'Let's face it, Mike, you've made a name for yourself as a bit of a cowboy around town, so . . . grab your lasso and trot along, will you?'

It sounds funny, runaway bullocks. It has echoes of cowboy films; stampedes, bulls in china shops. It's a cartoon image in most people's head, and to tell the truth it's the sort of thing I'd laugh at myself if I didn't know any better. But it's actually a very serious business. These beasts don't have to be malicious to cause mayhem. It's not so much that they're out to attack people as the fact that, once they start running, their mind is locked in the 'advance' position – and they don't particularly care whether they run into you, clamber all over you, or knock you down like a bloody ten-pin. And that goes for anything that stands in their way. Most of the time there's no malice involved, just a stubborn, brute will. They start running and they only have one thing on their mind and that is to keep going in a chosen direction until they can run no longer – nothing's going to stop them.

Still, at this point, when I set off for the market, I didn't quite know what to expect. It could've been a storm in a tea-cup. Some people will raise a hue and cry the minute they see an animal on the loose, but as often as not it'll be coaxed back into its pen, no trouble. After all, the Tuesday cattle market is crawling with people who spend their working day handling animals. Hopefully, by the time I got there, it'd all be under control and I could grab a bite to eat while I caught up on the latest gossip.

The first person I bumped into was Pete Jowett from out Bulmer way. He was sheltering under the shed where they have the auctions, the shoulders of his coat darkened by a steady drizzle. 'By heck, you've a job on, Mike,' he said.

There goes my cup of tea, I was thinking. 'Go on,' I said. 'Tell us the worst. You haven't let 'em get away, have you?'

'There was no stopping the buggers. They're gone, through the market place last I saw of them.'

219

'Christ, how far've they got?'

'Put it this way, Mike, if I was in your shoes I'd check t'fuel gauge before I set off after 'em.'

'Bloomin' 'eck – and how long they been loose?'

'Must be a good ten minutes, maybe fifteen.'

'That's just great, that is.'

As soon as I drove into the market place, people were sending me down the hill towards Yorkersgate. And that wasn't good news. It's a narrow street that takes all the through traffic heading east and west, being the old A64 Scarborough road. All it wanted was for the one of the bullocks to swerve in front of a car coming down the hill and we could have real trouble. It's a narrow road, and nowhere for a driver to go to avoid a collision, other than on to the pavement – and there isn't a great deal of that. Which meant that everyone – road-users and pedestrians – were in the firing line. And this, the busiest day of the week when people were in from all the villages doing their shopping.

As I prepared to turn on to Yorkersgate I had a quick look to left and right. Half the cars had their lights on, it was that gloomy. No sign of the runaways. But up the hill more people were waving at me, and pointing. It was one of the farmers, red-faced and brandishing a stick, who put me right. 'They've gone up past the war memorial yonder,' he called out as he stopped to catch his breath. 'Reckon the buggers are going blind.'

'Righto, matey.' He didn't mean they'd lost the use of their eyes. He meant they were thoroughly wound up. It's an expression they use. Panicking is what they mean. I didn't like the sound of it one little bit. If they had indeed gone blind, I wouldn't want to be there when they were cornered. They could charge you as soon as look at you. And although they're not fully grown, bullocks are hefty beasts.

By now I'd called for another car to be deployed further along to seal off the junction with the A64 where the by-pass meets the old road. If the beasts got that far, God knows what we'd end up with. Drivers come hurtling down the by-pass at 70 and 80 miles an hour, the road narrows to a single lane as the out-of-town traffic merges from the left, and when they're jockeying for position the last thing you'd want to throw into the mix is a couple of runaway cattle.

I put my foot down and sped out of town towards the industrial estate. Outside the BMW dealer the lads were on the forecourt in their suits and ties, pointing towards the by-pass. Christ, they surely couldn't have got that far, could they? But just as I was fearing the worst, I saw a cattle-truck pulled over on the roadside and three or four chaps in jackets and flat hats making their way across the verge towards a grass field. I recognized Mick Skinner, who farms out my way, just above Leavening.

'Now then Mick, are they yours?'

'Aye. Got worked up when we were unloading them, and some bugger hadn't fastened the barriers properly. They were away like shit off a stick. Couldn't hold 'em. '

I looked out into the field, and saw the two bullocks standing there, heads down, panting, steam rising off their backs. They were Limousins, their distinctive chestnut colour standing out against the drab wintry landscape. 'Still, you've caught them now. How'd you manage to get them in there?'

'God knows. We came haring down here in t'Land Rover and there they were. Must've got through t'thorn hedge up yonder.' As we spoke they backed the truck up to the gate and lowered a ramp into the field entrance. 'Wi' a bit of luck, we should get the buggers in now.'

A couple of four-wheel drives arrived, and out came the reinforcements, all carrying prods or sticks. It was at this point that the man from the *Gazette and Herald* showed up with his camera.

'Can you just hold it there, lads – as you were, with the bulls in the background.'

'Hey, we've a job on here, mate, so bugger off and leave us to get on wi' it. And they're bullocks, not bulls, so take note.'

'Do as he asks,' I said.

The men in the field were fanning out nice and slowly and gradually encircling the beasts. At first they stood their ground, then they started to trot down the hill as meekly as you please. They were handsome animals, a sort of chestnut red with white faces and curly hair on top of their heads, all matted and wet.

At first it all seemed to be going perfectly, but just as they approached the ramp the photographer, down on one knee and leaning against the gate-post, popped his flash. Well, that was that. One shot into the back of the wagon, but the other one stuck his front feet into the ground, snorted, then lurched to one side and was off along the hedge side with farmers hurling their sticks to the ground.

'Why, you daft pillock, what you do that for?'

'Gi' us that camera 'ere,' Mick said. 'I'll wrap it round your bloody head.'

'Steady on, lads,' I said. 'Let's stick to the task in hand, shall we? And you' – I turned to the photographer – 'I'd make yourself scarce if I was you.'

'Oh hell, now look at him!'

'Why, that's where he got in in t'first place.'

The bullock had smashed back through the hedge, and was out on the road, heading towards the by-pass into oncoming traffic. But not for long. As a line of cars slammed their brakes on and swerved to left and right he turned about and stood facing us. I was just thinking it was time I called for the Armed Response Unit when I heard the cameraman again. 'This'll make one hell of a shot,' he said, and blow me if he wasn't squatting down right beside me, fiddling with his lens. And there, 400 yards away, was the lone bullock, trotting towards us through the drizzle and murk with flecks of slaver dropping from his mouth. I've faced some hairy situations in my time.

I've tackled serial violent offenders at Millwall and Chelsea; I've broken down doors and been confronted with wild-eyed gunmen; I've been attacked by drunken women outside London pubs – only marginally less scary than the football hooligans, I might add. I've faced snarling Rottweilers in crack dens, runaway horses and I once ran into a python in a dead man's bathroom. I've had a rioter spit a mouthful of petrol at me and threaten to set fire to it; I've faced stones, iron railings, half-bricks, eggs, tomatoes and all manner of abuse which I wouldn't care to repeat in print. But I have never felt the urge to run so strongly as when that beast came pounding up the carriageway towards us with its head down. And as I stood there, wondering what the hell to do, matey with his camera was saying, 'Can you just go a few paces towards him and maybe get your truncheon out.'

'Hey, you go a bit closer, matey. This is one picture that ain't going to be hanging on my mantelpiece.'

It was time to get on to Control again. 'Listen,' I said, 'I'm not happy about this. At all. I want a firearms team out here. This bugger's getting excited. He's putting lives in danger. Get a couple of lads down here sharpish, will you.'

The beast was barely 100 yards away now, and showing no signs of slowing. He wasn't charging as such, but put it this way – he was moving with purpose. Looking around I saw that everyone was in his vehicle except me and David Bloody Bailey, but I was quite prepared to leave him to his fate. It would've been a popular decision. If he was hell-bent on getting the ultimate action shot, well, good luck to him. 'Get in the bloody car!' I shouted, but he wasn't having it. Give him his due, he was a real pro.

Some people just don't deserve what Fate dishes out to them. Just as it looked as though matey was going to get tossed over the fence like a hapless matador, I switched my blue lights on. Whether it was that, or a car that swerved out of his way and blared its horn, I don't know, but the runaway veered sharply to his left, took off like an overweight gazelle and leapt over the hawthorn hedge.

'By, did you see that!' one of the farmers shouted from the safety of his Subaru.

'Saw it? I bloody snapped it!' said the beaming newshound. 'What a beaut. Tell you what, this is going to the nationals.' A moment ago he was facing destruction. Now he was hugging himself with delight. 'They're gonna love this,' he grinned.

'Well, bully for you mate,' I said. 'Now we'll get on with capturing the bloody thing – if you're quite sure you've finished.'

The bullock had trotted across the field and was now halfway up the hill. He paused, turned and looked at us, then disappeared around the side of the woods. 'Well,' I said, 'that's bloody great, that is. He could go any direction from there.'

Still, we now had a squad car covering every road back into town, and out on to the by-pass.

'He's actually surrounded,' I said.

'But does the bullock know that? That's the question.'

'You want to fetch a megaphone,' the cameraman said, cupping a hand over his mouth. 'It's no good. You can't escape. Come on out with your hands up.'

As well as the squad cars we now had a posse of farmers ready to go after the runaway. There must've been a dozen of them. It was one bullock against the combined might of the cattle-market habitués. It didn't stand a chance. All we had to do was find it.

'So what's the plan, Mike?'

'Oh hello, Pete. I wondered when you'd make your way down here. This won't do the lunchtime trade much good, will it?'

'They'll mek up for it later, mate. Anyway, I hear you've got it cornered.'

'Had it cornered, you mean. Now he's got away again, up to

the copse yonder. He could be anywhere between us and the top road. Matter of waiting for him to show himself, I suppose.'

And so we waited, and waited. Nothing. A few more strays showed up – the usual suspects. They'd heard about the excitement and were hoping to see some action. The cameraman, having got his scoop, slipped away. On the road the traffic was now coming steadily, but cautiously. The Armed Response boys showed up – not one vehicle, but two – and were quickly on the radio getting clearance to load their guns. The drizzle turned to rain. The lads out on the by-pass called in, wanting to know what they were to do. Was it clear yet? Any chance of a cuppa? Then Control called me. Could we spare a car to go over to Rosedale – possible moorland fire? No, I told 'em. I'm looking for a bullock in the woods. The rain'll put your fire out.

'Well, we can't sit here all day,' I said to Pete as the posse set off across the field to scout around the woods. 'On the other hand we can't walk away.' This was maddening. 'We know the bugger's out there somewhere.'

From time to time one of the cars radioed in. 'How much longer?'

'How much longer?' I repeated. 'How do I bloody well know?'

'Well, have you seen owt?'

'No I haven't.' I usually have a pretty even temper, and bags of patience, but I was getting distinctly ragged. The bloody thing had simply disappeared.

One by one the farmers drifted back to town.

'Can't be missing our lunch, not on a market day.'

'Aye, gissa call if you see owt.'

'You'll be in t'King's Head, I s'pose?'

'Aye.'

And then, just when I was wondering what the hell to do

next, I got a call from the lads out on the Castle Howard road. 'Mike, get yourself over here. You're not gonna believe this.'

'You found him?'

'Oh aye, we've found him all right. You can call off the search.'

I left one of the patrol cars to keep an eye on things while I made way over there in convoy with the two Armed Response Vehicles. I didn't like the idea of the beast being shot, but I couldn't see any other result. 'Maybe there'll be a joint of sirloin in it for us,' one of the ARV lads said over the radio. 'Ages since I had a decent bit of roast beef.'

As it happened, we'd underestimated our four-legged friend. The squad car was parked by a gateway and there were Jayne and Ed grinning like idiots while the photographer beckoned me over. 'Come on,' he said, 'just one – for the record.'

'How'd you get here so bloody fast?' I said. 'And where's that bullock?'

'Oh, you been looking for it 'ave you?'

'Very funny, Jayne.'

'Yeah, we thought so too.' She jerked her thumb over her shoulder, and there in the field, milling around a hay-rick, was a gaggle of creamy white Charolais beef cattle, and in amongst them, nudging his way to the front of the scrum, was our chestnut-coloured friend, muddy, steaming, and probably very hungry.

'Well, I'll be . . . How'd he get in there?'

'Oh, it was nothing, Mike. A cape and a sword. Piece of cake.'

'Jayne . . .' I wasn't in the mood for her jokes.

'Yeah, okay. We flagged him down and flashed the old warrant card and he gave himself up.'

'We were just sat in the car and he ambled across out of the woods there,' Ed said.

'Anyway,' Jayne said, 'what happens now?'

'That's up to this fellow,' I said as Mick drove up, followed by a string of half a dozen muddy four-wheel drives.

Mick scratched his head. 'Well,' he said, 'I'll need to get a vet to him at some stage. He could've damaged himself ploughing through fences and what-not.'

'You don't mean he left his equipment dangling do you?'

'Jayne . . .'

'In the meantime, I'll have a word with the farmer here. Can't just remember his name. Do you know him?'

'No, can't say I do.'

'Well, anyway, I'll have a word with him, see if I can leave me-laddo there for a day or two till he recovers.'

I called Control and told them it was a wrap, collected up a few cones we'd put out on the York road, and made my way back to the station. On the way up the drive I bumped into Algy.

'Hell,' I said, 'I'd forgotten all about you. What happened?'

'I had what the old headmaster used to call a stern ticking-off,' he said.

That figured. Not only had he turned himself in, but he'd told the full story, had brought the missing property back with him to town, and had displayed obvious remorse. Yes, he'd committed an offence, but he had no previous criminal record. The custody sergeant had very wisely decided to stick with a formal caution.

• • •

To a man like Algy this had been a sobering experience. He'd been finger-printed, two samples of his DNA had been taken from the inside of his cheek by swab, and he'd been given a custody number to hold up while his photograph was taken. He would, quite literally, have felt the heavy hand of the law on his person, and for a man with no previous experience it would be chastening, to say the least. By the time I bumped into him he'd spent half a day at the police station and, in his own words, 'been processed like a . . . like a bullock coming to market.' Never mind the bullock, I thought, he actually looked a little sheepish as he left the building. And now, with the bike being returned to the lad who owned it, he'd realized that he'd left the Range Rover keys at home.

'You couldn't loan me 20 quid for a taxi fare, could you?' he asked.

'Course I can, Algy.'

'Golly, I hope I never have to go through anything like that again,' he said, and he gave a little shudder.

When I caught up with him in the Jolly Farmers later in the week, however, he was much perkier. He'd assumed the status of an outlaw hero with the locals. He'd 'had a go', struck a blow for the hard-done landlord against ne'er-do-well tenants. And he had news for me. I could have the cottage in Leavening in the New Year. But in return, he said, could I get him a copy of his 'mug-shot' so that he could frame it, or put it behind the bar with a great big WANTED sign under it. 'Tell you what,' I said, 'gimme my 20 quid back and I'll see what I can do for you.'

· Sixteen ·

It had been another wild and wet back end of the year, with the Derwent bursting its banks once more and trees coming down across back roads all over the county. But now at last we were having some proper old-fashioned winter weather. That's the way I prefer it – cold and still, with smoke coming out of the farmhouse chimneys, a nice white frost on the car in the mornings and old ladies grabbing your arms as they slither about on the pavements. We'd even had someone ring in to ask who'd nicked the salt out of the bins by the gallops on Langton road. There'd been a dusting of snow on the moors earlier in the week and someone had obviously panicked. You have to laugh.

It must have been half past eleven as I drove through Malton. Typical Friday scene: little knots of people turning out of the pubs, mostly young, the lads in their shirt-sleeves, girls in skimpy dresses; but with the amount of beer they put away these days they never seem to feel the cold. Some of them looked a bit unsteady on their feet but by and large they seemed good-natured and cheerful. The shops were all ablaze with coloured lights and tinsel, and as I drove up on to the estate the odd illuminated Santa on a roof-top threw a red glow over the tiles, all spangled with frost. High in the sky there was a half moon.

I usually try to forget about Christmas until the last minute. It's never going to be like it was when you were a kid, so why get worked up about it? Still, here we were with the holiday

229

season just a couple of weeks away, and even I was getting in the mood, whistling a carol to myself as I turned out of town towards the by-pass. I'd just started my shift, hoping against hope that nobody was out on the country roads driving under the influence. In some ways it's more of problem in a rural patch than in town. People set out for a quiet pint, maybe have one or two more than they've planned on, and suddenly realize they've got to get home. There's no bus, not many taxis cruising around like there would be in York or Scarborough, and the temptation is often there to slip into the car and drive home nice and steady. I do wish they wouldn't.

•   •   •

I'd just turned on to the Scarborough road when the message came over the radio.

'Can I have a unit to deal . . . Kirkbymoorside . . . Reports of a female fallen from a window. Unconscious. Ambulance on its way.'

As far as I was aware, Jayne was covering Kirkby with a young lass they'd sent over from Scarborough. I could hear them respond straight away. 'Romeo Papa 23.' I pulled over in a gateway. Should I get myself over there, or would they manage? They weren't that experienced. But then you don't like to go barging in taking control and find out they're perfectly capable of sorting it out themselves.

Then I heard one of them call in again. Just the tone of her voice told me all I needed to know. 'She's . . . she's stopped breathing.' I swung the car around, put on the blue lights and headed back to the roundabout. As I turned north the radio came on again. 'Got a crowd gathering. They're a bit rowdy . . .' There was no disguising her anxiety. I accelerated past Eden Camp and called in. 'Ten fifteen to Control. I'll back them up. Just leaving Malton.'

A lot of questions go through your head when you hear bits and pieces of information like that. You try to imagine what's happened, put a picture together. Was it a kid, or an adult? Badly injured or just knocked out? Did she fall or was she pushed?

'Are we getting an ambulance?' the WPC was on the radio again. She sounded rattled, and it didn't surprise me. First time you have to deal with something like that you don't want a crowd of youths, half of them drunk. Things can soon turn nasty. 'She needs help. We can't get her breathing.' In the background I could hear shouting. Someone screamed. This is where you have to be careful as a driver. You feel the adrenalin surging through your body, your foot's twitching on the accelerator, but you have to drive sensibly. Fast, but sensible. Luckily the roads are more or less empty at that time of night, and you can see oncoming lights a long way off. All the way ahead of me it was dark. I could see the outline of the moors, the tops glowing white in the moonlight. I was doing about 90 as I approached the turning for Flamingoland. There's a nice straight there, then you hit a series of bends and pretty soon you run into town.

I touched the brakes, and as I did so I felt that little shiver of trepidation. It's always the same: you're thinking about what you're going to find. This one could've been anything, but what I was getting over the radio made my heart sink. People go out at seven, drink all evening, and there they are, getting on for midnight, a crowd of them on the street, and half of them can't even stand up straight. It makes the job harder than it ought to be.

I was soon through Pickering and out on the A170. Five more minutes and I was in Kirkby. As soon as I approached the market place I could see the reflection of a blue light flashing off the side of a house, and there they were, 15, maybe 20 youngsters, some of them with drinks in their hands, standing outside some sort of boutique. Glancing up I saw the lights were on at the first-floor window, which was wide open. That never looks right, not in midwinter. There was a sort of balcony arrangement, maybe two or three feet deep and running the length of the shop front. I stopped the car, grabbed my hat and pushed my way through the crowd.

They didn't to want to move for me. They were pressing forward to see what had happened. There at the centre of it all I could see Jayne trying to push people back. But the kids weren't having it. 'She's our f***ing mate. We'll see to her,' someone was shouting. By the side of the road a lass was squatting on her haunches, covering her eyes with her hands. Another was sitting on the pavement, shaking her head. Some of the girls were crying; others were on their mobiles. I heard one speaking very deliberately, 'No, she was at the window reaching down . . .' Then, bizarre as it may sound, I heard someone laugh.

'Come on, lads, let me get through.' I was trying to shove my way forward to give Jayne a hand. 'Make room now, come on.' But they wouldn't budge. The fact is they were drunk, most of them, and those that weren't, were either in shock or hysterical. I grabbed one of the lads by his shoulders and yanked him to one side. 'What the f—?' he said, as he stumbled into the lad next to him. Then I heard someone say, 'Oh God, she's not dead is she?'

The girl was lying on the pavement, on her back, frighteningly still. She was wearing a sweatshirt and jeans. She had no shoes on, just a pair of red and black Dennis the Menace socks. She can't have been more than 18 or 20. There was another girl beside her on her knees, holding her hand and crying. The Scarborough lass was there, squatting down, giving the victim mouth-to-mouth. As I forced my way through, she broke off. She looked like a frightened rabbit, poor lass. 'Think I've got her breathing again,' she gasped.

I didn't like what I was seeing. There was fluid coming from the victim's ear, not blood but a straw-coloured liquid tinted with blood. I knew what that meant: damage to the brain. It wasn't looking good. I got down by her head and looked along her body. 'Yep, she's breathing,' I said. But hell, it was shallow. There was just the slightest rise and fall. 'Keep an eye on it though,' I said. 'Be ready to start mouth-to-mouth again if she stops.' I reached for the girl's wrist. I'd just found a pulse – but my goodness it was weak – when the ambulance arrived with a police van from Helmsley right behind it. The crowd was still pressing in. The paramedics were going to have the same job I had getting to the girl.

'Now then, back off will you, and let these lads through.' I'd dropped the girl's wrist and was leaning into them, forcing them back, but still they milled around. One of the lads even had his arm around me, breathing alcohol fumes in my face. 'You're all right, mate, I'll sort her out. Done first aid at college, me.'

'Move!' I shouted.

'Piss off, you four-eyed bastard.'

'Right . . .' I broke through, grabbed the lad, frog-marched him over to where the van had pulled up. 'Here,' I said, as the PC unlocked the back door, 'you can have this one for a start.' The lad's mate was trailing along behind me and was pawing my shoulder.

'Hey, what's he done?'

'Obstructing the police – and if you don't get out of my way you'll be joining him.'

'Nah, you arrest my mate, I'm going down with him, pal.' I threw him in the van too.

That seemed to quieten everyone down. The paramedics were able to get through now with a stretcher, which they laid down beside the girl on the pavement. 'Here, grab this and squeeze.' One of them passed me the black oval ball they use to force air into the lungs. I took hold of it and watched as she put a clear plastic mask over the girl's face and slipped the elastic band around her head. 'You know what to do?' she asked.

'Aye, squeeze, let it out—'

'Then count to two—'

'And repeat. I know.'

I was already doing it. At least the girl's chest was rising and falling properly now. Maybe . . . maybe . . . But then I looked at her eyes, which were half open. I knew right away what I'd seen, and I wished I hadn't. Sometimes you just have that sense – I never quite know what it is but I can only describe it as a sort of lostness.

As I squeezed, they prepared to lift her on to the stretcher. It needed the two of them, plus the WPCs. You have to be so careful – God knows what she could've done to her spine falling all that way. They got her on board, took the ball from me, then carried her towards the ambulance doors.

The PC who'd come from Helmsley in the van had grabbed a roll of blue-and-white tape. Together we forced everyone back and got an area cordoned off, tying it to a railing, then looping it out across the pavement, round a lamp-post and back again. The girls were getting names and addresses of witnesses, picking up bits and pieces of the story. We now had a crime scene established. But was it a crime, or just an accident? Everyone seemed to have something to say about it.

'We told her not to . . .'

'She was just climbing out of the window . . .'

'She wanted to talk to Mike . . . he was down here like . . .'

'She was trying to get down.' The lad was pointing to the balcony.

'She just . . . lost it, like.'

'Slipped.'

'Lost her balance.'

Bit by bit, we pieced together a version of what seemed to

have happened. It wasn't a party. The girl had been out with her friends. They'd been in the pub, just down the road, and she'd got into an argument with her boyfriend. It had escalated into a full-blown row, and she ended up threatening to dump him. Both of them had had plenty to drink, and she'd gone back to her flat above the boutique with a couple of friends. One or two others had gathered there, then her boyfriend came by. She wouldn't let him in, so he started calling to her from the street, making a bit of a fuss. There were things he wanted to say. She opened the window and they started talking. Come down here, he said. No, it was bloody freezing, and she was nice and warm upstairs. Then one of the neighbours called out to keep the noise down. Rather than carry on shouting she said she'd come down to him, but instead of going indoors and using the stairs she climbed out on to the balcony. God knows why, but it's the sort of daft thing people do when they've had too much to drink. Some of her friends in the flat were urging her to come inside, she could fall. Others thought it was a bit of laugh. The boyfriend offered her a cigarette, tried to throw one up to her. This is where the stories differed. Some said she was trying to climb down; others said she reached out for the cig. Whatever the truth of it, that's where it all went wrong. There was no malice, just stupidity – and alcohol. The usual story. She slipped. It could've been the frost, could've been spilt beer, could've been a simple misjudgement.

By the time we'd heard the various witness statements I was coming to the conclusion that this was an accident, not a crime. A stupid, avoidable accident, and now the poor girl was in the ambulance on her way to Scarborough.

The PC from Helmsley came over. 'What about those two lads you've got in my van?'

'Oh Christ, forgotten about them. They weren't doing anything. Just verbals. Needed to get 'em out of the way.' I went across and unlocked the door. They looked pretty sorry for themselves. Couldn't have been more than 18. One of them was drying his eyes on his T-shirt.

'Come on, you two. Get yourselves home.'

'Thanks, officer. We didn't mean—'

'I know you didn't. You were upset. We all are.'

It was time to check out the girl's flat. In theory it was still a potential crime scene. Nothing had been proved one way or the other. The street door was half open. I went up the stairs beside the shop and opened the door. No one told me she had a dog, a little black-and-white mongrel. I just about tripped over it, but the poor thing was more startled than I was. It shot across the living-room and dived behind a sofa. I looked around for signs of what might have happened. Had there been a struggle? Was there a suicide note? You have this mental check-list. You can't go assuming anything. But there was nothing out of the ordinary. A half-drunk bottle of Stella on the coffee-table, her coat carelessly thrown over a chair, keys on the floor, purse beside it with the trainers she'd kicked off. It could've been any young girl's place, anywhere.

By the time I came back down people were drifting away. Some of them were still carrying the bottles they'd had in their hands when they'd come out of the pub. There were empty cans lying in the gutter. It was as if a street party had just ended – and in a sense it had. One of the girls was leaning into the tape, looking at the pavement, inside the area I'd cordoned off, where the fluid from the girl's head was reflecting the light from the street-lamp. Her boyfriend came and put his arm around her. You always feel as if you want to get a hose-pipe and wash away the evidence. It looks obscene, but it has to be left there for the scene of crime officers. They were still on their way from Scarborough. We were expecting them any minute, then we'd be done.

It was past one o'clock. We'd got our list of people who'd been in the flat, the witnesses who'd been in the street. Now someone had to go and wake up a middle-aged couple and tell them what had happened to their daughter just a couple of weeks before Christmas.

It turned out her parents only lived a few hundred yards away. I looked at Jayne and the lass from Scarborough. It had been a hell of a shock for them, I could tell. Someone had fetched them each a mug of tea and they were hunched under the lamp-post blowing the steam off. Jayne had the parents' address in her notebook. 'Don't worry,' I said to her, 'I'll go.'

'Thanks,' she said, shaking her head. 'I don't think I could face them right now.'

It barely took me a minute to drive there. As I walked up their front path and prepared to knock on the door I was going over what I would say. You have to be so careful. They know as soon as they open the door that something's happened.

The house was in darkness, of course. The church bell in the town centre was just striking the quarter hour. I leant on the buzzer. Gave it one decent ring to wake them, then another to make sure. Christ, I just hoped they wouldn't go to pieces on me. For the first time that night I was feeling the cold.

First the landing light – I could see it through the frosted glass on the front door. Then the porch light. Then the door opening, and there was Mum, still working her shoulder to get her dressing-gown on properly, blinking in the glare.

'Mrs Bryon?'

'What is it? What's happened?'

'I'm ever so sorry to disturb you at this time of night, Mrs Bryon, but there's been an accident—'

'Who? Is it Julie?'

'Do you mind if step inside?' I wanted to get her sat down. You never know – sometimes people just pass out on you.

'But what's it all about? It's Julie, isn't it?'

Her husband was at her side now. 'Yes, what is it?'

'If I could just come in a moment—'

'No, tell us now. What is it?'

She was on the verge, I could see it.

'I'm afraid there's been an accident. Your daughter Julie, she's had a fall.'

'Oh God, no. What fall? Where is she? Where'd it happen?'

'She's in good hands, but she is rather poorly, I'm afraid. She's on her way to Scarborough Hospital.'

She was in tears already. It was him I was talking to. You're sorry for them, of course you are. If you could stop and think about it, you'd feel dreadful, but you can't allow yourself to feel. You're in charge – they expect you to know what has to be done. What I was actually thinking was, would they be fit to get themselves over to the hospital or would I have to offer to drive them? Practical stuff – that's what you think about.

'No no, I'll be all right,' the father was saying. 'I'll get dressed and get the car out.'

$$\bullet \quad \bullet \quad \bullet$$

'Units to Malton, fight outside the Assembly Rooms.'

I was back outside the little shop. Jayne and her mate were still in shock, effectively, but they'd sort themselves out. The Helmsley lad had already responded to another call, someone who'd gone and rolled his car over out at Rosedale. That left most of Ryedale in my capable hands. 'Aye, ten fifteen. I'm on my way.'

You really don't want to be sorting out a fight on the back of an incident like that. But you manage. You just switch on to automatic. You wade in, drag a couple of likely lads out of it, calm everything down, and try to get them to settle their dispute some other way. And of course they're mostly so full of pop they aren't good for more than a couple of swings. It was all wind and wild threats and what one would do if he ever caught the other bloke talking to his girl that way again. I dished out a couple of warnings, took a few names, and hung around until the main contenders had staggered off towards home. Last thing I wanted was to be clogging our cells overnight with some drunken oik who'd throw up all over his bed.

Back at the station I managed to write up my notes, then it was back on the road. Somebody had rung in about the alarm at the sand quarry. Miles from anywhere, and the bloody thing was always going off of its own accord, but it had to be seen to. Then it was all the way out to Foxholes to check out a car parked outside the pub – 'at an odd angle'. Had it crashed? Stolen? Was it a suicide? No, it was none of the above. There was a note on the window to say it had broken down and the owner would be back to it in the morning.

As I drove back to Malton, along the valley that takes you through Weaverthorpe and Helperthorpe, the moon was lighting up the bare Wolds, the trees casting vivid shadows. It seemed a strangely peaceful scene, miles removed from the turmoil and tragedy outside the shop in Kirkby. I wondered when I'd get to talk it through with Jayne, the lad from Helmsley, the lass from Scarborough. And what had happened to the girl after she was shipped off to the hospital? I shrugged mentally. I was feeling very weary. If it was to be bad news, I'd rather not hear it till the morning.

I got away from the station about seven, was back at Walt's for twenty past. He'd been up an hour or so and had a pot of tea on the go. What sort of a shift had I had? I somehow managed to squeeze it all into about 20 words over half a cup. He didn't push it. He knew when not to ask questions. Ten more minutes and I was in my bed. I hoped I would get off quickly. It'd soon be time to get out there and start all over again.

· Seventeen ·

As Christmas approached I started to wonder what had happened to the legendary Pannett luck. Had it deserted me? The way I saw it, my first meeting with WPC Ann Barker had gone quite well. We'd discovered that we had a few things in common, she seemed to have enjoyed chatting with me, and in my mind's eye I kept seeing the little half smile that had lit up her face when she realized I was watching her rather than the scenery as we drove towards the moors that time. There was hope there, surely. Trouble was, I hadn't had a chance to chat with her since then, what with being away on the wildlife course and one thing or another – like being off for a week with a rotten cold. Of course, I kept an eye on the roster to see whether there were any last-minute changes, but we were always stuck on different turns, just bumping into each other at shift hand-over with no chance for a private moment. Meanwhile Chris was starting to angle for payment on our bet. I'd stalled him for long enough, and in the end we'd agreed I had till the year end to get a result. Still, with the annual outbreak of flu starting to make its seasonal inroads there was always a chance Ann and I would be rostered together. Then I would make my move. Not that I knew how I was going to play it if we did. I knew what I wanted to do, but actually getting round to it – well, that was going to be a different matter. As I said, a good-looking woman has the power to do what few other people have ever managed to do to Michael Pannett – namely, shut me up. Still, the festive season would soon be upon us, the time of year when everybody likes to get out. I'd be working most of the time, which suited me fine, being on my own. I'd be having Christmas dinner with my brother and his family, and I'd been invited over to Walt's for Boxing Day. There was also a party planned up at Algy's place, and I was thinking that maybe I could ask Ann to come with me. Question was, how to broach the subject when I never seemed to see her?

Just when I was starting to think I might have to drop an invitation in her work-tray – and was consequently spending my spare moments on the beat composing everything from brief, off-hand notes to passionate declarations of undying love – the chance I'd been waiting for dropped into my lap. I seem to remember it was the shortest day of the year – and I'd just come in for a 10 p.m. night shift. I'd got changed and was in what we call the parade-room, but is actually a combined office and briefing room. There were five of us on duty, plus Chris Cocks, the duty sergeant, all sitting with our cup of tea. It was a Friday and somebody had brought a bag of Eccles cakes in – although all that remained on the plate when I breezed in was a pile of crumbs and a last, solitary specimen, slightly squashed, which I immediately grabbed.

'We one short?' I asked through a mouthful of currants, looking round the table. Normally on a night we've six PCs and three cars, all double-crewed.

'We are now,' Chris said, screwing up the remains of the bag and lobbing it neatly into the waste-paper bin.

'No, I meant bodies,' I said, licking the sugary bits off my fingers. I love Eccles cakes, always have done.

'Oh, that's very nice, that is.' Everyone turned around, and there was Ann walking in carrying a briefcase in one hand and a mug of tea in the other. She looked very trim indeed in her uniform. 'What was the last thing I said when I put them on the table?'

Chris stifled a laugh. 'Er . . . to save one for you,' he said. Ed was grinning at me behind his hand. I felt my face colour up. I tried to speak, but nothing came out – except a shower of crumbs.

'Well, thanks a lot,' she said, as she slammed her case on the table and sat down.

I swallowed – twice – and started to explain. 'I thought—'

'No, *I* thought,' she said. '*I* thought if there's one place you'd be safe from thievery it'd be in a blooming cop shop.'

'He's like that, Ann,' Ed said, nodding at me. 'Sees sommat he fancies and just, you know, can't keep his hands to himself.'

'Aye, so be warned, lass,' Chris added. ''Cos you're doubling up with him tonight.'

● ● ●

'What brought that on?' I asked Chris after the others had trooped out.

'What d'you mean?'

'Well, you've 20 quid riding on me getting a date with Ann, and you send us out together. You've blown it. You know that, don't you?'

He shook his head. 'What are you going to propose – afternoon tea in Betty's, so that you can pay her back the cake you nicked? Listen, Mike, I was feeling generous. You don't deserve it, but I'm giving you a chance. Call it a Christmas present.'

It hadn't been a good start, I was thinking as I trudged across the car park with her ten minutes later. My big chance to cosy up to the best-looking WPC I'd ever clapped eyes on and I'd made a complete balls of it.

'Don't worry about it,' she said as she leaned into the car and threw her briefcase on to the back seat.

'Worry about what?'

'The cake.' She stretched and yawned.

'Oh. I'll make it up to you. I'll bring some Jaffa cakes in tomorrow—'

'No, it doesn't matter. Really.' I'd been burbling, and she knew it.

'You sure?'

'I'll survive. Good for my figure to go without. Mind, I could've done with upping my blood sugar tonight. I thought I'd finished my run of nights, so I stayed up today, then the phone goes to say Jayne's gone down with the flu. Tried to have a couple of hours' sleep this aft, but I couldn't get off.'

'Well, let's hope we have a nice quiet night, eh?'

'Yes let's,' she said as she wriggled into her seat and made herself comfortable. 'So where we off to?'

'Well, there's the rugby club do across the road there, there's a disco up at Kirkby, another in town, so we may get called in to help out there if there's any trouble. Apart from that, I was planning to see if we could nab a turkey rustler or two.'

'Oh, seasonal crime-busting. No crack gangs or hostage takers then? I was in the mood for a bit of excitement. Keep me awake.'

'I tell you what, the day that sort of thing starts happening in Ryedale I'll sling my hook. Had enough of that in the Met. Didn't you?' She didn't answer. 'Anyway, there's been the usual complaints from poultry farmers. Birds going missing. Same every year.'

'Hell,' she said. 'You've just reminded me. I promised my Mum I'd see to the turkey and I still haven't got one organized.'

'You'll be popular . . . And lucky. Four days to go?'

'I'd best see to it in the morning, before I get to bed, I suppose.'

'Tell you what,' I said. 'Try the market. They have the auction tomorrow if I'm not mistaken.'

'Yeah, that's an idea. Anyway, what's the plan for tonight? How we going to catch these poultry rustlers?'

244

'Nothing very sophisticated. Just sit up in a likely location. See if owt comes by. Mind, that won't be till later on. Till then, most of Ryedale is at our disposal.'

It was a bitterly cold night, starry, with a frost already forming on the pavement. It was the sort of night when a lot of people would stay home. At least, that was what I was hoping. I wasn't in the mood for breaking up fights outside pubs.

'You'll know this area pretty well, then?' I said as we headed towards Pickering. 'Being from Huby, like.'

'Used to. But I tell you what, after eight years in London it's surprising how much you forget. Didn't you find that?'

'I did. But then I soon realized that I'd never known it that well in the first place. Just a few villages around Sheriff Hutton. We never strayed far from home when I was a lad.'

'No, neither did we.'

'Always on that horse of yours, eh?'

'Yes,' she said. Then silence. I don't like that – not until I really get to know someone. It makes me feel awkward. I hoped something would happen – anything. There was precious little traffic on the roads. We took a tour round Pickering, but it was all quiet there. Moved on towards Kirkby for chucking-out time – nothing doing there either. We were in Helmsley by about one.

'Tell you what,' I said, 'why don't we get into position outside Hovingham? Then we can have our grub. Or is that too early for you?'

'No, I'm ready for mine. Haven't eaten since lunchtime.'

We climbed out of Helmsley and turned off the main road at Sproxton. A few hundreds yards on, where the road drops down, I pulled over into a gateway and switched the lights off.

'Something up?' Ann asked.

'No,' I said.

'You seen something?'

'Look over there,' I said. The field had had a crop of turnips in it. They'd been dug up and left lying on the surface. And there, behind a line of netting, was a flock of sheep, their breath coming in clouds as they worked their way along the rows. I wound down the window. 'Just listen,' I said. You could hear them munching through the frozen roots. Otherwise it was as quiet as it was still. And there on the horizon, towards Ampleforth, the sky was lightening perceptibly.

'Any minute now,' I said.

'Any minute what?'

'The moon'll come up. Should be full too. I was on this shift a fortnight since and I sat and watched a new moon over Blakey Ridge.'

'You're really into all this, aren't you?' she said as I closed the window and turned my coat collar up. It was freezing out there.

'The great outdoors, you mean?'

'Yes,' she said, 'the countryside.'

'I am. It's what brought me back from London really.'

'Yeah, me too,' she said, sort of quiet and thoughtfully. I glanced across at her as a car approached from Hovingham direction, illuminating her face. She had a real gentle expression, as if she was remembering something or someone she loved. She looked very young. 'Aye, you missed all this when you're down south. Loved the work, mind, but you never had time to get out in the country. Proper country, I mean.'

'I know what you mean,' I said. 'I used to get out on the Surrey Downs on a weekend, but you were never far from a motorway. There's some right nice country – well, pretty country anyway – but there was always the noise of traffic. It would've driven me mad in the end.'

I looked towards the horizon. I wanted that moon to come up, and I wanted it to be full. 'How about hiking?' I said. 'D'you ever do any of that?'

'Love it . . . when I get the chance.'

246

'That makes two of us.'

'Oh, have you done much?'

'Get out when I can. Done a few long-distance ones in my time.'

'Oh yes?'

'The Wolds Way, Hull to Filey; and the Cleveland Way, Helmsley round to Scarborough. That's hard work when you're out of condition. What about you?'

'Lots of day hikes in the Dales. But I've never done a long-distance one. It's not easy for a woman on her own, you know.'

'No, that's true. Well,' I said, as the moon finally showed itself through the woods along Caulkley Bank, 'maybe you'd like to take a walk with me some time.'

There was a pause, then she said, 'You know, you're quite right.'

'Fantastic,' I said.

'It is a full moon.'

'Oh.'

· · ·

We got to Hovingham and parked up in the woods there, right by the road that cuts across to Easingwold.

'Why here?' Ann asked, as I got out my sandwiches and flask.

'Just a hunch. This is the kind of short-cut someone would take – well, I would anyway, if I wanted to cut across to the A19. And we can keep an eye on the road through the village too. Worth a try, anyway.'

We ate in silence. The radio was still pretty quiet. Nothing for us at least. Ann yawned a couple of times. I thought for a minute she was going to nod off. I was wondering whether to bring up the hiking business again. I should've pressed the point, but she'd caught me off guard with that remark about the moon. Damn – it would've been easy if I'd come right back with it. Now I'd have to start all over again. Of course, she could have been winding me up. I wouldn't have put it past her.

'Well,' I said, as I polished off the last of my sandwiches and snapped my bait tin shut, 'if there's any thieves out and about, are you ready for 'em?'

'In a minute,' she said. Then I felt her nudge me in the ribs, 'How about one of these first?' She was holding out her sandwich box and there inside it, lying on a paper towel, were three Eccles cakes.

'You crafty little . . .'

She laughed, her eyes glinting, reflecting the light of the dashboard. 'Well,' she said, 'they told me you liked sweet things.'

'I do,' I said, as I helped myself, 'and I tell you what . . .' She was looking at me, with one dark eyebrow raised, and I blurted it out before I had time to think. 'I'm starting to like you too.'

There was a moment's silence before she said, 'Thank you.'

We sat there for another quarter an hour or so. I don't think we saw a single vehicle. 'What shall we do, give it another ten minutes?' I said. Before she could answer the woods around us were lit up as a vehicle turned out from the village, lights on full beam, and headed towards us.

'Look at that,' I said, as a grubby old Sherpa van roared past. 'Run the check, will you?' I slung the car into gear and set off after it.

It didn't take more than minute or two before the answer came over the radio. Leeds. Nothing on it.

'Leeds,' I said. 'So what they doing out here at this time of night?'

We followed the van for a mile or two before I swung out, put the blue lights on, and signalled them to pull in. I got out, approached the driver's door and shone my Dragon light inside the cab. 'Well, well, well,' I said to myself. Three lads, all

248

in their twenties by the look of them. And as the driver wound his window down, what did I see in the cab? 'Take a look at this, Ann,' I called to her as she came up behind me. The seats, the floor and the shelf behind them were all covered in feathers. The driver was even pulling one out of his hair.

'Evening, officer,' he said.

'Evening. Where we off to, then?'

'Easingwold, mate.'

'Oh aye, and where have you been?'

'Driff.'

'Driffield, eh? Care to explain the . . . er, feathers?'

'Oh aye, them'll be t'turkeys.'

'And which turkeys are those?'

'I never asked 'em their name. Seen one you've seen 'em all, right lads?'

He got the laugh he was after. 'Okay,' I said, 'care to tell me what's in the back of the van?'

'Oh, no good askin' me. I'm just the driver, mate.'

'Well, I'm going to ask you to open it up, if you'll hand me the keys.'

He took the keys from the ignition and passed them to me.

I wouldn't say I was over the moon, but I was certainly feeling a warm glow inside. This would look good in the papers. Ryedale Police strike a blow against raiding parties from the West Riding as they try to make off with our Christmas dinners. I unlocked the door and opened it carefully. Just a crack – I didn't want the whole flock spilling out on the road. I was remembering the time I let half a dozen whippets out of the back of a Range Rover. We spent an hour rounding them up, and the owner threatened to sue us. Still, I was thinking, by the time your average turkey is fattened up for market it's hardly in the greyhound category. I swung the door wide open.

Nothing. Not a sausage. And certainly no gobblers. The van was as clean as a whistle. Not a feather to be seen. 'Well, where's

249

the bloody birds?' I said. The driver was loving this now. He was grinning from ear to ear, and Ann was looking at the ground, trying not to grin back at him. 'We don't transport 'em,' he said. 'We just pluck 'em.'

'What do you mean, you pluck 'em?'

'We pull their feathers out – it makes 'em easier to carve. You should try it.' Then he laughed out loud. 'We're pluckers, mate.'

I still wasn't entirely convinced. The fact is, I didn't want to be. They could easily have nicked the birds and delivered them to some market trader. Well, it was a possibility, surely. 'So what you doing on the road this time of night?' I asked. 'You can't have finished your shift yet. It's only one o'clock.'

'Piece-rate, mate. We go in, pluck 'em, and get on to t'next job sharpish. We're off to some place up the A19 right now. Sixteen hundred geese to see to. Here, I'll show you.' He walked up to the cab and shouted to the lads, 'Now then, giss the ticket for that next job, will you.' One of them reached into his overalls pocket and pulled out a couple of pieces of scrunched-up paper. 'Here y'are, officer . . . and here's the paperwork for t'job we just done.'

It all made sense now. They'd been to a farm out near Sledmere. I knew the place well. I walked past it one time on the Wolds Way. 'They used to do ostriches, didn't they?' I said – to myself as much as anyone. Matey hadn't a clue what I was on about. He just scratched his head, pulled out another feather and gave Ann a quizzical sort of look as if they were sharing the same thought – that I was off my rocker.

'Right,' I said, handing back the papers, 'you want to be getting along then. And drive steady. These roads are slippery as hell tonight.'

'Would you believe it?' I said as we got back in the car.

'Thought you'd copped one there, didn't you?'

'Bunch of stupid pluckers. Still, just goes to show, doesn't it?

Never assume anything. I tell probationers that time and again, then I go and fall into the trap myself.'

The rest of the shift we kept busy enough. There were a couple of false alarms in Pickering, a cyclist with no lights on the A64 making his way home to Huttons Ambo – stone-cold sober, but, as we pointed out to him, stark-raving mad – and a call from my old mate John the milkman in Sheriff Hutton to report a suspicious-looking character trying the side window of a house on the edge of the village. Turned out it was the owner's son, home late from a party and scared to wake his parents. Thought they'd be angry with him. They certainly were when we banged on the door at 5 a.m.

By the time we set off back to the station, Ann was struggling to stay awake, yawning like a good 'un. ''Scuse me, I'm shattered.' Then she groaned. 'Oh, and I've got to sort this turkey lark out when I get home.'

'Well,' I said, 'it doesn't kick off till about two.'

'What doesn't?'

'The Farmers' Market thing.'

'Listen, I'm going to need about ten hours the way I feel.'

'Okay then, I tell you what. Let me do it. I'm two days off now. Doubt I'll have more than an hour or two in the easy chair. I'll be in the Spotted Cow lunchtime for a quick pint, then I can pop across the market and snap you up a bargain.'

'You sure?'

'How big a bird do you want?'

'Oh, now you're asking. Sort of average, I suppose. I've never had to buy one before.'

'Well, shall I say ten, twelve pounds, sommat like that?'

'That ought to do it.'

'Right. Leave it to me. Oh, how'll I deliver it?'

'Good point. How long you going to be in town?'

'I'll be back to the pub after tea. Meeting a couple of pals . . . well, Chris and Ed.'

'Okay then. We'll make it a date, shall we? A quick one before I go to work. About seven?'

•　　•　　•

To say I was walking on air that afternoon as I made my way to the cattle market would only be a slight exaggeration. Of course, I'd had a couple of hours' sleep, a huge fried breakfast in town and a pint of beer in the Spotted Cow. And that evening I had a date with WPC Ann Barker – well, not a date as such, so to speak, but at least a little time together in a sociable environment. I'd called the lads and told them I couldn't make it till eight, so that gave me an hour alone with her. If I couldn't get a result there I'd be handing over £20 to Chris – and he'd be grinning all the way to the bank. Well, first things first. I was going to have to pave the way by getting her the best turkey she'd ever eaten at a knock-down price.

The birds were all set out, some plucked and dressed, some still in their feathers, on tables in the big draughty shed at the top of the market. Lucky it wasn't raining, because the old place leaks like a sieve, and if there's any wind it fair whistles through it. There must have been 150 prospective buyers gathered around, and I should think 80 per cent of them were dressed the same as me: waxed jackets and flat caps. I shouldn't have been surprised if they all had their thermal underwear on too. I certainly did. It was perishing, with the puddles on the roadside frozen solid, the cold seeping up from the concrete and through my leather-soled shoes.

The birds were all numbered, clearly marked with their weights, and labelled as to who had reared them. To judge from the knowing comments I overheard as I passed along the rows, reputation counted for a lot.

'I bought one off matey three years ago, y'know.'

'Who's that?'

'You'll know him. Big lad. Comes from out Kirkby Grindalythe way.'

'Oh aye.'

'Aye. Weren't nowt but feathers and skin. Died of starvation, most like.'

'We allus stick with 'er they call Pig Woman.'

'From Terrington way, that who you mean?'

'That's her. Right plump and tasty.'

'Aye, and they reckon her poultry ain't bad neither.'

'Tell you who you want, that old girl from Duggleby. By, she can't half raise a tasty bod.'

'What they call her?'

'Ooh, now yer askin'. Bradshaw, is it?'

Bradshaw, Bradshaw . . . I made my way along the tables. Bradshaw – ah, there they were, as nice a selection of birds as you could hope to see. I found a nice plump one, plenty of breast meat, and made a note of its lot number: 134. They'd only just started the auction so it'd be a while before it came up. I might as well have a walk around the market square. It was a lovely sight, the crowds of shoppers at the fruit and veg stalls, the coloured lights strung across the street, the rows of rabbit and pheasants hanging up outside the butcher's shop. I wondered briefly how many of those had been bagged on the sly. Outside the bookshop on the corner, the White Star Brass Band, 100 years old and still going strong, were playing all the old favourite Christmas carols. Below the church were the steam organ and the kiddie rides, the toddlers looking up in wonder at the Christmas-tree lights. It was the sort of Yorkshire scene I used to think about when I was patrolling around Battersea on the run-up to Christmas, alone, on my guard, as often as not recovering from a run-in with some knife-wielding nutter.

I bought some hot chestnuts from a guy with a little brazier, and stood there soaking it all up. It had been a funny old year, what with settling into the new job, then moving in with Walt, and now I could look forward to moving into Algy's cottage in Leavening. On balance it had been a good year. But something was missing, and I knew what it was. I was tired of being alone. If I had one hope for next year it was to put that right. And who knows, I thought, if I could get a proper date with Ann . . .

Back in the shed, the auctioneer, in his white coat, with the sleeves of his chunky sweater sticking out at the wrist, was rattling through the lots. 'Now then, ladies and gentlemen. 129. Eight birds from Mrs Halford of Thorpe Bassett, all of them about the 12 lb mark I'm told. What are we bid here? Do I hear six pounds? Five? Start me off at four then, lady over there. Yes sir, you're in at four-fifty . . . and five . . . and fifty . . . and six . . .' And so it went on until he knocked them down at £14 apiece as I stood there chewing my chestnuts.

All too soon it was my bird – at least, the bird I meant to buy. Ann's Christmas dinner. 'Lot 134, ladies and gents,' he started, and then he was off at a canter and I could hardly hear him. 'Four, four-fifty, five, five-fifty, six . . .' and he kept nodding in my direction even though I hadn't raised a hand yet. Then I realized – it was the chap standing next to me, little squat fellow about 70 in a belted mackintosh and a cloth cap, puffing on a pipe, the bowl of it dipping down and back up as he nodded his response to the auctioneer's every glance.

'Six-fifty, seven, seven-fifty, eight . . .' Blow this, I thought, I need to get in. I stuck my hand up.

'New bidder on my left, ladies and gentlemen . . . with you at eight-fifty, sir, and nine over here, nine-fifty.' Hell, I wish I'd done my sums. What was it, 11 lb at £1.10 . . . That's 11 times 11, isn't it? Never was any good at my tables.

'Ten pounds with you, sir. Ten-fifty, eleven . . .' It was me and this old codger now and it was a fight to the death. What gave him the right to step and bid for my bird, that's what I wanted to know. The auctioneer had finally slowed down, and was staring at matey with the pipe. 'The bid's against you at £14, sir.' Another of his blasted little nods.

'Fourteen-twenty it is, then.' I shoved my hand up again.

'Fourteen-forty . . .' Another nod.

'And sixty, eighty . . . and . . . is that fifteen, sir? Fifteen pounds with the gent in the flat hat.'

'They've both got a flat hat,' someone shouted out. 'Aye, and not a lot underneath it, either of 'em,' someone chipped in.

'With the pipe. Gentleman with the pipe. It's your bid, sir.'

Surely now he would give up.

'Fifteen-twenty . . . and forty . . . fifteen-sixty.'

I'd had enough of this. 'Sixteen pounds,' I called out.

'All done at £16, is it?'

I looked around, braced for another onslaught, but he'd gone. Simply vanished. 'Thank God for that,' I muttered under my breath.

Down came the hammer. 'Name, sir?'

'Pannett, Mike Pannett.'

'Ah, good to see our local bobby supporting the hard-pressed poultry farmer in his hour of need.' A ripple of laughter ran through the crowd.

'It's a good job I'm thick skinned, that's all I can say,' I told the auctioneer's clerk, as I coughed up the money a few minutes later. 'Advertising my name to all and sundry. And I tell you what, if I'm daft, what about that other old bugger bidding against me? Who was he?'

'I think they call him Bradshaw.'

• • •

I showed up at the pub for seven as arranged, with my parcel under my arm. I'd just managed to get a table and was re-arranging the seating so that we'd be nice and cosy when she showed up – bang on time. What an entrance. Apart from

255

that time she'd nicked my parking spot I'd only ever seen her in uniform. She was wearing a pair of dark trousers, a beautiful silky magenta blouse with short sleeves – and a gorgeous, warm smile.

'Well!' I said – and then nothing else came out. Pannett, stumped for words – again. Just what was going on?

'What you having?' she asked, putting her coat over the back of a chair and dipping into her purse.

'No, no, this one's on me,' I said. But she was past me and at the bar.

'Look,' she said, 'you've got me out of jail, you have. If I'd let my Mum down, I'd never have heard the last of it.'

'Go on, then. I'll have a pint of bitter.'

She was just about to order when she stopped in her tracks. 'You have *got* a turkey?'

'Course I have. I'm a man of my word, I am. And it's a beaut. It's under the table there.'

'Right then.'

I watched her as she was getting served. Trim figure, neat little waist, and I couldn't help noticing a shapely rear end as she reached forward to hand over the money. But more than that, she had a real confident style about her. I wondered whether Chris the sergeant was right – maybe she was out of my league. She was certainly up there.

'I'm on the wagon I'm afraid – back in to work tonight,' she said as she placed my pint on the table and took a sip from a glass of orange juice. 'Anyway, did you manage to swing it?'

'Swing what?'

'Why, you said you'd get me a good deal.'

'Oh hell aye. Bargain of the year. An absolute beauty. Big plump . . . er . . .'

'You mean a full figure?'

'Aye, that's it. And bang on 11 lb, just like you asked for.'

'So how much do I owe you?'

'Er . . . well, it was £1.10 a pound, so that's 11 times 11 . . .'

'Twelve pounds and ten pence.'

'I'm impressed.'

'So'm I. That's a hell of a price.'

'That's what they told me at the auction. They said, "you've paid a hell of a price for that bird." Course,' I continued, supping my pint, 'you have to understand the auction game. It's no place for a novice. The trick is to watch and wait, set your limit, and then pounce.' I banged the table and rattled the ice in her orange juice. 'Whoops, sorry. Like a cobra, I was.'

'Well, don't think I don't appreciate it. 'Cos I do.'

We only had time for the one drink. She hadn't had any supper yet and wanted to be in at work nice and early. I carried the bird out to the car for her. She'd parked in the market place, deserted now apart from one or two people scurrying off to the King's Head, shoulders hunched against the cold night. 'Well,' I said as she opened the boot of the Merc, 'I hope you enjoy it.'

'I'm sure I will.' She gave that little smile again. Sweet, but ever so slightly shy – like the smile I got when I told her I was starting to like her.

'Listen,' I said, 'I've been invited to a party out in the country, New Year's Eve, and I'm on me own. Would you . . . would you like to come with me?'

'New Year's Eve?'

'Aye.'

'Yes, I'm free then. Yes, that'd be really nice.'

'Oh, that's . . . that's great. Look, if I don't see you while after Christmas, have a lovely time.'

'You too.'

She was about to get in the car, but she seemed to hesitate. 'Well then,' I said, and stopped.

'Well what?' That smile again, the one where she knew bloody well what I was thinking.

'Do I deserve a Christmas kiss?' I said.

She stood there for a moment, then her eyes twinkled as she said, 'Yes, I'd say you've earned one.'

•   •   •

Ten minutes later I walked – no, I floated – into the Spotted Cow. Chris was there with Ed, three-quarters of the way down their first pints.

'What you having, lads?'

'Oh, good call,' Chris said. 'Another pint'd just hit the spot nicely.'

'Right,' I said, holding out my hand. 'But first give us that 20 quid you owe me.'